Foundations of Black Epistemology

ADEBAYO OLUWAYOMI

Foundations of Black Epistemology

Knowledge Discourse in Africana Philosophy

TEMPLE UNIVERSITY PRESS
Philadelphia • *Rome* • *Tokyo*

TEMPLE UNIVERSITY PRESS
Philadelphia, Pennsylvania 19122
tupress.temple.edu

Library of Congress Cataloging-in-Publication Data

Names: Oluwayomi, Adebayo, 1981– author.
Title: Foundations of Black epistemology : knowledge discourse in Africana
philosophy / Adebayo Oluwayomi.
Description: Philadelphia : Temple University Press, 2025. | Includes
bibliographical references and index. | Summary: "This book makes the
case for the concretization of a subdiscipline of Black Epistemology
within Black and Africana Philosophy. As the first book-length
consideration of various Black thinkers, specifically as Black
epistemologists, this volume critically engages self-epistemologies and
political epistemologies offered from a Black philosophical
perspective"— Provided by publisher.
Identifiers: LCCN 2025003088 (print) | LCCN 2025003089 (ebook) | ISBN
9781439925478 (cloth) | ISBN 9781439925485 (paperback) | ISBN
9781439925492 (pdf)
Subjects: LCSH: Philosophy, Black. | Knowledge, Theory of. | Black
people—Intellectual life.
Classification: LCC B808.8 .O58 2025 (print) | LCC B808.8 (ebook) | DDC
120.89/96073—dc23/eng/20250324
LC record available at https://lccn.loc.gov/2025003088
LC ebook record available at https://lccn.loc.gov/2025003089

The manufacturer's authorized representative in the EU for product safety is
Temple University Rome, Via di San Sebastianello, 16, 00187 Rome RM, Italy
(https://rome.temple.edu/).
tempress@temple.edu

To Temi, my lovely wife.

To Eni, Moni, and Bami, my wonderful children.

Your support and love mean the world to me.

Contents

Preface

The idea for this book was conceived during my graduate studies in philosophy when I began to critically examine the substance of knowledge formation in my formal training in philosophy. I grappled with the realization that this discipline fundamentally centers *whiteness* as the foundation of knowledge by positioning and canonizing Western thinkers as "principal" intellectuals across different philosophical traditions and areas of inquiry. However, as I probed deeper into the construction of knowledge within these cultural philosophical traditions, I discovered a major flaw, which is the fact that Black thinkers were firmly erased from the philosophical discussions within these traditions. I also discovered a dark truth about philosophy: that it is mostly considered a provincial discipline, and an exclusive preserve of white (and mostly male) thinkers. In many philosophy departments in the United States, core courses and seminars are typically framed around thinkers like John Locke, Thomas Hobbes, Rene Descartes, Frederick Nietzsche, David Hume, Søren Kierkegaard, Georg Hegel, and Immanuel Kant, just to a mention a few. It does not help that many of these white philosophers were virulently racist and published books and essays where they expressed horrible anti-Black ideas. But these philosophers have now been thoroughly sanitized or "whitewashed" and presented as important thinkers that one must study seriously in order to earn terminal degrees in philosophy.

I similarly discovered the preferential and selective manner in which the scholarship of these philosophers was approached, such that many of the horrific ideas that contradicted their widely "celebrated ideas" were de-emphasized so as to present a one-sided account of their intellectual contributions. I took this as extra motivation to explore these traditions more broadly to unearth the roots of this exclusion of Blackness from the discourse of knowledge. As I read and researched deeper into the broad history of ideas within philosophy, I began to notice the systematic exclusion of Black philosophers who had published important works at the same time that many of these "recognized" or canonized white philosophers were actively writing and publishing. For instance, a typical seminar on twentieth-century philosophy may include white/European thinkers such as Ludwig Wittgenstein, Jean-Paul Sartre, Martin Heidegger, Simone de Beauvoir, Hans-Georg Gadamer, and so on. Given that the lines of demarcation of ideas are typically drawn by historical period, why are Black twentieth-century thinkers such as W.E.B. Du Bois, Ida B. Wells-Barnett, Thomas Fortune, Carter G. Woodson, Ralph Ellison, and Ella Baker, to mention a few, not considered part of this group?

This was the question that troubled my mind. The simple but deeply disturbing answer to this question is that they were not considered because they are Blacks and, as such, do not qualify as brilliant minds to be regarded in the white academy as philosophers, nor were they to be taken seriously just as any of these other white/European thinkers. Black thinkers are generally not considered as philosophers whose thoughts and ideas deserve disciplinary specialization. In other words, the ideas of Black philosophers have not been taken into account in the canonization of philosophical contemplations. But a robust study of Black intellectual history would reveal that they wrote volumes exploring the Black lived experience, which indicates their in-depth understanding of the human condition, especially their insistence that the myriad of problems affecting the human condition can be improved through philosophical principles and knowledge categories.

The idea of "canonization" within philosophy can be thought of as a consecration of systems of thought and the individual thinkers who produced them. It is basically a system of treating something, ideas, or individuals as having great relevance and significance. Ultimately, this decision regarding who is included in the canon, or excluded from it, is made by a group of people and—in the case of philosophy—by white scholars who themselves reify and reinforce the structure of thought and the systematization in which they were trained. Thus, the practice of excluding or putting Black thinkers outside the canon of philosophy is mainly a signification that they are not central to the development of ideas. It also portrays the incorrect notion that only white philosophers (mostly males) have made significant contributions to the history of human ideas. No wonder, then, that most discussions on African American or Black thinkers are typically considered an aside or not part of core philosophy. This explains why seminars that somewhat consider the works of Black thinkers are labeled with denigrating terms like "New Perspectives on the (white/European) Canon," "Non-European Philosophy," "Nontraditional," and "Philosophy from Elsewhere." All of these titles point to their subordinated and undervalued status within this discourse. Furthermore, when the works of Black thinkers are selected under such a subordinated status or designation, the Black thinkers themselves are mostly discussed as "activists," "protesters," "agitators," or "disruptors," among many other negative connotations. They are not considered primarily as philosophers who were making important contributions to the history of human ideas. This reality led me to raise a question that I was persistently troubled by: What would a work that engages seriously with Black thinkers as philosophers by examining the knowledge systems they produced look like?

For a long time, I searched for books that primarily focused on Black people as philosophers because I was strongly convinced that the centering of *whiteness* as knowledge cannot be the complete story of philosophy as chronicled within the history of ideas. So, I rummaged research institutions, archives, libraries, and bookstores searching for philosophical works that would highlight the important contributions Black thinkers have made in the vocation of knowledge production or the discourse of knowledge within the discipline of philosophy, but I could not find any. My search proved futile and led me to write this book.

Acknowledgments

Since I began working on this book, I have had the opportunity to share my thoughts and excitement about its objective with numerous people, including friends, family, and colleagues. To everyone who listened patiently, offered counsel, and uttered words of encouragement and enthusiasm toward this project, I offer my deep and sincere thank-you. I particularly want to thank all my family members, including my siblings and in-laws, for their love and support of my scholarly pursuits. I also want to thank my wife and children for their understanding and endurance for the many days I had to be away from home to work on this book. I would not have been able to complete this book otherwise. I have been truly blessed to have such a supportive community. I typically think of writing as a journey with many twists and turns; at every juncture where I encountered challenges, there were people along the way who provided helpful suggestions and guidance. I am grateful to Sándor Paull, for his encouragement and for visualizing the completion of this book even before I actively started writing. I thank Tim and Margaret Pappoe, John and Dina Kamas, Winston and Kristin Bryant, and Terry and Mary Howard for their friendship and support. My brother-in-law, Tobi Abereoje, deserves special recognition for his constant interest in my work broadly and his contribution to this book. My discussions with him, while I was writing Chapter 5, helped clarify some of my thoughts on Ida B. Wells-Barnett.

I want to thank Dr. Tommy J. Curry, Personal Chair in Africana Philosophy and Black Male Studies at Edinburgh University, for believing in this project from its initial conception to this stage of completion. I thank him for providing commentaries on earlier drafts of this work, which helped sharpen some of my ideas. I also want to thank Dr. George Yancy, Samuel Candler Dobbs Professor of Philosophy at Emory University, for his support of my scholarship. I am grateful to Dr. Huaping Lu-Adler, associate professor at Georgetown University, for her encouraging words after I presented aspects of this work at the Extending New Narratives in the History of Philosophy conference, organized by the Social Sciences and Humanities Research Council of Canada. I also have to thank Dr. Jacoby Carter, associate professor at Boston College and former chair of the Department of Philosophy at Howard University, for his continuous support and interest in this work.

Doing research on the Black intellectual tradition, an extremely rich tradition, has its own unique challenges. Apart from the fact that I had to grapple with a broad spectrum of materials to draw from, I was also faced with the difficulty of narrowing the scope of inquiry to fit into my vision for this book—a vision of intellectual engagement within Africana/Black philosophy that centers Black thinkers as Black epistemologists. My search for resources and research materials on the different representative thinkers whose ideas are explored in this work was made easier by many librarians and institutions. I am especially grateful to the staff of Chester County Library in Exton, Pennsylvania, for their assistance in locating materials through the interlibrary loan system. I am indebted to the following institutions for facilitating my research for this book: Cecil H. Green Library at Stanford University, the Library of Congress, Schomburg Center for Research in Black Culture, Robert W. Woodruff Library, Cornell University Library, Elmer Holmes Bobst Library at New York University, and the Historical Society of Pennsylvania. I am especially grateful to the staff at Brooklyn Public Library in Brooklyn, New York, for providing me with crucial materials for the chapter on Kathleen Cleaver.

This book would not have come to fruition without the patient, persistent, and perceptive advice of my editor, Shaun Vigil, at Temple University Press. Shaun's drive for clarity and concision made this book better. Some of his thoughts and suggestions allowed me to think more broadly about the impact and implications of my work. I want to thank my colleagues at West Chester University for their support of my teaching and scholarship. I especially thank Professors Joan Woolfrey and Dean Johnson for their support during the process of drafting this book. Dr. Jen Bacon, dean of the College of Arts and Humanities, has been very supportive of my scholarly work, and I am indebted to her. I am grateful to Professor Jacqueline S. Hodes, chair of the Educational Leadership and Higher Education Administration Department, for her enthusiastic support of my research. I also want to thank Dr. Tammy James, faculty associate for student engagement and retention, for her encouragement and support of my scholarly pursuits.

Many people and institutions provided support at different stages of the development of this work. I received a fellowship from the American Council of Learned Societies (ACLS), which provided funding for my research work on the first two chapters of this book. This funding opportunity also allowed me to engage in research work at Dartmouth College as an Emerging Voices Fellow. I am grateful to the ACLS for this opportunity. I want to thank my colleagues and friends, Dalitso Ruwe, assistant professor of Black political thought in philosophy at Queen's University, and Andrew Soto, professor of philosophy at Hartnell College, for reading earlier drafts of this work and providing very useful feedback. I am grateful to Dr. Denise Meda-Lambru for her constant encouragement. I want to thank Dr. Kelisha B. Graves, chief research, education, and programs officer at the Martin Luther King Jr. Center for Nonviolent Social Change, for her constant support of my scholarly initiatives.

I also want to thank Drs. Benjamin McMyler, Michael Collins, and Amir Jaima for reading earlier drafts of this work and offering constructive criticism. I am grateful to my friends Rene Hamilton, Peter Williams, Willie C. J. Harmon, Kiyadh Burt, and Derefe Chevannes for all their support. My gratitude goes to Temitope Oluwayomi for reading sections of this work and providing suggestions for improvement. To everyone who contributed to this project in one way or another, I am eternally grateful.

Foundations of Black Epistemology

Introduction

*The Necessity of Framing a Black
Epistemological Discourse in
Africana Thought*

My goal in this book is to make the case for Black epistemology as a new subdisciplinary focus in contemporary Africana or Black philosophy. It is a strategic move to focus on Black thinkers as social epistemologists, whose philosophical deliberations deserve serious intellectual consideration, especially within the discipline of philosophy. This approach is a deviation from the extraverted epistemological posture through which philosophical production by Black scholars has been characterized in current Africana/Black philosophical scholarship. This book engages in a rigorous historical study of Black intellectual history in a bid to reveal that Black thinkers have been interested in and have engaged with questions concerning the phenomenon of human knowledge and questions around human agency, including practical considerations regarding the social and political values of knowledge. These are important considerations that offer a different perspective on how the philosophical works of Black thinkers should be understood and assessed both historically and contemporaneously. This book addresses the problem of the extraverted epistemological posture of the discourse of knowledge in Africana/Black philosophy by centering the embodied subjectivity of Black subjects and the Black lived experience as the basis for a Black epistemological inquiry within Africana philosophy.

This book examines what it means to think of Black thinkers as epistemologists, especially concerning the creation and dissemination of knowledge in particular areas of the Black experience. It aims to show that epistemological considerations are not the prerogative of thinkers within Western philosophical praxis; they are something that Black thinkers have given a great deal of thought to within Black intellectual history as well. In this work, Black thinkers are not considered as mere commentators, critics, activists, or insurgents offering "sheer ideological" critiques to hegemonic systems of knowledge and practices, but primarily as social epistemologists. They are engaged as serious intellectuals who are writing about the importance of knowledge toward achieving individual and social transformation in an anti-Black world. Thus, this book maintains that African-descended or Black people cannot be defined only by their oppression, struggle, and resistance to hegemonic forces but also, and more importantly, by their self-conscious creation of knowledge geared toward achieving both individual and social change in the context of extreme anti-Black oppression and racialization. Its distinguishing feature consists of the propagation of the view that the future of intellectual engagement within Africana/Black philosophy should be geared toward the creation of new vistas of knowledge exploring the richness of the historiography of Black intellectual thought. This is the justification for the development of "Black epistemology" as a new subdisciplinary focus within Africana thought.

Knowing While Black: Dimensions of Black Epistemology in Africana Thought

The fundamental problem at the center of my work is how Blackness was written out of the discourse of knowledge (the deformation of Blackness) in the nineteenth century following the anthropological assumptions of white ethnologists and social epistemologists who used physiological categories to determine the intellectual capacities of Black people. I demonstrate how the biological racism that was disguised as social epistemology became the dominant framework of ascribing epistemic status to subjects in the discourse of knowledge through the twentieth century. It is important to note that the scope of this book does not cover the breadth of the epistemology of selected systems, broad theories, approaches and movements in an extremely rich intellectual tradition of Africana thought. Rather, it explores the thoughts of key Black figures (both men and women) within this intellectual framework as representative philosophical voices across the broad periods under examination.

The Black figures explored in this book have been selected because their life and times, including their intellectual work, directly rupture and challenge the assumptions of biological racism and inferiority that were disguised as social epistemological schemes during those periods. In other words, this book challenges the assumptions and posture of knowledge in the racialized social epistemology by highlighting selected figures in Black intellectual history from the nineteenth and twentieth centuries who are viewed, through an anticolonial framework, as social epistemologists. It explores how the exploits and achievements of Black intellectuals not only refute these assumptions but also serve as the grounding for their status as Black social epistemologists.

Frederick Douglass and Phillis Wheatley have been selected because they were former slaves who, against all odds, proved that even though the education of Blacks was made illegal through antiliteracy laws in nineteenth-century America, Black thinkers (who were slaves) demonstrated genius and avowed epistemic claims—in the first person—as authorial agents that made nonsense of the canonization of knowledge as a characteristic of whiteness. Ida B. Wells-Barnett and W.E.B. Du Bois have been selected for employing an anticolonial epistemological framework to develop an empiricist approach that challenged the false conclusions propagated in nineteenth-century ethnology about the Black race and the imaginations of new visions for Black humanity in the twentieth century. The selection of both Frantz Fanon and Steve Bantu Biko is based on their determination to extend the framing of anticolonial epistemology to Blacks in the diaspora. This is particularly evident if one considers the sociogenic principle in Fanon's philosophy as an extension of Du Bois's unparalleled sociological and empirical work on the Black lived experience, while also considering Steve Biko's Black Consciousness philosophy as an attempt to realize, on a practical level, some of the aspects of Fanon's sociogenic principle. Finally, Huey P. Newton and Kathleen Neal Cleaver have been selected as representative figures (representing Black men and women) within the Black radical tradition. The epistemological achievements of these Black philosophers are constructively explored throughout the chapters in this book.

Chapter 1 traces the historical roots of the crisis of knowledge—the derelictical crisis in Africana philosophy—by examining how this crisis contributed to the undermining of Black intellectuals within the discipline of philosophy and how it reinforced the erasure of Black subjects from the discourse of knowledge more broadly. It argues that an anticolonial methodological inquiry into Black intellectual history, through the examination of the works of representative thinkers within the Black intellectual tradition, would reveal the philosophical underpinnings of their thoughts and ideas that orient us toward an epistemological discourse. In this chapter, the works of these thinkers are considered as systematized bodies of knowledge that show the genius contributions that Black people have made to human liberation, and particularly to the advancement of the progress of the Black race within a sociological context that historically has not placed much value on Black intellect and Black lives. Chapter 2 explores how biological racism was framed as a social epistemological scheme in the anthropological and ethnological theories developed by white scientists in the eighteenth and nineteenth centuries and how these theories were considered "proof" of the inferiority and intellectual handicap of the Black race generally. It explores the historical construction, or "destruction," of the notion of *Blackness* in Western epistemologies, rooted in nineteenth-century ethnological science and theories of racial hierarchy in the United States as propagated by figures such as Buckner H. Payne (writing under the pseudonym "Ariel"), Samuel George Morton, Houston Stewart Chamberlain, and so on. This historical investigation aims to excavate the impediments to the formation of Black epistemologies of the self within the discourse of knowledge.

Chapter 3 looks at the genius of Phillis Wheatley, the prodigious and intellectually gifted Black female slave who was the first African American to be published as a poet or writer in the United States. The subtleties of Wheatley's written poems were engaged with epistemological thought systems about various themes, including reflections on nature, life, death, and humanity's pursuit of meaning in a meaningless world. Wheatley is considered an unlikely Black female epistemologist, especially in the context of slavery, one of the most dehumanizing and evil institutions ever created by humans. The chapter also specifically considers the significance of Black self-knowledge from the standpoint of Wheatley, a Black woman in this period, emphasizing how she challenged the notion that "reason" in its historical configuration was grounded in whiteness. Chapter 4 highlights the violence involved in the process of eschewing Black people from the domain of learning during slavery, through the eyes of Frederick Douglass, and argues that we can derive a plausible notion of self-knowledge and a framework of anticolonial epistemology from his philosophical thoughts. It also shows that Douglass understood mental darkness— the realm of the *unknowing being*—as a mark of colonial oppression; throughout his life he strove to develop a distinctive notion of Black epistemology that was directed at developing the political consciousness of Black folks and marshaling ideas toward the future of the Black race.

Chapter 5 considers the contributions of Ida B. Wells-Barnett to Black epistemology. As a Black woman in the twentieth century, Wells-Barnett is popularly known for her antilynching activism, which has been widely discussed in historical and contemporary scholarship. However, this chapter offers new ideas in the scholarship about this Black intellectual by highlighting the unique and groundbreaking method of knowledge that she produced (the empiricist model of knowledge) and established as a framework for understanding social phenomena (the racially motivated but illegal killing of human beings) in the late nineteenth through early twentieth century. It also underlines the complexities and complications of the principles of white feminism in the twentieth century, specifically her confrontation with suffragists and abolitionists such as Frances Willard and the women from the Women's Christian Temperance Union regarding their injudicious support of the lynching of Black men. Chapter 6 explores the development of an empiricist epistemology by W.E.B. Du Bois that investigates Black subjects as beings in the world and the articulation of an embodied experience that negates the categories of ignorance projected on them by racialized science in the twentieth century. This chapter focuses on the ways in which Du Bois developed principles of Black epistemological thought to provide a systematic understanding of the Black condition and to imagine a positive vision for Black humanity grounded in the socioepistemic perspective of the Black experience.

Chapter 7 draws a connection between the thoughts of Frantz Fanon and the legacies of W.E.B. Du Bois. It explores Fanon's most penetrating and powerful critiques of Western/colonial logics as a form of anticolonial epistemology. Fanon diagnosed Western/colonial epistemes and accretions as the prime causative of mental disorder and the psychological feeling of inferiority among colonized Black folks, including all forms of self-estrangement, in the same manner that Du Bois discerned the color-line to be the problem in the twentieth century that generates the phenomenon of double consciousness as well as self-alienation. This chapter also emphasizes how Fanon challenged the colonial epistemological categories that erased Blackness from the space of "reason" and unleashed a new vision for Blackness in an anticolonial space of "reason." This is a state of awareness where the Black subject exhibits its epistemic authority by "acknowledging no other authority" for cataloging the lived experience, which constitutes grounds for visualizing a new image of Black humanity. Chapter 8 attempts a reading of

Steve Biko's Black Consciousness as an anticolonial epistemology that embodies a form of Black resistance aimed at demolishing the structures of colonial hegemony and psychopathologies, including oppressive epistemologies that confront the lived experience of Black people in the African diaspora. It examines Biko's revelation, in his diagnosis of the Black condition under white colonial repression, that the prime objective of the colonialist is to conquer the Black mind. It also explores two epistemological dimensions that are present in Biko's philosophy of Black consciousness, namely, affective and political epistemologies. They are both considered from a philosophical angle and the position of praxis, in terms of Black social mobilization and the transformation of oppressive social mechanisms and social structures.

Chapter 9 moves beyond the common but sensational view of Huey P. Newton as the leader of the Black Panther Party, which gained notoriety from its inception in the late 1960s for organizing Black men and women to resist America's oppressive power structure and the systematic injustice against Black folks. This chapter explores the deeply philosophical views of Newton, the principal theoretician of the Party, and places particular emphasis on the philosophical basis of his conception of the notion of Black self-determination and how this orients us toward his views on Black epistemologies of the self. Chapter 10 considers the convergent lines between Black knowledge, Black feminism, and Black resistance by focusing on the ideas of Kathleen Neal Cleaver. Her advocacy of self-determination and the importance of community as necessary elements for organizing and achieving social change is explored to show the connections between knowledge and the transformation of social reality. This chapter also offers an epistemology of Black liberation within the Black radical movement that does not replicate the denigration of Black male revolutionaries often found in aspects of Black feminist scholarship about the Black Panthers.

Currently, in Africana philosophical scholarship, there is no book that explores Black intellectual thought under the rubric of Black epistemology. This book fills that void by making a case for a subdisciplinary study that focuses primarily on Black epistemological thought. It explores two broad categories—namely, Black epistemologies as personal or self-epistemologies, and Black epistemologies as political epistemologies. The first category, Black epistemologies of the self, explores the affective ways in which Black thinkers have conceived of the notion of Black agency concerning thoughts and actions while expressing individual power, and the choices made to transform arduous existential conditions. This exploration investigates the conscious construction of the *knowing self* by Black folks against the assumed episteme of the natural inferiority of an adjudged "worthless" race in the imaginary of Eurocentric and Anglo-American norms of rationality. The second category, which looks at Black epistemology as a form of political epistemology, focuses on the connections between the axes of knowledge and social power, especially emphasizing how Blacks have developed political epistemologies to drive, initiate, and sustain the process of social transformation and the project of racial uplift. The emphasis on the discourse of Black epistemologies is designed to arrive at a new imagination of Blackness—a humanizing vision of Blackness.

This vision entails the encapsulation of the relational connection between the conditions of human knowledge and the conditions of human freedom, as developed by the representative thinkers within the Black intellectual tradition who are explored in this book. The Black epistemological schemes examined here look toward both self-transformation and the sociopolitical reordering of structures of power. This work expands on the phenomenon of human knowledge as a site of Black social and personal transformation. These dynamics between knowledge, self, and social transformation reveal a long tradition of Black epistemological reflections that are currently underrepresented within Africana thought. This book is not just for researchers, instructors, or professors working within the academy; it is also for the general reader who is interested in developing a more robust understanding of the genius contributions of Black people to intellectual history more broadly. I hope this book will serve as a definitive resource that highlights Black thinkers as philosophers who have made significant contributions to the area of philosophy that concerns itself with the phenomenon of human knowledge known as epistemology. The acquisition of authentic knowledge brings freedom from the chains of ignorance. Although the current posture in society seems to glorify ignorance, unfounded emotional reactions, and appearance over the factual representation of reality, there is still freedom in pursuing the truth of history for those that dare to know. My hope is that every person who reads this book will have the courage to face the truth and become free.

1

Black Epistemology and the Derelictical Crisis in Africana Philosophical Thought

From its inception in the early 1970s, formalized discourse in Africana philosophical scholarship in the United States has been plagued by two distinct but related issues. The first concerns the quest by Black intellectuals to fashion a unique philosophical orientation with a vision of disciplinarity that is focused primarily on the thoughts, travails, and lived experiences of African-descended people. The second deals with the delineation of a contextual framework that is required for the evolution of such disciplinary engagement, one that is particularly focused on the articulation of what it means for a philosophy to be born of struggle. In the late twentieth century, classic publications such as "Crisis in Philosophy: The Black Presence" and "The Legitimacy and Necessity of Black Philosophy: Some Preliminary Considerations" by William R. Jones and Cornel West's "Philosophy and the Afro-American Experience" were pivotal in highlighting the issues that confronted Black philosophical scholarship during this period.[1] While Jones, in his 1973 and 1977 publications, argues for a philosophical paradigm that expressly centers the Black experience, West argues for the assimilation of the Black experience within disciplinary theories and Eurocentric canons of thought. For Jones, the urgent task before Black philosophers is to understand that philosophy, by its very nature, is particularized. As such, "Blacks dehumanize themselves if they fail to initiate a philosophical statement that faithfully expresses their experience and culture."[2] In contrast to Jones's suggestion, West maintains that "certain philosophical techniques, derived from a particular [Eurocentric] conception of philosophy, can contribute to our understanding of the Afro-American experience."[3]

The philosophical praxis (that of Martin Heidegger, and later, of Ludwig Wittgenstein and John Dewey) that West recommends for Africana philosophy is fundamentally centered on an extraverted epistemology or an epistemological framework that is dependent on Eurocentric accretions and merely straps along the Black lived experience as an apron string to the Eurocentric experience. Jones vehemently disagrees with West on this point. As Jones sees it, what is at stake here is the power and epistemic authority of *the subject of knowledge* to define reality. Thus, he considers Blacks to be dehumanizing themselves if they do not insist upon the right to make their history the point of departure for philosophizing.[4] The disagreement here on the nature of Black philosophical engagement is not merely about methodology or the appropriate philosophical praxis to document the history of Black intellectual thought; it is also, at its very core, a disagreement on the vision of Blackness or Black humanity held by these thinkers.[5] This disagreement continues to reverberate through the ways in which classical and contemporary Africana or Black philosophers conceive of the thrust of Africana philosophy and the methodology for the documentation of Black intellectual thought.

Other notable Black scholars such as E. Franklin Frazier, Vincent Harding, and Harold Cruse have weighed in on this issue concerning which epistemological framework should frame Black intellectual pursuits. Frazier is famous for his characterization of the African American family as a unique sociological unit that lacks any peculiar cultural model other than the one imposed by white culture. This assumption is contingent upon the consequences of slavery, which, for him, is primarily responsible for the destruction of the African social and cultural heritage. In *The Negro Family in the United States*, Frazier portrayed varying instances of the cultural dislocation that Black slaves experienced to show how difficult it was for slaves, who had retained a memory of their African background, to find a congenial milieu in which to perpetuate their old way of life. That is, this dislocation occasioned a crisis of the self and of *being* that led to other forms of pathological and socially or culturally discordant behaviors and nonassimilationist practices.

Although the conclusions drawn by Frazier highlight the devastating consequences of slavery on the Black experience of dehumanization and the rupturing of authentic African values for Black slaves, they also offer a narrative that portrays the Black experience as encapsulated by white cultural ideals. This is particularly true of his depiction of white cultural models as the "normative" vehicle for cataloging the human experience, or more specifically, for interpreting the Black experience. Frazier's conclusions also raised questions regarding whether Black intellectuals should concern themselves with assimilationist or nonassimilationist approaches to the cataloging of the Black experience in the New World. In the latter parts of the twentieth century, Vincent Harding challenged some of the hypotheses Frazier put forward in his earlier sociological studies, warning against the uncritical acceptance of the wisdom of white America or white cultural ideals as a prism for understanding and interpreting the Black experience. For Harding, the characterization of the Black experience should not be subsumed under the hegemonic knowledge schemes or "wisdom" of white America because "once we recognize and admit that the mass of black[6] people live as unmistakably colonized victims (yet courageously as more than victims) of white America, there is no escape from the knowledge that white America and its systems of domination are the enemy."[7] Harding thinks of the vocation of the Black scholar as the sum of the intellectual efforts that strive to document how the gifts of Black minds are meant to be fully used in the service of the Black community and to combat the various forms of anti-Blackness in society at large.[8]

In *The Crisis of the Negro Intellectual*, Harold Cruse describes the role or vocation of the Black intellectual as a preoccupation that is trapped in a double-bind. This double-bind consists of "the peculiarities of the American social structure, and the position of the intellectual class within it, make the functional role of the Negro [Black] intellectual a special one. The Negro [Black[9]] intellectual must deal intimately with the white power structure and cultural apparatus, and inner realities of the black world at one and the same time."[10] The idea of crisis that Cruse emphasizes here hinges on the complexities embedded in the social reality, including class subtleties or stratifications that invariably influence the framework in which the Black intellectual theorizes. For him, therefore, "the functional role of the Negro [Black] intellectual demands that he cannot be absolutely separated from the black or white world."[11] However, if the causative element of what Cruse refers to as "the cultural identity problem" is the hegemonic imposition of white American values and ideologies as a heuristic for categorizing the Black experience, then an argument can be made that scholarly efforts to break away from this may be viewed as a positive intellectual engagement toward fashioning authentic Black cultural perspectives in a plural world. The foregoing analysis indicates how Black thinkers have visualized the thrust of Black intellectual engagement in the New World. Although these philosophers differ in terms of how and what they conceive as the thrust of Black intellectual engagement, as well as the designation of the task or vocation of the Black scholar, they are united in their efforts to provide some form of conceptual clarification on the nature, scope, and substance of this field of inquiry.

In his classic essay titled "Africana Philosophy,"[12] Lucius Outlaw describes his vision for this field of inquiry as "a gathering notion under which to situate the articulations (writings, speeches, etc.), and traditions of the same, of Africans and peoples of African descent collectively, as well as the sub-discipline- or field-forming, tradition-defining, tradition-organizing reconstructive efforts which are (to be) regarded as philosophy."[13] Although Outlaw maintains that the thrust of this field of inquiry should focus on Africans and peoples of African descent collectively; he would go on to claim that Africana philosophy should also "include the work of those persons who are neither African nor of African descent but who recognize the legitimacy and importance of the issues and endeavors that constitute the philosophizing of persons African or African-descended and who contribute to discussions of their efforts, persons whose work justifies their being called Africanists."[14] What Outlaw is proposing, in more explicit terms, is that the works of European or Caucasian philosophers can be adequately regarded as works of Africana philosophy, insofar as they can justify such works to pertain to the lives of Black people. This means the gamut of scholarship that pertains to the lived experience of Black people can then take on a Eurocentric posture. This onerous position by Outlaw is even more pronounced in his work *On Race and Philosophy*, where he describes the task of Black philosophy as the "quest to revise the philosophical canon to include articulations by African and African-descended thinkers."[15] In the first instance, the revisionist imaginary that Outlaw talks about here plays on the thinking that the hegemonic posture of the "philosophical canon," more specifically the Eurocentric and Anglo-American canon, will wholeheartedly embrace the "inclusion" of Blacks or African descendants within its "hallowed" circles. The racialized and hierarchical epistemological setup of these alien philosophical praxes, which places knowledge schemes produced by white thinkers over and above those produced by people classified as "others," will always be averse to the revisionist-integrationist project that Outlaw had in mind.

Outlaw's proposal that works produced by European or Caucasian philosophers could be counted as works of Africana philosophy was informed by his attempt to escape the challenge of particularity and embrace a more universal appeal in his imagination of a disciplinary focus for Africana philosophy. However, it is difficult to imagine the viability of such kinds of intellectual production envisioned by Outlaw, given the fact that non-Black scholars will not and cannot have a tincture of the Black experience to draw from to make their contributions useful in tackling problems confronting the Black community. Furthermore, Outlaw's description engenders the problem of "epistemological masquerading" described by Carter G. Woodson in *The Mis-Education of the Negro*. Epistemological masquerading is the problem that ensues when Black philosophers and scholars parrot the thoughts of European thinkers as grounds or fodder for studying Black people as a pseudouniversal lens for viewing the world. Woodson acknowledges that the same thought process that inspires and motivates the oppressor with the thought that he is everything and has accomplished everything worthwhile will invariably crush, simultaneously, the spark of genius in Black people by making them feel that their race does not amount to much and will never measure up to the standards of other people.[16] This understanding is what reinforced his position that the anthropological and ontological assumptions of European science such as economics and modern European history deeply misunderstand the actual condition of Black people and cannot address their existential conditions. As Ama Mazama observes, "Eurocentric assumptions of African intellectual inferiority and inadequacy have deep and pervasive roots in modern European intellectual history and concepts."[17] For this reason, Woodson considers the systems of thoughts and intellectual frameworks that are external to the Black lived experience as problematic.

This intellectual debate on the appropriate methodological approach to utilize in the study of Black people within Africana philosophy is also topical in contemporary scholarship. For instance, in "Disciplinary Decadence and the Decolonization of Knowledge," Lewis Gordon articulates a definition of Africana philosophy that he imagines would subvert what he characterizes as the problem of disciplinary decadence—"an inward path of disciplinary solitude."[18] For him, the thrust of Africana philosophy should be on the "the exploration of modern life as understood through contradictions raised by the lived-reality of African Diasporic people. Because such people are often linked to many other communities whose humanity has been challenged, Africana philosophy is also a philosophy that speaks beyond the Africana community."[19] The justification that Gordon cites as the basis for projecting the substantive focus of Africana philosophy beyond Black people has to do with the desire to emphasize the notion of existential plurality and the nexus of human social relationships. However, this may end up obscuring the specific issues and problems of Black people in a world where the devaluation of Blackness is marshaled into the social fabric. There is also the unmistakable, albeit implicit, reference to the specter of universalism or pluralism in the characterization and vision of Africana philosophy within the definition that Gordon articulates, especially the emphasis on "the nexus of human social relationships."

This approach to conceptual universalism in Gordon's scholarship is evident in *Bad Faith and Antiblack Racism*, where Sartrean existential ontology is employed to attempt an "analysis of Blackness as a mode of being beneath the scheme of whiteness in an antiblack world. Yet a conclusion of a Sartrean analysis is that antiblack racism is a contingent (though accidental) feature of our world. There could very well have been an interpretation of Blackness as fullness and whiteness as the emptiness that threatens it."[20] The exploitation of Sartrean existential ontology in this work was aimed at characterizing the specter of anti-Black racism as a form of bad faith. In this imagination, what is considered "existential about racism is that it is a form of bad faith, which is a phenomenological ontological or existential-phenomenological concept."[21] This then brings up the larger issue of the applicability or plausibility of deploying Eurocentric conceptual and philosophical frames, such as Sartre's existentialism, to characterize the Black experience. While it is quite common to see Africana/Black philosophers arguing for the significance of Eurocentric and Americanized ideas in characterizing and qualifying the Black experience, it is rare to see European and American philosophers making similar arguments about using the ideas developed by Black philosophers or intellectuals to interpret existential problems within such a cultural framework.

It is important to note that Gordon's exploration of such a "pluralistic" methodology is motivated by the hope that people will come to the understanding that "these considerations bring us to a matter in which the relationship between bad faith and antiblack racism is of great importance: the problem of legitimacy in the human sciences."[22] What this line of reasoning implies, if followed to its logical conclusion, is that it does not matter what specific philosophical framework, model, or orientation is utilized to represent the Black experience; what truly matters, for Gordon, is the type of questions that are being asked, especially the question of the human—the true kernel of existential philosophy. For him, "existential philosophy addresses problems of freedom, anguish, dread, responsibility, embodied agency, sociality, and liberation; it addresses these problems through a focus on the human condition."[23] He sees Sartre as a philosopher, whose philosophy speaks to and beyond the Africana community. As he argues in *Existentia Africana*, Sartre stands as an unusual catalyst in the history of Black existential philosophy. He describes Sartre as an intellectual-genealogical link or a forerunner of the ideas between Richard Wright and Frantz Fanon (undoubtedly the twentieth century's two most influential Africana existentialist "men of letters") and the historical forces that came into play for the ascendance of European philosophy of existence in the American academy.[24] One wonders how to reconcile this Eurocentric existential philosophical method advocated by Gordon as a framework for understanding Fanon's critical and anticolonial philosophy. We know, for instance, that in *Black Skin, White Masks*, Fanon emphasized "Black Consciousness" as an alternative model of theorizing about the Black lived experience in an anti-Black world. Fanon sees Black consciousness as "immanent in itself," which means that it is its *logos*, episteme, and existential grounding for Blackness, and as such does not require any Eurocentric philosophical frames for interpreting the Black experience. Therefore, Fanon argues that Black consciousness helps him to see that he is fully human; he does "not have to look for the universal."[25]

In a similar vein, Derek Kelly, in "The Logic of Black Philosophy," argues from the perspective of assumed philosophical universalism that since "the point of philosophical theorizing is simply to find some general regulative principles which form a foundation for rationality,"[26] then there could be "no philosophy worth its name [e.g., Black philosophy] which is conditioned by contingent idiosyncrasies such as the color of a man's skin, or of his historical or geographical or social position."[27] That is, if Black philosophy, through an assimilationist imaginary, does not imbibe Eurocentric epistemes and values—as its foundation of *rational inquiry*—it cannot be considered as a system of philosophy that is worth its name. The allusion to the specter of *rationality* as a universal prism for philosophical investigation and experiential documentation, here, is unmistakable. The allusion is akin to aping Eurocentric and Western modes of thinking, with their humanist pretensions, disguised as a mode of studying the reality of the Black experience in an undetached fashion. It is a hegemonic system of thought that is inimical to Black progress because its philosophical starting point does not prioritize the Black lived experience and does not take seriously the thought systems produced by Black intellectuals.

The Politics of Knowledge and the Derelictical
Crisis in Africana Philosophy

The derelictical crisis in Africana/Black philosophy is a crisis of knowledge: a knowledge crisis that is generated by intellectual commitments within Black philosophical scholarship that does not primarily center Black ideas and thought systems as the groundwork for representing Blackness or cataloging the Black experience. Such approaches to Black philosophical scholarship that do not prioritize the intellectual productions of Black people as the groundwork for reasoning and thinking through the problems that confront Black people in the world have been criticized in contemporary Africana philosophical scholarship. In this respect, Tommy J. Curry has been consistent in his critiques of such modes of paradigmatic considerations within the field of Africana/Black philosophy that do not privilege Black people as the grounding for theorization and, consequently, constitute an obstacle to the historiography of Black ideas and systems of thought. Curry refers to this problem as "the derelictical crisis." This consists of the failure of African American philosophy "to inquire seriously into the culturally particular epistemologies of African-descended people, preferring instead to read into Black thought decidedly European philosophical continuities."[28] Curry utilizes the term "epistemological convergence" to highlight this problematic. In his view, "epistemological convergence [is] the phenomenon by which Black cultural perspectives are only given the status of knowledge to the extent that they extend or reify currently maintained traditions of thought in European philosophy."[29]

So, the arguments for the racial normativity of the idea of universal humanism care more about aligning cultural worldviews as structured epistemological systems or epistemological homogeneity of Eurocentrism than privileging the pluralism in cultural-epistemic perspectives. This idea of "normativity" of Eurocentric modalities as the acceptable matrix for codifying human experiences in the world depicts the politics of knowledge such that this epistemological scheme becomes racialized and normalized. On one side, the Eurocentric world view is normalized as the structure for characterizing human knowledge, although it is often framed using the broad language of "normativity." On the other side, the racialized component of the idea of normativity as it pertains to knowledge acquisition explains why it is quite difficult to make sense of the suggestion by some Black intellectuals that the Black lived experience should be subsumed into Eurocentric modalities under the guise of achieving universalism. Using such Eurocentric philosophical schemes to frame knowledge attributions can lead to the erasure of Blacks from being considered serious epistemic subjects.

This problematic also highlights the need for Black intellectual works that take a detour from the epistemological imposition of Western or Euro-American philosophical hegemony on thought systems related to people of African descent within Africana philosophy and reinforce the need to focus the thrust of Black scholarship on Black people. As Molefi Kete Asante notes, the struggle for the disciplinary focus on Black people is not merely a struggle against reactionary forces but also the struggle for the advancement of such kinds of intellectual commitments.[30] Since the hegemonic knowledge regime that reifies traditions of thought in Eurocentric philosophy is extraverted in its orientation, intellectual production and cultural-logic reflections of Black people cannot, under such a system, obtain the status of a fully developed theory of knowledge. Herein lies the relevance of the interventions proposed in this book, which argues for the necessity of a Black epistemological discourse as a new subdisciplinary focus under Africana Philosophy.

The term "Black Epistemology," as I imagine it, primarily focuses on the concerns of Black intellectuals about the phenomenon of human knowledge as it pertains to the questions of the nature, origin, limits, and application of knowledge to the human condition. It engages with the question of who can acquire knowledge, perspectives of truth, and the categorization of epistemic authority in regard to the articulations of the goals of knowledge acquisition. It underscores the importance of considering questions of belief formation from the Black perspective, especially within a discourse community that has, for too long, erased this perspective. It is an approach to epistemological inquiry that takes the Black subject seriously as an epistemological agent capable of engaging in sophisticated deliberations about topics such as the formation of belief, emanating truths, and contesting the idea about whose truth deserves to be granted validation, as well as who gives such validation to knowledge. Put differently, the Black epistemological perspective pursued in this book emphasizes the social epistemological apparatus that draws primarily from the thoughts of Black intellectuals (including figures unlikely to be considered as such) to characterize the spectrum of knowledge systems, thought patterns, and culturological epistemological categories developed in a world that undervalues the intellectual contributions Black people have made to human civilization.

This book posits that knowledge is a site of power as well as a site for transformation. These are the two important Black epistemological axes that are examined here—the *power of knowledge* and the *knowledge of power* exhibited and explored by Black people, both in diasporic contexts and in the New World, aimed toward self-transformation and social change. Thus, the Black epistemological discourse embarked upon in this book explores how Black people, on the one hand, have mastered the *power of knowledge* in extreme conditions of racial, structural, and intellectual oppression to attain self-transformation through the understanding and application of personal epistemologies or self-knowledge, to ultimately achieve the humanization of Blackness.[31] On the other hand, it explores Black people's demonstration of the *knowledge of power* as a heuristic tool to transform their social conditions or change their sociopolitical destinies in a world steeped in endemic doses of anti-Blackness.

This Black epistemological perspective considers the discourse of knowledge as crucial to the question of defining the human, especially the connections between ascriptions of agency and epistemic power regarding how the knowing subject is characterized as the standard for shaping reality, truth, and the world as we know it. In "A Black Studies Manifesto," Sylvia Wynter makes a case for the centrality of the discourse of knowledge when envisioning the future of Black studies. She argues that because the question of knowledge occupies a central place in the definition of what it means to be human, Black studies needs to focus on the discourse of knowledge to undo the dehumanization of Blackness in hegemonic discourses of knowledge. Wynter specifically argues for "a Black Studies hypothesis [which] redefines the human in the following terms: that although *being human* is implemented by the physiological processes of the body—how else? . . . *Being human* can therefore not pre-exist the cultural systems and institutional mechanisms, including the institution of knowledge, by means of which we are socialized *to be* human."[32]

Wynter's arguments emphasize the importance of positioning the epistemological commitments within Africana/Black philosophy toward humanizing Blackness. In other words, taking the thoughts and intellectual contributions of Black folks seriously as epistemological constructs has the potential to undercut hegemonic, cultural, and institutional structures while moving the discourse of knowledge toward the humanization of Blackness. As Jason Ambroise and Sabine Broeck point to in their recently published anthology, *Black Knowledges/Black Struggles,* there is an urgent need to develop a discourse of Black knowledge that transcends the present order of knowing acquiescent to the reification of the Western memory or imaginary—a sort of epistemic disloyalty to the present otherization of knowledge. This epistemic disloyalty should lead to the emergence of a "formidable tradition or strain of 'Black' epistemic work."[33] The discourse of knowledge within the conventional theory of knowledge or epistemology (the present order of knowledge in the Euro-American praxis) has, for the most part, not taken Black epistemic work and Black thought, as well as Black agency, seriously.

The mechanisms of epistemic discourse within this hegemonic framework project epistemological issues and problems as those which primarily concern the analysis of knowledge, questions concerning epistemic agency or doxastic epistemic features, collective mentality, and epistemic authority within a limited Western or Eurocentric individualistic understanding of knowledge and epistemology. These issues are mostly codified and rendered through the de-bodied articulation of such issues, such that knowledge is often abstracted from racial categories of embodied subjectivity and ultimately leads to the erasure of Blackness. What this reveals is that the derelictical crisis includes the politics of knowledge that implicates the allotting of epistemological status to subjects within the present order of knowledge, which tends to frame Black subjects as victims rather than progenitors of knowledge. In *The End of the Cognitive Empire*, Boaventura de Sousa Santos describes this politics of knowledge as a situation whereby "dominant politics becomes epistemological when it is able to make a credible claim that the only valid knowledge available is the one that ratifies its own dominance."[34] In other words, white subjects of knowledge are deemed authorial because they are able to ratify their dominance through the recognition or ratification of their own agency.

This endorsement of the white subject as an authorial credible source of knowledge is well pronounced in Miranda Fricker's popular book titled *Epistemic Injustice: Power and the Ethics of Knowing*. In this text, Fricker explores the social context of knowledge generation and distribution in such a way that Black subjects were represented as victims but not as progenitors of knowledge—in lieu of calling out systems of epistemic injustices and oppressive knowledge practices. However, she maintains that her focus is on "epistemic practices as they are, [and] of necessity, played out by subjects that are socially situated."[35] Black people are only included in her discussion of the intersections of power and the ethics of knowing as "victims" of systems of epistemic injustice (broadly construed as testimonial and hermeneutic injustices). Although Fricker's work has been rightly credited for its emphases on the discriminatory epistemic practices that emanate from different social contexts, including the systems of epistemic injustice or wrongs individuals suffer in their capacity as the subject of knowledge, which is essential to their human value, she locates Black subjects in the position she regards as having a "credibility deficit" without necessarily interrogating the deeper implications of such epistemic assumptions concerning the Black subject.[36]

Fricker's description of the Black subject as an epistemic subject suffering from "credibility deficit" was drawn from her analysis of certain aspects of Harper Lee's *To Kill a Mockingbird*, which she utilized to frame Black people (or "Negroes" as she colloquially cites) as epistemic subjects suffering from deeply rooted anti-Black racist prejudicial attributions of epistemic worthiness, primarily in relation to the "dominant" and authorial white subject. Fricker does not pay critical attention to the signification of the discrimination experienced by the Black subject portrayed in the section she cites from Harper Lee's work. She rehearses a courtroom scene in the fictional text where a young Black man named Tom Robinson, who was falsely accused of a crime he did not commit, was brought to trial. From this scenario, Fricker concludes that "[t]he trial proceedings enact what is in one sense a straightforward struggle between the power of evidence and the power of racial prejudice."[37] However, there are certain faulty assumptions inherent in this conclusion that Fricker draws from the court scene. The first has to do with Fricker's assumption or imagination that Robinson was even considered a human (not to speak of an epistemic agent) within the social context of Jim Crow America and the extreme ways in which Black humanity was undermined under such anti-Black systems of oppression.[38] The historical reality of Black suffering, especially the erasure of Black humanity through violent deaths (lynchings) that were imposed on Black people during this period by the white community, is not reflected in her conclusion. This assumption on the part of Fricker consists of the idea that there is an "intuitive relationship between racial oppression and the character (trustworthiness, truthful, etc.) attributed to the members of racial groups."[39]

The second, faulty assumption concerns other dimensions of discrimination suggested by the scene in question, such as anti-Black misandry, that are absent in Fricker's analysis of the text.[40] That is, the fact that Robinson is Black and male makes him an easy target for being molded into any fantasy that the white court imagines him to be—a malleable epistemic agent that takes on whatever negative stereotypes are projected onto him. Thus, both of these assumptions that Fricker draws from her reading of Harper's text, in an epistemological fashion, are deeply problematic. They fail to account for the undermining of Black agency that makes it impossible for the systems of structural racism embedded in white institutions of power, such as the court, to recognize the humanity and epistemic agency of Robinson, who symbolizes Black folks in the text. Fricker also ignores the problem of Black male vulnerability that is present in the analysis of Robinson's case. He was primarily targeted for being a Black male; he was believed to be guilty of a crime he did not commit because the mere perception of criminalization projected onto Black males is enough to get them convicted or killed. This makes the question of *epistemic failure* based on the prejudice that Fricker highlights irrelevant.

This type of negative ascription of victimhood to Black subjects, present in current epistemological scholarship, is what I like to refer to as "victimhood epistemologies." This phenomenon is also visible in José Medina's "Toward a Foucaultian Epistemology of Resistance." In this work, Medina discusses Black subjects as suffering from credibility deficit (just like Fricker), and the failure of attributing epistemic virtues to Black subjects. He highlights all kinds of mechanisms in white epistemic practices that have contributed to maintaining the repudiation and blocking of Black subjectivities from giving testimony and exercising an epistemic assumption against its credibility. Medina describes the goal of his epistemic project as an attempt to explore multiple venues of epistemic interaction in the white world, from the streets of white suburbs to the lecture halls of the academy, through which Black voices have been traditionally minimized and heavily constrained in their ability to speak about their own experiences.[41] What the works by Fricker and Medina have in common here is the negative standpoint from which Black epistemic subjects are characterized or studied—the standpoint of victimhood epistemologies. Such epistemological works that study Black people from the place of deficit-epistemologies are antithetical to the goal of humanizing Blackness through the discourse of Black cultural, self-expressive epistemologies that is of primary concern in this book.

If the project of humanizing Blackness is going to be achieved, then there has to be a deliberate strategy to move away from such intellectual projects that negatively portray Blackness from a place of epistemological deficit. This strategy should also focus on the rejection of ideas that do not consider Black subjects as primary but secondary epistemic agents, object with effect, only in white schemes. The story of Blackness cannot merely be the story of deficiency, insufficiency, and death. It cannot also be a story of dependency, epistemological decency that may reinforce the stereotype that Black people are not intellectually creative. This book takes a detour from such negative approaches to the study of Blackness in an anti-Black world by exploring the historical intellectual experiences of Black folks, while also presenting a nuanced discussion of the unique postulations of knowledge and systems of thought that they have contributed to the quest for racial uplift and human civilization. History shows that Black intellectuals have been progenitors of knowledge, epistemologists in every sense of the word, even though their written reflections on the nature of knowledge and the use of knowledge to promote human understanding, self, and social transformation—as well as the use of knowledge to break the chains of enslavement, racialized violence, and ignorance—have not been adequately characterized in contemporary Africana/Black scholarship. Thus, this Black epistemological project is crucial to the vision of humanizing Blackness.

Humanizing Blackness: Beyond the Deficit-Epistemological Portraiture of the Black Experience

This book advances an epistemological mode of studying Black people that upholds a humanizing vision of Blackness such that the intellectual productions, knowledge, and thought systems of Black people are taken seriously and considered as foundational principles or social epistemes for navigating the world. In a world where Blackness is thought to be laced with endemic backwardness and human deficiencies, this work becomes crucial in its insistence that the epistemological schemes and principles developed by Black thinkers constitute a veritable resource for forging a humanizing vision of Blackness. It takes a departure from current trends or orientations in Africana philosophical scholarship, antiracist studies, and other critical scholarship that seek to limit Black intellectual production to mere critiques of hegemonic knowledge systems, including systems of structural oppression and anti-Black racism. This book also departs from forms of scholarship that seek to deny the Black epistemological perspective on the assumption of "objectivity."

Such denial is portrayed in Stephen Ferguson's work documenting his reflections on the condition of Blackness and epistemology, with a chapter provocatively subtitled as "the 'Death of Epistemology' in African American Studies."[42] This work depicts an undisguised denial of Afrocentric [Black-centered] ways of looking at the world in favor of a more Eurocentric and alien perspective and describing the place of

Blackness within such a realm, which Fanon refers to as the Manichean world. For Fanon, the Eurocentric-Manichean world is one that is devoid of reason and logicality, and replete with varying forms of epistemic violence disguised as objectivity, truth, normativity, and other idealistic categories. Ferguson argues (albeit incorrectly) that "the Afrocentric notion regarding a Black epistemology and science has to be rejected."[43] His rationale for this position lies in his Eurocentric and hegemonic conceptualization that any forms of knowledge that characterize a people's experience must meet the criteria of "objectivity" and "scientific truth." However, he fails to subject the sources of his assumptions about the notions of "objectivity" and "scientific truth" to critical assessment.

Ferguson primarily derived this notion of a "criterion of objectivity" from the philosophy of Karl Marx. In a section of his work in which he strongly criticizes Afrocentricity as a value-free science, he articulates why he finds Marx and Marxism attractive. As he puts it, "The unity of science and ideology, for Marx, is grounded in an ideology's capacity to approximate objective material reality correctly."[44] Regarding the assumptions that Ferguson makes in reference to a Marxist interpretation of the notion of objectivity and the dismissal of the particularity of the Black experience, we can raise the following critical question: why should Karl Marx be the epistemological grounding for cataloging the material reality of the Black experience? Ferguson does not provide a rationale or any substantive arguments for privileging such Eurocentric philosophical praxis as the theoretical prism for articulating the Black experience. However, we can also flip the question around and ask whether the thoughts of Black intellectual stalwarts like W.E.B. Du Bois can constitute the epistemological grounding for the "objective" articulation and expression of the epistemological worldview for all Europeans. This clearly shows Ferguson's acquiescence to hegemonic scholarship and Eurocentric dogma, disguised as "critique." In my view, this type of trite scholarship does not help to humanize Blackness; in fact, it dehumanizes Blackness through the subjugation and substitution of how Black people have cataloged their own experiences into alien interpretive frames like those of Marx, as suggested by Ferguson.

Some sociologists of knowledge and social epistemologists have flippantly reduced the rigor of Black scholarship to mere "analysis." The emphasis on the "analysis" of the harrowing and dehumanizing conditions of Black folks in the New World has led some sociologists of knowledge like Joe Feagin to characterize Black thinkers, in a reductionist fashion, not as creators or producers of knowledge but as "activists," "critics," or "analysts." For instance, in *Racist America,* Feagin describes Black intellectuals such as Frederick Douglass, W.E.B. Du Bois, Anna Julia Cooper, Ida B. Wells-Barnett, and Kwame Ture as activists (as troublemakers).[45]

He also argued that one of the "gifts" of Black folks to white/Western civilization is the development of the "critique of institutional racism." It is quite interesting to note that he sees these gifted Black intellectuals not as creators of knowledge but as thinkers who were mainly focused on critiquing the flaws and racism within Western civilization. Feagin essentially offers a narrative that erroneously characterizes Black thinkers as merely interested in pointing out the problems and contradictions of white civilization. This undermines the greater commitment to Black self-development and social change that overwhelmingly informs the intellectual commitments of these Black thinkers. It also does not take into consideration the plethora of scholarship produced by these Black thinkers that goes beyond mere critiques and analyses of white people's moral/racist flaws, especially the aspects of their intellectual works that are primarily focused on improving the lived experience of Black people. Even within Black intellectual history, works that are promoted as offering "new perspectives" on the Black intellectual tradition describe Black thinkers and scholars in an essentialist fashion as "activists."[46]

Similarly, in *The Epistemology of Resistance,* José Medina discusses the criteria for knowledge, with an idea of resistance subjectivity and resistant subjects. As he describes it, resistant subjects are active subjects who exert resistance. They live under conditions of oppression, however they happen to inhabit contexts of domination.[47] Within this analytical frame of reference devised by Medina, Black subjects would only be able to achieve some epistemic justice or attain some kind of epistemic virtue if and only if they are embroiled in some perpetual mix of struggle within everyday praxis. There is a negative orientation attached to this conceptualization of resistant subjects such that Black subjects cannot be imagined as creators of knowledge but as subjects struggling to be perceived as "worthy" epistemic agents. The limitation of ascribing knowledge production to the axis of a struggle between the oppressed and the oppressor suggests a loop that does not mirror other considerations and possibilities of knowledge production.

Scholarship of this kind, which advocates an intellectual preoccupation with Black philosophy focused on "sanitizing" racist ideas, or which privileges epistemological categories within Western, Eurocentric, or American philosophical schemes, contributes to the deficit-epistemological portraiture of the Black experience. It is important to emphasize that within intellectual history, Black thinkers have not merely been responding to these pathological narratives, victimhood characterizations, and caricatures masqueraded as "social truths" or framed in the tainted language of "objectivity"; they have been more interested in showing aspects of the Black lived experience that emphasize dimensions of knowledge and learning, which are crucial in the project of racial uplift. The works and thoughts of the Black intellectuals pursued in the subsequent chapters reveal that Black intellectuals have been concerned with epistemological questions and their application to the Black condition in a world that is set up to perpetually negate Black humanity and relegate the Black experience to the dustbin of history. It is only when we look at the actual writings, reflections, and philosophical ruminations of Black intellectuals that we can fully and deeply appreciate the gamut of epistemological contributions they have made to human progress. This highlights the importance of the advancement of an epistemological perspective that humanizes Blackness by focusing on the knowledge schemes created by Black people within the Black intellectual tradition.

2

The Erasure of the Black
Subject in Eighteenth- and
Nineteenth-Century Racialized
Discourse of Knowledge

In the manner that the discourse of knowledge was structured in the eighteenth and nineteenth centuries, Blackness was deemed a conceptual impossibility and an erased specter owing to the fact that the epistemological lens used to measure the criteria for knowing and the credence given to a knower were mainly restricted on the basis of membership of the white race. It was basically a period when the articulation of the phenomenon of knowledge was racialized. The conceptual schemes upon which categories of human thought were constructed were decided based on fixed markers of identity such as a person's ethnic affiliation, race, age and gender. This order of knowledge was designed to achieve the erasure of Blackness from the discourse of knowledge. This is invariably an erasure of the humanity of the Black subject, since part of what it means *to know* is deeply connected to the question of being. That is, to be human is to be able to avow systems of thought, consciously project categories into the world, and to demonstrate epistemic authority over naming *what is* and *what is not*. As such, if the Black subject does not feature in the imaginations of what it means to possess such power to avow knowledge claims in the realm of existence, the humanity of the Black subject is considered deficient in some form, or deformed in this imaginary.

It is often taken for granted that the characterization of knowledge frequently assumes that the knower is always rational, intelligible, and possesses the capacity to claim awareness of observable and abstract realities. This was not the case for Black subjects within the historical context under consideration. The eighteenth and nineteenth centuries were a time when Blackness was erased because it could not participate in the "space of reason." The "space of reason" is a metaphor that alludes to the Eurocentric order of "objective" knowledge that grounds epistemic authority and the power of knowledge in the "rational self," mainly abstracted but powerful subjects. These subjects are constructed to be powerful because they are categorized as possessing an ontological status that naturally emits attributes such as reasonability, knowability, discernment, and judgment. Under this imaginary, the "space of reason" becomes a site of struggle that generates the crisis of knowledge between the *ontologized being* and the *deontologized (negated) being* in terms of the criteria for ownership of the process of knowledge production. In such a rational "space of reason," only one system of bifurcated logic exists, and this is premised on the division between the knowing subject (rational being) and the unknowing subject (irrational being). This suggests that the philosophical foundations of rationality in Western philosophical praxis have serious ontological implications for the conception of the Black subject in relation to knowledge or knowing.

Such ideological constructions aim to produce self-consciousness as this enables subjects to know what they are capable of doing and becoming. Boundaries must be known, and a free subject would be able to desire and achieve what can rationally be expected, given the limitations.[1] The underside of this is that it places the Black subject outside the limit of knowledge based on the overemphasis on bodily markers of identity and being rather than the functions of the mind that the Eurocentric "abstracted" subject, or *ego*, enjoys. In other words, the physical features of the Black subject, such as skin coloration and other pseudo-scientific, physiological projections, obstruct any considerations that may envision Blackness with knowledge. The ontological erasure of Blackness is not only abstract but also material, such that the Black subject is seen as the negative pathology, the Other who is placed outside the margins of the community of life.[2] The critical question to raise here concerns how, in the absence of genuine and irrefutable knowledge, Blackness became associated, in this ideological framework, primarily with somatic features, to the point where the three other categories— the idealistic, rational, and ontological status—have been reduced to somatic characteristics as a purported way of knowing with certainty.[3]

In *On Reason: Rationality in a World of Cultural Conflict and Racism*, Emmanuel Eze considers the reduction of the Black subject to somatic or bodily features as something that is realized through the overemphasis on "reason" in an attempt to glorify the "heroism" of interventions of Western scientific methods while grappling with the pathologies often generated through a race-based lens. By implication, all interventions developed to grapple with the outcomes of such a method become fundamentally tainted, since they are developed through negative racial stereotypes. This is how knowledge construction is associated with the deformation of Blackness through the overemphasis on bodily makers in hegemonic contexts. It is the construction of a state of existence that perpetually seeks to categorize Black subjects as social problems rather than as knowledgeable subjects. In such a society, Eze argues, the Black body is adjudged to be the signification of experience of the racialized Other, such that it is considered a legitimate practice of intellectual work to "treat" Blackness as the ontological and biological harbinger of negative pathologies.

After all, from a racialized mind or a racialized philosophical standpoint, such as that of Western epistemology, the connection between the moral problem of social ills and other negative realities is easily attributable to the existence of bodies that are deemed to be outside of the bounds of humanity.[4] This exposes the grounds for anti-Blackness and the pathologizing of Blackness in contemporary epistemological discourse. This phenomenon is what Calvin Warren, in "Black Nihilism and the Politics of Hope," describes as anti-Black epistemology. For Warren, "anti-black Epistemology is somewhat schizophrenic in its aim: it at once portrays blackness as an anti-grammatical entity—paradoxically, a *non-foundation*-foundation that provides the condition of possibility for its own existence—and at the same time, and in stunning contradiction, it forces a translation of this anti-grammar into a system of understanding that is designed to exclude it."[5] This characterization of dominant epistemology that favors anti-Black codification is inherently violent—this violence consists of the attempt to advance a discursive and linguistic unification—to establish a unifying ground of language or reason—that places Blackness outside the customary framework of life and culture, and outside the domain of avowal of epistemic states in the world.

The overemphasis on bodily markers of the Black subject in the discourse of knowledge can also be considered as a form of both epistemic violence and deadly objectification that may lead to a violation of the integrity of the Black body. This objectification raises the issue of Black invisibility and hypervisibility as modes of further erasure of the body's integrity; it also raises issues around the constitutive and constructive semiotic, material, and sociopolitical processes that hail and fix the white body as normative, thus reinforcing the importance of the social "ontological space white *ego* generates and maintains, that requires the eluding of the humanity of Black people."[6] What is being explored in the foregoing is the notion that the undermining of the humanity of Black people in Eurocentric/Anglo-American knowledge spheres was achieved through empirical and nonempirical arguments—emphatically, through embodied and disembodied framing of the Black subject as ontologically defective and incapable of possessing knowledge.

In *The World and Africa*, W.E.B. Du Bois describes this tendency to merely glorify the humanity of Europeans through the denigration of people of non-European descent in the study of the history of human civilization as the greatest tragedy of the world, especially in the later parts of the nineteenth century and earlier periods of the twentieth century. As Du Bois argues, this tragedy, which led to the collapse of Europe in the early twentieth century, ought to be astounding because of the boundless faith which was hitherto accorded to European civilization. This is the long-held belief, held without argument or reflection, that the cultural and intellectual status of people of Europe and North America represented not only the best civilization that the world had ever known but also a goal of human effort destined to go on from triumph to triumph until the perfect accomplishment was reached.[7] By implication, this assumption of the supremacy of European civilization over and above non-European civilizations further reinforced the contemporary binaries that are drawn between the knowledge systems produced within Eurocentric cultural praxis and those produced "outside" of that praxis. It also reinforced the idea of the distinction between inferior and superior beings in terms of epistemological achievements.

So, Du Bois's reflection illustrates how Blackness was eschewed from the considerations of the historical-genealogical documentation of ideas and intellectual schemes because of the hegemonic centering of what it means to be "human" and "civilized," which does not include the Black subject, when simultaneously considered. This notion that Black people were rightly excluded from the chronicling of knowledge in cultural history on intellectual grounds was generally accepted as common and indubitable knowledge in the nineteenth century. However, Du Bois rubbished this notion of excluding Black folks from the chronicling of historical contributions to human civilization by arguing that although it is almost universally assumed that history can be truly written without reference to Black people, this assumption is scientifically unsound and also dangerous for logical social conclusions.[8] But how was this exclusion achieved, rationalized, and justified? I engage with this question by tracing the roots of the idea of the Black subject as defective or deformed within the Eurocentric regime of knowledge rooted in eighteenth- and nineteenth-century race theory.

The Deformation of Blackness: The Disguise of Biological Racism as Social Epistemology in Eighteenth- and Nineteenth-Century Race Theory

The predominant social epistemologies developed in the context of eighteenth- and nineteenth-century race theory by American theorists, anthropologists, and scientists deployed a "master narrative" that caricaturized Blackness as an unformed or deformed category of being. That is, the collective epistemologies formed in this period about Black subjects were aimed at the denial of Black intellectual gifts and abilities as well as the denial of Black humanity. During this period, ethnology was regarded as the eminent science in American culture because it created a classification system that categorized the human and established a hierarchy among the races through an overemphasis on physiological features as well as through the deducing of personality traits and the measurement of intellectual abilities through cranial information. For instance, in an essay titled "Some Observations on the Psychological Differences Which Exist among the Typical Races of Man," published in the journal *Transactions of the Ethnological Society of London* in 1865, Robert Dunn argued that because the anterior lobe of the brain in Blacks is larger than that of the European, in proportion to the middle lobe, Black folks are intellectually and morally inferior to the European. He affirms that when the cranial differences of the Negro are contrasted with the complexity, irregularity, and asymmetrical character that is presented on the brain of the European, it warrants "a legitimate inference, that unlike in the Negro and the Indian, the nervous apparatus of the perceptive and intellectual consciousness falls short of that fulness, elaboration [of the European], and complexity of his manifestations, both intellectually and morally."[9]

What is clear from Dunn's argument is the systematic attempt to perfect the argument for the inferiorization of the so-called "inferior races" (Negro and Indian) through scientific conjurations built from cranial measurements in nineteenth-century ethnology. Melissa Stein expands on this in *Races of Men: Ethnology in Antebellum America*, arguing that this systematic inferiorization had serious racial and masculinist implications since, "in the antebellum period, when racial scientists spoke of a race or races, they usually meant men specifically, although that was not always immediately apparent. Much of the literature in the field was written in what psychologists and linguists refer to as the 'masculine generic'—that is, 'man' and 'mankind' to mean all of humankind."[10] What this means is that ethnology's development as a field was one in which masculinity was simultaneously central and implicit, even though most of the discussions about the hierarchy of being were conceived from the standpoint of the white-black binary, such that, "in the black-and-white world of antebellum ethnology, the white race was normative whereas the black race was scrutinized for evidence of difference and deviance."[11]

Ethnology, as understood by nineteenth-century anthropologists, limited its investigations to the rudimentary beginnings of human society. Essentially, ethnology was the comparative and developmental study of "social man and his culture." Concerned with the science of culture, the ethnologist enumerated the conditions and modes of existence of specific non-Western peoples and only touched tangentially upon the contemporary problems of Western life.[12] The work by Buckner H. Payne, who wrote under the pseudonym "Ariel," titled *The Negro: What Is His Ethnological Status?* is a good example of a document that shows how ethnologists focused their racializing science on characterizing the modes of existence of non-Western peoples. In this work, Ariel presented a defense of the ontological distinctions between the white race and the Black race (the two races of men existing on earth), which he believed were largely manifested in the physiological distinctions that are more accessible to "empirical" investigations and measurable "scientific" conclusions. In Ariel's description, ethnologically speaking, the prominent characteristics and differences of these two races are as we now find them—peoples of the white race have long, straight hair, high foreheads, high noses, thin lips, and white skin. Peoples of the Negro or Black race are woolly- or kinky-haired and have low foreheads, flat noses, thick lips, and black skin.[13]

Ariel eventually moved from the presentation of arguments of physiological differences between the Black and white races to construct an argument for the superiority of the white race by divine design in his exegetical musings.[14] Ariel argued that God, in making Adam to be the head of creation, intended to distinguish, and did distinguish, his creation with eminent grandeur and notableness over and above everything else that had preceded it. Thus, the Black race is merely the background of the picture that concretizes the power of the white race in the world, signifying its dominion over the earth, as the darkness was the background of the picture of creation, before and over which light, God's light, should forever be seen.[15] What we see from the assumptions imbued in Ariel's writings (and similar writings of this kind) in the eighteenth and nineteenth centuries in the United States are the foundations of the deformation of Blackness.

These types of thinking were pervasive during the antebellum period and were generally held as socially formulated truths, acceptable knowledge that was used to shape the regimes of rewards and punishment within society as well as to distinguish the domain of the human. Samuel George Morton, a highly regarded American paleontologist and medical director, who was one of the leaders of ethnology in the nineteenth century, compiled a "scientific" manuscript published in 1855 titled *Types of Mankind*, where he argued that, based on cranial data collected from mostly human skulls, Black people were biologically inferior to Europeans.[16] This work was praised for containing well-executed lithographic plates of numerous crania, of natural size, and for presenting a highly regarded specimen of American art. The text includes accurate measurements of the crania, especially of their interior capacity; the latter was calculated using a plan peculiar to Morton, which enabled him to estimate with precision the relative amount of brain matter in various races.[17] Even though he specifically stated that a large part of the skulls he collected for his research came from dead birds and reptiles, his conclusions about the inferiority of Blacks, believed to have been deduced from cranial data, were not rendered invalid. Morton's work was highly praised as one of the most sophisticated scientific (ethnological) studies on the inequality of the human races. His study was not discredited because it aligned with the social epistemologies and scientific assumptions in antebellum America. The work tremendously contributed to shaping the nature of collective knowledge, including common sense, consensus, and common group, communal, and impersonal knowledge, within the context of nineteenth-century ethnological theory.

At the time of its publication, Morton's work on biological racism was hailed as the most extensive and valuable contribution to the natural history of mankind that had yet appeared on the American continent and it was cordially received by scientists, not only in the United States but in Europe. It became the socially accepted episteme in regard to the determination of what kinds of humans can possess knowledge and can demonstrate intellectual abilities. It also became the widely accepted view of the differences between human personality traits and other natural tendencies. Houston S. Chamberlain, another prominent ethnologist, would advance the thoughts of Morton and his fellow race theorists, at the turn of the century, to argue that other racial groups are inferior to the white race, which makes it impossible for them to assimilate into Western culture. In his seminal work titled *Foundations of the Nineteenth Century*, Chamberlain argued that inferior races such as Blacks and the American Indians possess limited knowledge and are an inadequately developed civilization. His prejudiced analysis of European culture, which accords the greatness and creativity of Europe to Western Aryan peoples but characterizes Jewish peoples as having a negative influence on European civilization, greatly influenced Hitler.[18]

Since the very idea of the ethnological theories developed by white biologists in the nineteenth century was aimed at erasing nonwhite peoples from the domain of the human, it follows that the concept of human progress during this period was primarily restricted to a European and Anglo-American cultural matrix. As such, the biological racism that was developed within the context of nineteenth-century race theory in America largely shaped society's newfound social epistemology, which holds that human uniqueness has had an enormous impact upon the world because it has established a new kind of evolution to support the transmission across generations of learned knowledge and behavior. In *The Mismeasure of Man*, Stephen Jay Gould describes this phenomenon as the upshot of social Darwinism. He argues that the concept of evolution transformed human thought during the nineteenth century because nearly every question in the life sciences was reformulated in its light. No idea was ever more widely used, or misused ("social Darwinism" as an evolutionary rationale for the inevitability of poverty, for example). Both creationists and evolutionists could exploit artifacts such as cranial data to make invalid and invidious distinctions among groups.[19] What Gould mentions here concerning the invidious distinctions among groups is instructive because of the horrible history of American enslavement of Blacks, which was justified within a culture that espouses "Christian values" using such "false" scientific ethnological theories.

The exploration of how biological racism informed the dominant social epistemologies in the eighteenth and nineteenth centuries is important in this chapter because it exposes the set of concepts used to rationalize and help justify the value system upon which the idea of racial inferiority rested in American thought. The idea of racial inferiority as the upshot of this racializing science—the science of ethnology and paleontology—was to make concretized conclusions about the inferiority and superiority of the races during this period that were primarily geared toward the deformation of Blackness. During this period, the notion of "reason" became the hallmark of intelligibility and the ultimate consideration for membership or classification in the human community. In this regard, "reason" was not considered an innate human attribute that is possessed by "all" humans; rather, it was considered as a socially ascribed attribute belonging primarily to those who have European cultural heritage and nothing more. In other words, the idea of "reason" was not regarded as something that all humans innately possess, rather, it was designed as something to be allotted based on group associations. So, "reason" or "reasonability" became the foundational precept in social epistemology by which nonwhite individuals or subjects were removed or erased from the domain of knowledge as well as from the domain of being.

This biological racism espoused by Euro-American ethnologists and social theorists was informed by the dominant racialized epistemologies developed by the early modern philosophers, especially the works from the mid-seventeenth century through the eighteenth century that focused on the concept of human understanding. During this period, "reason" and "reasonability" (understood as the prerogative of Europeans), were considered the greatest value of humanity. Early Modern philosophy, in line with the manifest racism in Western sciences of the human and social epistemologies, projected "rationality" as the hallmark of intellectual superiority while restricting this to white subjects alone. For instance, David Hume (1711–1776), the eighteenth-century Scottish philosopher, was among the first noted authors to profess the polygenic theory of racism. He did so as part of his "inductive" naturalistic philosophy, or experimental philosophy. It was such racial prejudice that inspired Hume to write in the footnote to his essay "Of National Characters" (1753), that nonwhites, especially Blacks, are naturally inferior to whites.[20]

Hume, who is considered among the most important figures in the history of Western philosophy and the Scottish Enlightenment, advocated the separate creation and innate inferiority of nonwhite peoples.[21] In his *Essays and Treatises on Several Subjects*, published in 1758, Hume argued thus:

I am apt to suspect the negroes, and in general all the other species of men (for there are four or five different kinds) to be naturally inferior to whites. There never was a civilized nation of any other complexion than white, nor even any individual eminent either in action or speculation. No ingenious manufacturers amongst them, no arts, no sciences. On the other hand, the most rude and barbarous of the whites, such as the ancient GERMANS, the present TARTARS, have still something eminent about them, in their valour, form of government, or some other particular. Such a uniform and constant difference could not happen, in so many countries and ages, if nature had not made an original distinction betwixt these breeds of men. Not to mention our colonies, there are NEGROE slaves dispersed all over EUROPE, of which none ever discovered any symptom of ingenuity; tho' low people, without education, will start up amongst us, they talk of one negro as a man of parts and learning; but 'tis likely he is admired for very slender accomplishments, like a parrot, who speaks a few words plainly.[22]

Apart from the fact that Hume's expressed thoughts cited here are virulently racist, it laid the groundwork for the ideas concerning the assumed inferiority of nonwhites using markers of racial hierarchy like "skin complexion," "artistic or literary productions," and other physiological markers that were formulated and concretized in nineteenth-century race theory. When Hume talks about education, he thinks of it as inextricably tied to the ability to reason. So, he sees education, or the lack thereof, as a marker of racial superiority or inferiority between whites and nonwhite peoples. In this regard, he is signifying "reason" as the ultimate marker for what it means to be human. Following in Hume's footsteps but adding and enveloping similar racist ideas into a whole system of philosophical thought, Immanuel Kant essentially created a racist anthropology based on skin color. Kant, who is acknowledged as one of the most influential philosophers of the Enlightenment, is also regarded as the father of the modern concept of race and scientific racism.[23] Kant's theory of race corresponded to intellectual ability and limitation. He included the typical color-coded races of Europe, Asia, Africa, and Native America, differentiated by their degree of innate talent. In Kant's theory, the "pure" nature of the white race guarantees its rational and moral order, which is why they are in the highest position of all creatures, followed by yellow, Black, and then red peoples. Nonwhites cannot exhibit reason and rational moral perfectibility through education.[24]

J. C. Lavater, the acknowledged physiognomist, drew from the "philosophical" and anthropological teachings of Kant (which he regarded as excellent) regarding the distinctions of the races to construct a discourse of difference, where non-Europeans (including Blacks), were characterized as inferior to Europeans.[25] Blackness, in the manner that J. C. Lavater's Kant-inspired imagination conceives of it, is nothing but a collection of odious sensory or bodily reactions and characterizations. The restriction of Blackness to this realm suggests a limitation of Blackness to the domain of the irrational and unintelligent, which is made apparent in Lavater's assertion that "[t]he Guinea negroes are extremely limited in their capacities. Many of them appear to be wholly stupid; or, never capable of counting more than three, remain in a thoughtless state if not acted upon, and have no memory."[26] Basically, Lavater invokes Kant as one of the intellectual sources for his thoughts to achieve two ends. The first is aimed at maintaining the unity of the conclusions drawn in the eighteenth century and reinforced in nineteenth-century ethnology that reduce Blackness to somatic features, and the second is geared toward the reinforcement of the racial hierarchy between the white race and other races in the world through an overemphasis on physiological differences construed in physiognomic terms as "defects."

Kant was one of the philosophers whose writings significantly shaped the Enlightenment period, which later became known as "the Age of Reason" for its apparent emphasis on the value of reason in shaping human existence.[27] During this period, "reason" was considered the principal essence of human existence, albeit exclusive to beings. So, the notion of rationality during this period was not aimed at an inclusive humanism; it was aimed at divining the notion of exclusive humanism, where all nonwhites can be categorized outside the classification of the human. Although Kant wrote about and taught lessons in philosophical anthropology for a long time (over forty years) in Königsberg (also known as "the State of the Teutonic Order" in eastern Germany, before 1945), where he espoused views about the intellectual and biological inferiority of Blacks, there was no historical record of him physically seeing a Black person in his lifetime. Yet, he was considered one of the authorities in modern philosophical anthropology and an expert on the geography of human races. In *Menschenkunde: oder Philosophische Anthropologie (Human Science: or Philosophical Anthropology)*, Kant writes that "the race of the Negroes, one could say, is completely the opposite of the [white] Americans; they are full of affect and passion, very lively, talkative and vain. Even though they lacked the capacity of reason, they can be educated but only as servants (slaves); that is if they allow themselves to be trained."[28] It is clear from this assertion that Kant does not think of Blacks as humans who possess the "gift" of reason who can make knowledge claims just like the white subject.

In "The Struggle to Define and Reinvent Whiteness," Joe Kincheloe argues that the Enlightenment's idea of reason was so hegemonic that it sought to construct Europeans/beings/humans as entities that transcend the geospatial notion of time and space and grounded itself as the foundational precept for knowing the world as it is. Kincheloe makes the following argument:

> A dominant impulse of whiteness took shape around the European Enlightenment's notion of rationality with its privileged construction of a transcendental white, male, rational subject who operated at the recesses of power while concurrently giving every indication that he escaped the confines of time and space. In this context whiteness was naturalized as a universal entity that operated as more than a mere ethnic positionality emerging from a particular time, the late seventeenth and eighteenth centuries, and a particular space, Western Europe. Reason in this historical configuration is whitened and human nature itself is grounded upon this reasoning capacity. Lost in the defining process is the socially constructed nature of reason itself, not to mention its emergence as a signifier of whiteness. Thus, in its rationalistic womb whiteness begins to establish itself as a norm that represents an authoritative, delimited, and hierarchical mode of thought.[29]

Perhaps one of Kincheloe's most instructive assertions is this: "Reason in this historical configuration is whitened and human nature itself is grounded upon this reasoning capacity."[30] In other words, the ability to reason is only ascribed to humans if they belong to the white racial group—it is not even a function of biology or science per se—rather, it is a function of what has been socially accepted as the normative principle behind the ascription of knowledge. However, it does not stop at affirming the agency, knowability, and humanity of those who belong to these group associations; it goes further to lay this down as the foundational qualitative yardstick for measuring humanity as a whole. This is what Kincheloe meant by the term "socially constructed nature of reason." It can also be regarded as a form of social epistemology, one that utilizes the preset mechanism of "reason" or "reasonability" as the ultimate measure of what it means to be human and what it means to be something else—"not-human," the Other, and other fictional categories that can be imagined within this system of thought.

Blackness Unbound: Beyond the Deformation of Blackness

What this historical exegesis shows is that epistemology, as developed within the Western philosophical canon, has been more about constructing a social system of knowledge or dialogical formation, often backed by the authority of science, that captures the ruminations of the Western/European man/human/being, as well as the attributions of the functions of the mind. This social system of knowledge production was historically constructed to eschew Blackness from the domain of knowledge and make it impossible to negotiate the conditions of livity for Black folks. It reveals how anthropological assumptions—functional and structural arguments made by European social biologists, ethnologists, and paleontologists within this cultural praxis—were informed by the epistemological preoccupation of philosophers, especially regarding how the notion of "reason" was constructed as a mechanism for humanism and social power. So, it is not the attributes of the mind that take preeminence in the questions about what can be known, but essentially who has the power to determine *what* can be known. It is about epistemic power—the power to affirm as well as the power to negate. Western anthropologists took the liberty of constructing "scientific" theories to "prove" that Blacks cannot develop rational faculty or intellectual competence to grasp the abstract realities of nature. They went as far as advancing these views as the ultimate social reality or truth, even though most of the conclusions they reached were drawn out of sheer imaginative, fictitious, and unfounded assumptions where Black people were often constructed as "unfortunate" victims of the knowledge acquisition process.

This historical exegesis on the racial origins of social epistemology explains why it is unreasonable to make inquisitions under this Eurocentric regime of knowledge. The ultimate objective of the biological racism that was peddled as social epistemology in the eighteenth and nineteenth centuries was to ensure the deformation of Blackness. It gave birth to the generally held belief of Black inferiority based on the criteria of "reason," which was used to ultimately determine those to whom the gift of intellect and the classification of "human" would be either denied or extended. In academic circles today, a commonly expressed view on the racial origins of knowledge discourse holds that even though nineteenth-century race theory was primarily focused on destroying Blackness, through the force of sheer intellectual and epistemic violence, such a disparaging legacy ought to be "sanitized" to accommodate previously excluded communities, such as Blacks. This position reeks of intellectual arrogance because it presupposes that those Western hegemonic ideas, theories, and theoretical assumptions should be the "privileged" lens through which Blackness should be framed in the pursuit of knowledge. It is also an extension of the logic of the epistemic violence that seeks to propagate the erasure of Blackness from the discourse of knowledge through the use of the tainted notion of "rationality."

This historical legacy that thrives on the exclusion of Blackness also manifests in contemporary discussions about the foundations of knowledge and other aspects of knowledge attribution generally. As constructed in the present order of knowledge, epistemic power to avow knowledge claims in the world is mainly characterized as the exclusive privilege of the "self" or the "authorial abstracted self," whose signification is the white/European/Anglo-American subject that ascribes rationality to *itself* and establishes its authority to universally avow epistemic categories. From Hegel's *absolute spirit* to Cartesian *ego cogito*, the historical and ontological trajectory of philosophical ideas propagates this idea of the exclusivity of "rationality." This is the ontological side of the attribution of "reason" to the knowing subject that is concealed in contemporary analytic epistemology. As John Agnew observes in "Know-Where: Geographies of Knowledge of World Politics," "knowledge creation and dissemination are never innocent of at least [some] ontological commitments, be they provincial, class, gender, identity, or something else."[31] This human subject is often characterized within this praxis as self-evident and abstracted from the body, which is essential to maintaining its epistemic power or "authorial dominance" even within metaphysical or transcendental realms. Lindon Barrett, in *Racial Blackness and the Discontinuity of Western Modernity*, argues that this schematic, where knowledge is said to consist of self-evident abstracted forms, is how Blackness was systematically erased from the discourse of knowledge in Western modernity because Blackness is relegated to the realm of a material agency or bodily functions.

In Barrett's view, the distinctions between the human subject and the human body are precisely the enabling and exclusionary inventions of the modern episteme, rather than self-evident forms of worldly agency. He argues further that the epistemic space and the disjunction between epistemes cannot be explained through recourse to the human subject as a given and the human body as a constant. For Barrett, René Descartes's *Meditations on First Philosophy* exemplifies this erasure of

Blackness through the abstraction of forms of knowledge in the mid-seventeenth century, especially the Cartesian emphasis on the human subject as that which is not a "natural" phenomenon at all, but rather the confounding, animating abstraction always ascertainable by its contradistinction to the natural, as most immediately represented by the material agency of the human body.[32] In one of his key philosophical writings, "On the Principles of Human Knowledge," Descartes articulates his emphasis on the primacy of mental properties in the process of knowledge acquisition by putting forward the argument that since we certainly observe many more qualities in our mind than in any other thing, such as the body, the consciousness of thought that is produced by the mind is more exciting and significant than any consideration one may have for the body.[33]

Here, Descartes describes why he thinks the knowledge of "a knowing mind" is better than that of a "body," thereby laying the foundation for the bifurcation between the human subject/knowing subject as an abstract entity, distinguished from the material agency of the human body within the Eurocentric discourse of knowledge that was popularized in the mid-seventeenth century. This later became the marker of existential distinctions between human subjective experiences, which turned out to be premised upon the binaries of "Self" and the "Other," where the "Self" is believed to possess the dominant or authorial epistemological features like intuition, rationality, and basic foundational beliefs, and the "Other" is considered as incapable of exhibiting such distinguishing features.

This shows the subjective need to establish control over the processes of the mind, in terms of its intuitive capacities, while at the same time projecting control over the external world via the social construction of reality. In his collection of essays published under the title *Knowledge, Power, and Black Politics*, Mack C. Jones emphasized the point that such knowledge, which is dichotomized in this binary of "Self" and "Other," mostly serves a people's needs for anticipation and control to the extent that people or even societies construct certain epistemic positions to meet their needs, by any means necessary.[34] Thus, it is through the postulation of this idea of "Self" consciousness or the "abstracted self" that the Black subjective process of knowledge acquisition is undermined in the present discourse of knowledge. The fact that the European and Anglo-American philosophers put themselves in the position of knowledge avatars that can give the status of knowledge to intellectual productions within this frame is a depiction of tremendous epistemic power. This is a self-ascribed epistemic power that leads to metaphysical determinism and epistemic discrimination, such that "what counts as knowledge is determined not to the extent that it accurately depicts the set of relations in the world, but to the extent that it takes up an ideological perspective from which the world is to be viewed. This consideration does not necessitate that Black thought derives from European thinkers but maintains that for Black thought to gain a philosophical status, it must be describable by an established European philosophical stream of thought."[35] This subordination of Black epistemological perspectives is akin to what Fanon describes as the imposition of an existential deviation on Blacks by white/European philosophical streams of thought and culture.

A confrontation of this imposition of existential deviation is essential through the exploration of the notion of the "Black knowing self." One of the cardinal issues that is under consideration in this chapter concerns how the historical legacies of biological racism, purveyed as social epistemology and the scheme of contemporary discourse on knowledge, was deployed to deny the "gift" of rationality and humanity to Black subjects. This also contributed to undermining the value of the tomes of works and philosophical reflections produced by Black thinkers, in which they developed epistemologies of the self from a Black perspective. The articulation of Black epistemologies that emphasize the significance of the Black self and knowledge attributions is an important way of humanizing Blackness within a society that thrives on and profits from varying degrees of anti-Blackness.

3

Phillis Wheatley

The Unlikely Black Female
Epistemologist in the
Eighteenth Century

S ocial reality in America, from historic times to the present, has
always been driven and shaped by contradictions, reflected in the
persistent espousal of ideas, beliefs, and ideals that are illogically
inconsistent or rationally conflicting. Examples of such contradictions
abound. For instance, the American Declaration of Independence of
1776, Bill of Rights, and Constitution all emphasized the ideals of
equality for all, universal human rights, and unfettered freedom. Yet
it is within the same social structure where all of these ideals were
professed and practiced that slavery, the worst institution ever created by man, was designed and maintained for over four centuries.
The contradiction also exists in how many people in America think of
themselves as Christians, even though their lives and actions, especially
toward those who are deemed as outsiders or people who identify as
non-Christians, are a far cry from what a life lived by a true Christian
ethic should look like. This is the same disposition that has led to the
upsurge of vocal deniers of scientifically proven facts and conspiracy
theories within a nation that boasts of the best scientific minds and
intellectually gifted people. These contradictions are typically normalized instead of being seen for what they are: a symptom of something
deeply broken in the psychology of the individual within the American
social fabric. It is such moral bankruptcy that has made it impossible
for people to see through the propaganda of history and the cunning of
education that has portrayed members of the Black race as a footnote to
the discourse of knowledge in the history of human ideas. Perhaps those

who uphold such contradictory and false beliefs engage in such folly because it makes them feel a sense of superiority, power, or dominance.

In this chapter, I explore how the life and achievements of Phillis Wheatley stand as an existential contradiction to the widely held view that Blacks and people of African descent were intellectually, spiritually, physiologically, psychologically, and rationally inferior to whites in colonial America. The genius of Wheatley, a Black slave, the first published African American writer, and the first Black female epistemologist, flourished at a time when the American founders were still debating the question of slavery and its codification within the imagined independent state that was to be created after the Revolutionary War of 1775–1783 fought against the British, a war whose philosophical and ideological justifications were founded on the ideals of freedom, equality, and liberty. These ideals were enshrined in the founding documents and the United States Constitution even though slavery, which was a contradiction to those ideals, was instituted side-by-side in order to sustain the economic, social, and political prosperity of the nation. The founders were well aware that slavery contradicted the idea of "self-evident truth" proclaimed in founding documents such as the Declaration of Independence, or the promise of equality, liberty, and freedom enshrined in the Constitution of the United States, but they normalized such inconsistencies because it was both economically and politically advantageous for them to do so. Many of the major founding fathers, such as George Washington, Thomas Jefferson, and James Madison, were notorious for owning numerous slaves. There were those, such as Benjamin Franklin, who owned only a few slaves, while others, such as Alexander Hamilton, married into large slave-owning families to achieve financial prosperity and gain massive political influence.

In most cases, the normalization of these contradictions was made possible by categories of stratification such as racism, ethnocentrism, sexism, nationalism, patriotism, antiscientism, and other forms of prejudicial dispositions or predilections, including the consideration of the benefits that are derivable from them. It is such a contradiction that led to the denial of the exceptional knowledge created by Wheatley in the eighteenth century in order to maintain the falsehood that white maleness, as a racial category or group identity, is the only criterion for the designation of the knowledgeable human subject. Such normalized contradictions reveal how racist prejudice prevented many influential whites from acknowledging the genius of Wheatley, whose many intellectual accomplishments, including being the first published African American author, contradicted the dominant beliefs held in eighteenth-century America about the intellectual inferiority of Black people.

The structure of knowledge production in eighteenth-century America was very individualistic, such that epistemologists focused mostly on an individual's articulation of their experience, thoughts, and ideas about the external world or their mastery of understanding of a subject. But the emphasis on the *knowing individual* was either abstracted as a normative category or placed on a specific criterion of white maleness. This notion was propagated in much of the respected literature produced in this period stressing the view that on matters of knowledge, the white person and the Negro (Blacks) are unrelated because the former belongs to a "nobler race."[1] In fact, the Black race was reduced to a category of underage children or wards, persons who by reason of incapacity (such as being a minor or mental illness) were placed under the protection of a superior entity, namely their white guardians or owners.[2] These categories had lasting implications for Black lives and how the dehumanizing institution of slavery was established and preserved for so many years. Such categories of differentiation on the basis of race and gender contradiction were utilized to deny the humanity of Black slaves who were held captive, dehumanized, bruised, and exploited for white comfort and for the economic and political prosperity of the nation. However, I think the case of Wheatley reveals how the trajectory of history can be considered as somewhat brutal. White men in America spent many decades conjuring and making up false theories of Black inferiority to support their nefarious goal of building a "new" nation out of the British colony in North America, which they imagined would be free from the oppression of the British authorial monarchical system. But it took a Black female slave (a young girl) owned by a white man, John Wheatley in Boston, to put asunder all of these conjurations and expose the incongruity of these false but widely held beliefs.

While there have been numerous studies on Wheatley's life, experiences, religious beliefs, social connections, and penmanship, no research has been conducted that considers her place in history as a creator of knowledge—a Black epistemologist. This is a novel attempt to specifically consider Wheatley as a Black female philosopher in the eighteenth century who is distinguished for her efforts in the creation of social knowledge. It deserves to be stated that during the period of Wheatley's life in America (c. 1753–December 5, 1784), women (not to mention a female slave) were not permitted or expected to be intellectually gifted or smart. It was a period that was significantly shaped by the structures of patriarchy, sexist dominance, and structural power that considered intellectual genius as an exclusive prerogative of white maleness.[3] Black female slaves were deemed merely useful for subservient roles such as maids, nannies, laborers on the plantation, the actualization of the white male sexual fantasy, and as general domestic servants caring for and tending to the children and wives of their slave masters. They were not considered valuable for the quest and development of useful knowledge in this period. In fact, by the time Phillis arrived in Boston in the summer of 1761, most Blacks throughout the colonies had long since been forcibly fixed into lowly positions of servitude and slavery in the white social imagination and social fabric.[4] This was a social context that had consolidated the idea of race and racial difference, as well as the practices of racialization that upheld white supremacy and made acceptable the logical justification offered to sustain the legacies of the transatlantic slave trade in the Western Hemisphere.[5]

In the preceding chapter, I emphasized how the Enlightenment's idea of reason became the axiomatic matrix for measuring knowledge attribution and the acknowledgment of the kinds of people or subjects that can be regarded as capable of possessing, creating, and disseminating knowledge. It is on the basis of this idea of reason that the genius of the first Black poet, Phillis Wheatley, was denied in the eighteenth century. She could not possibly participate in the social order of knowledge that acknowledged only white subjects (mostly white men) as authority figures in terms of knowledge acquisition and dissemination. Wheatley, who was purchased as a very young slave, developed her literary genius at a time when the majority of Black folks in the United States were held in bondage. Since this was also a period where white law and social practice prohibited slaves from learning to read and write, it is a sign of genius that Wheatley was able to cultivate the skill of writing, even in such difficult circumstances. Possessing at first no materials, she improvised some for the occasion. Not being supplied with pen and paper, she found ever-ready substitutes in a piece of chalk or charcoal and a brick wall. According to G. Herbert Renfro, "in her twelfth year, Wheatley was able to carry on an extensive correspondence about the most important and interesting topics of the day with many of the wisest and most learned in Boston and London."[6] Wheatley's genius was widely considered to be shocking (if not impossible) because the predominant belief in eighteenth-century colonial America was that Blacks were incapable of displaying the talents of reason that come with such great intellectual achievements. This made Wheatley attract an unusual kind of Boston audience, the powerful kind that subjected her to a trial and oral examination.[7]

The publication of Phillis Wheatley's book of poetry enunciated doubts about the true authorship of this text, so much so that her slave master was summoned to bring her to a trial. In *The Trials of Phillis Wheatley,* a very insightful work describing this summons, Henry Louis Gates Jr. argues that the panel that was assembled, consisting of the most respectable characters in Boston, had the primary task of verifying the authorship of her poems and to find the answer to a much larger question: was a Negro capable of producing literature?[8] To put this question somewhat differently: is a Black person capable of exhibiting the genius of knowledge production in literature? This question not only probed the genius of Wheatley in producing masterful literary pieces, but it also raised a deeper inquiry about whether any member of the Black race could possess such knowledge and intellectual ability to write a book of poetry. Gates's assessment here is very revealing because it depicts why Wheatley's oral examination was so important. In particular, he notes that if she had indeed written her poems, then this would demonstrate that enslaved Africans were human beings and should be liberated from slavery. If, on the other hand, she had not written or could not write her poems, or if indeed she was like a parrot who speaks a few words plainly, then that would be another matter entirely. Essentially, she was auditioning for the humanity of the entire African people.[9]

An example of such censure is one that Thomas Jefferson leveled against the genius of Phillis Wheatley, which was aimed at undermining her humanity as well as reinforcing the widely accepted belief that Blacks were intellectually inferior to whites. Jefferson, like many white Americans at that time, believed that even though Africans have human souls, they cannot be compared to other members of the human race because he believed that they lacked the intellectual endowments of other races.[10] In *Notes on the State of Virginia*, Jefferson stated that when Blacks are compared to whites "by their faculties of memory, reason, and imagination, it appears to me that in memory they are equal to whites; in reason much inferior, as I think one could scarcely be found capable of tracing and comprehending the investigations of Euclid: and that in imagination they are dull, tasteless and anomalous."[11] Here he is echoing the same stereotypical views that were predominant in eighteenth- and nineteenth-century race theory in America. He made further allusions to biological racism in this text by advancing the view that physiological differences between whites and Blacks in terms of skin pigmentation, hair, and symmetry of form mark the circumstance of superior beauty of whites, as well as their intellectual superiority.

So, Jefferson's denigration of the intellectual genius of Phillis Wheatley was consistent with his espoused view of a world where intellectual acumen can only be demonstrated by members of the white race. He would go on to argue in *Notes on the State of Virginia* that "religion indeed has produced a Phyllis Whatley [*sic*]; but it could not produce poetry. The compositions published under her name are below the dignity of criticism."[12] Even though Wheatley had been subjected to the most rigorous forms of vetting to confirm that she was truly the author of the numerous poems that were published under her name, Jefferson (along with other prominent white men) refused to acknowledge her genius and her epistemic accomplishments. His denial of Wheatley's genius and knowledge amounts to a denial of her humanity, as well as a denial of the possibility that any Black person could possess such qualities that are mainly "reserved" for whites. This infelicitous remark by Jefferson prompted a strong counterargument from Dr. Samuel Stanhope Smith, who was himself a slave owner like Jefferson. Smith, in his "Essay on the Causes of the Variety of Complexion and Figure in the Human Species," writes in response to Jefferson's critique of Wheatley, "The poems of Phillis Wheatley, a poor African slave, taught to read by the indulgent piety of her master are spoken of with infinite contempt. But I will demand of Mr. Jefferson or any other man who is acquainted with American planters, how many of those masters could have written poems equal to those of Phillis Wheatley?"[13] This question reveals, on the one hand, the ridiculous nature of the denial of Wheatley's genius and, on the other hand, the danger of prejudiced white arrogance that leads to the denial of Black knowledge.

White Arrogance and the Denial of Wheatley's Genius

When Wheatley completed her manuscript containing a considerable number of carefully crafted poems in 1772, she could not find a publisher in all of Boston that would agree to publish it. John and Susanna Wheatley, her slave master and mistress, decided to search in England for a publishing company. They eventually found a publisher that agreed to publish the manuscript in London, but they wanted evidence that the work was truly written by Wheatley. So, in the first edition of *Poems on Various Subjects*, published on September 1, 1773, by Archibald

Bell, two sets and attestation of proof were provided. The first was written by the author's master to the publisher, and the second was written by those regarded as the most respectable characters in Boston to the public. The second attestation to Wheatley's book, written as an open letter "To the Publick" [sic] that served as a preamble to her book, reads in part:

> We whose names are under-written, do assure the World, that the Poems specified in the following Page, were (as we verily believe) written by Phillis, a young Negro Girl, who was but a few years since, brought an uncultivated Barbarian from Africa, and has ever since been, and now is, under the Disadvantage of serving as a Slave in a family in this town. She has been examined by some of the best Judges, and is thought qualified to write them.[14]

The fact that the attestation is needed in the first place speaks volume about white racist attitudes and the unfounded perception about Black subjects as incapable of exhibiting highly exceptional intellectual abilities, especially those required in the writing of a book. In other words, a knowledgeable Black person (not to mention that she was a Black female slave) was the strangest thing that could ever be conceived of in the white mind. This explains why John Wheatley, Phillis's master, attempted but failed to find a publisher for the manuscript in 1772. He had to travel all the way to Britain to find publishers who were willing to publish it, but not without a signed attestation by some of Boston's most respected and powerful white men such as Thomas Hutchinson, governor of the British North American Province of Massachusetts Bay (1771–1774); Andrew Oliver, who served alongside Hutchinson as lieutenant governor; and the Honorable Thomas Hubbard, who served as treasurer of Harvard University from 1752 to 1773 and as commissary general of the Province of Massachusetts Bay from 1759 to 1771, among others. Thus, if white men were unable to verify or validate claims of knowledge for Black subjects, then the white public could not accept such claims as valid sources of knowledge. Many commentators on this section of the text typically gloss over the insidious racism in this attestation, as it is generally assumed that the positive support for the book is a more important point of emphasis than the deep anti-Black racism that undergirds it.

The allusion to Africans as "uncultivated barbarians" who do not belong to an enlightened or civilized community of humans reveals the depth of the prejudiced ignorance that informs white arrogance and the white racist imagination. It is an imagination that had consumed most Europeans since the beginning of the sixteenth century, raising concerns about whether or not the African "species of men," as they were most commonly referred to, could ever create formal literature, or if they could ever master "the arts and sciences." The implication of answering this question in the affirmative, stating that they could, would mean, then, that the African variety of humanity was fundamentally related to the European variety. If not, then it seemed clear that the African was destined by nature to be a slave, a member of the so-described "uncultivated barbarian" race.[15] This is why Wheatley directly responded to these uninformed views about the Black race from Africa in many of her writings. She forcefully and directly responded by identifying all Blacks as belonging to the "blameless race," and called slavery a deed most "ungenerous," maintaining that if virtue is allowed to take dominion, then an American military and political victory over Britain, during the revolutionary war, necessarily should indicate that Blacks will subsequently and necessarily receive for themselves "generous freedom."[16]

Wheatley was very proud of her African heritage despite some of what could be considered as her irregular ambivalence toward it. In "The Pan-African and Puritan Dimensions of Phillis Wheatley's Poems and Letters," Babacar M'Baye argues that most studies on Wheatley fail to show how her writings project a humane image of Africans and Blacks seeking to dismantle the bondage of slavery.[17] Yet, in many of her writings Wheatley continued to identify herself as an African. For instance, in "To Maecenas," she describes herself as a person from "*Afric's* sable race" that can be compared to the Black literary genius who was himself a Black young male slave.

> The happier Terence *all the choir inspir'd,*
> *His soul replenish'd, and his bosom fir'd;*
> *But say, ye Muses, why this partial grace,*
> *To one alone of* Afric's *sable race;*
> *From age to age transmitting thus his name*
> *With the first glory in the rolls of fame?*[18]

This passage reflects Wheatley's admiration and pride in how Terence, a Roman poet of African descent, was able to use his oratorical skills to inspire the world and achieve his freedom. This reference, found in Wheatley's poem, is a reference to Black genius, Black knowledge, and the outstanding intellectual achievement of the Black race ("*Afric's* sable race") generally. It does not and should not be subsumed under the validation of whiteness. As such, the attestation by this group of powerful white men reveals white arrogance as an epistemic problem because it stems from a misperception that Black knowledge is always subservient to white validation and that Black subjectivity does not or cannot exist outside of its relation to whiteness. This white arrogance is also highlighted in the letter sent to the publisher of Wheatley's book by her master.

The following is a Copy of a LETTER sent by
The Author's Master to the Publisher

PHILLIS was brought from *Africa* to *America* in the Year 1761, between Seven and Eight years of age. Without any Assistance from School Education, and by only what she was taught in the Family, she in sixteen Months Time from her arrival, attained the English Language, to which she was an utter Stranger before, to such a degree as to read any, the most difficult Parts of the Sacred Writings, to the great Astonishment of all who heard her.

As to her WRITING, her own curiosity led her to it, and this she learnt in so short a Time that in the year 1765, she wrote a Letter to the Rev. Mr. OCCOM, the *Indian* Minister, while in *England*.

She has a great Inclination to learn the Latin Tongue, and has made some Progress in it. This Relation is given by her Master who bought her, and with whom she now lives.

JOHN WHEATLEY
Boston, Nov. 14, 1772.[19]

This letter, written as an attestation to the publisher, was intended to characterize Wheatley as a prodigy that deserves to have her work in a reputable white publishing outlet whose main audience is mainly white and middle class. It reflects more than a proof of validation of Wheatley's creative genius. It shows the power of testimony and testimonial knowledge offered by a white subject (more specially, a white male subject) in the eighteenth century. In fact, the very condition for agreeing to publish Wheatley's manuscript was contingent on whether there were white male voices that were ready to provide testimony that could serve as a validation of the knowledge claims contained in the manuscript. In other words, the white publishers could not accept the genius, knowledge, and testimony of Wheatley in themselves; they had to be validated by white men. In the same vein, the white public would not take the work seriously if it was not authenticated by other white voices. This reveals how white arrogance can be seen as an epistemic problem, especially the appreciation and valuation of Black knowledge on its own merits without any emphasis on white validation. As Wheatley began to gain recognition as a genius poet, she would reject this white validation that subjected her to the description of servitude used in advertising her books. For instance, in May of 1774, after receiving three hundred more copies of her books from the London publisher, she advertised them for sale in the *Boston Evening Post* and *Advertiser* as the work of Phillis Wheatley/A Negro girl, not, as subsequent advertisements would state, as the poems of a servant of Mr. John Wheatley of Boston.[20] This was a powerful demonstration of self-consciousness and self-attribution of knowledge production.

Even after the book was published, some of the criticisms directed at Wheatley and the content of her published work in the British tabloids continued in this frame of white arrogance. The *London Magazine: Or, Gentleman's Monthly Intelligencer*, a prominent periodical at the time, had this to say about her poems in the September 1773 edition (XLII, 456): "These poems display no astonishing power of genius; but we consider them as the production of a young untutored African."[21] Similarly, in December of 1773, *The Monthly Review* of London was less concerned with the poems than with the fact that their author was a Black slave, saying among other things, the following:

> If we believed, with the ancient mythologists, that genius is the offspring of the sun, we should rather wonder that the stable race has not been more distinguished by it, than express our surprise at a single instance. . . . The poems written by this young negro bear no endemial marks of solar fire or spirit. They are merely imitative; and, indeed, most of those people have a turn for imitation, though they have little or none for invention.[22]

Wheatley's intellectual aptitude was even more impressive when one considers that she continued to write and express her intellectual ideas or thoughts, even though she was faced with such frames of racial hatred, sexism, provincialism, and anti-Black racism masked as critiques. These types of criticisms did not deter her from avowing her genius and demanding respect based on her own self-recognition and intellect. This is clearly evident in her letter to John Thornton Esqr., Merchant of London in 1770, where she states that "the world is a severe schoolmaster, for its frowns are less dang'rous than its Smiles and flatteries, and it is a difficult task to keep in the path of Wisdom. I attended and find exactly true your thoughts on the behavior of those who seem'd to respect me while under my mistress's patronage: you said right, for some of those have already put on a reserve."[23] She challenges those white people who appeared to "respect" her on the basis of her former owners, not on her own accord as a gifted poet and sage of *"Afric's* sable race." In what follows, I consider Wheatley as a sage who developed an aesthetic understanding of Black knowledge in many of her essays, poems, and other writings that expose the misperception of Black slaves as inferior and ignorant for what it is—an empty falsehood.

Wheatley's Development of Black Aesthetics as Knowledge

The criticisms and opprobrium put up against Wheatley's writings do not in any way diminish her place in history as one of the brilliant minds of eighteenth-century America. Even at a time in American history when powerful white men were busy laying the foundation for the racial myth of Black inferiority to justify the institution of slavery, there were Black individuals such as Wheatley whose genius and life contradicted these myths. But this reality was not enough to rupture the scheme of things. I consider Wheatley a pioneering figure who developed the concept of Black aesthetics as knowledge in a period when Blackness and knowledge creation were thought to be contradictory. Black aesthetics as knowledge involves the investigation and cultivation of the epistemological aspects of Black creative expression in literature and other forms of artistic expression. Aesthetics, in this sense, is more than philosophy of art or the theory of beauty and the pursuit of abstract categories. It is a way of life, more specifically, expressions that speak to the vagaries of human experience. This includes the demonstration of an individual's understanding of concepts such as "beauty," "pain," "virtue," "good," "sorrow," and "compassion" not as mere abstract concepts but as applicative realities that contribute to human good. In the manner in which this notion evolves in the elegies and poems written by Wheatley, words were transformed from isolated blocks of rhythmic lines into affective and perceptual states that speak profoundly to the human condition. So, in her writings, including her letters, extant poems, and verses in *Poems on Various*

Subjects, Wheatley offers an aesthetic understanding of Black knowledge to emphasize two major themes: the *beauty in* Black humanity and the *beauty from* Black humanity.

For instance, in her letter to Reverend Samson Occum, an American Indian minister, in 1774, Wheatley goes against the weight of scientific racism in her day to offer different knowledge about the *beauty in* Black humanity, defending it against the institution of slavery by citing the dehumanizing characterization of Black humanity within this institution as a contradiction to the natural law theory - the "vindication of their natural rights."

> I have this Day received your obliging kind Epistle, and am greatly satisfied with your Reasons respecting the Negroes, and think highly reasonable what you offer in Vindication of their natural Rights: Those that invade them cannot be insensible that the divine Light is chasing away the thick Darkness which broods over the Land of Africa; and the Chaos which has reign'd so long, is converting into beautiful Order, and [r]eveals more and more clearly, the glorious Dispensation of civil and religious Liberty, which are so inseparably Limited, that there is little or no Enjoyment of one Without the other.[24]

The fact that Wheatley was no legal scholar, yet referenced the principles of natural law to defend the biological and ontological worth of Black humanity as vindication or evidence of the moral depravity and legal contradiction of this institution of slavery, is a testament to her incomparable genius. Further, she described those who perpetuate and support the slavery system as "insensible" and wallowing in darkness, a kind of celestial darkness that prevents them from appreciating or coming to the knowledge of the "beautiful order" that broods over those from "the land of Africa." She uses this expression, "land of Africa," and "*Afric's* sable race," in many of her writings to refer to her place of origin, the ancestral home of all Black people before they were kidnapped, captured, and sold in the transatlantic slave trade. This feat is very remarkable because Wheatley was about eleven years old when she wrote this letter. She utilized her creative genius in Black aesthetics to construct arguments against subjugating Blacks on the basis of race. She expresses her condemnation of slavery, arguing that "for in every human Breast, God has implanted a principle, which we call Love of Freedom; it is impatient of Oppression, and pants for Deliverance."[25] The emphasis on love of freedom being implanted in every human soul means that slavery was an unnatural institution that was created to despoil the pristine beauty in Black humanity.

Wheatley's goal for writing this letter was, as she puts it, to speak directly to the white colonists, "not for their hurt, but to convince them of the strange absurdity of their conduct whose words and actions are so diametrically, opposite."[26] This statement is a direct indictment of the hypocrisy of white, slave-holding, Christian ministers who supported the institution of slavery. She concludes this letter to Occum by highlighting the contradiction between the colonists' own demands for freedom from Britain and their determination to uphold slavery. This is captured in the following lines expressed in her letter, "How well the Cry for Liberty, and the reverse Disposition for the exercise of oppressive Power over others agree,—I humbly think it does not require the Penetration of a Philosopher to determine."[27] It does not require the deep thinking of a philosopher to see the hypocrisy of the white colonists who are clamoring for freedom from the British while at the same time enslaving Black people.

She would express similar thoughts in one of her extant but unpublished poems, "On the Death of General Wooster," that was written to Mary Wooster, the wife of the general who fought in the American Revolution and was killed in the Battle of Ridgefield.

> For we combat on the field of fame
> Without her presence vice maintains full sway
> O still propitious be thy guardian care
> And lead Columbia thro' the toils of war.
> With thine own hand conduct them and defend
> And bring the deadly contest to an end— . . .
> But how, presumptuous shall we hope to find
> Divine acceptance with th' Almighty mind—
> While yet (O deed ungenerous!) they disgrace
> And hold in bondage Afric's blameless race?
> Let virtue reign—And thou accord our prayers
> Be victory our's, and generous freedom theirs.[28]

Although this was an elegy that laments the passing of the general, Wheatley raises serious questions about the rationale for the deaths occasioned by this revolution in the first place, which, in her mind, still needs to respond to the question of Black humanity ("Afric's blameless race") and slavery. She considers it presumptuous that white colonists would engage in the toils of war in pursuit of freedom during the

American Revolution and hope to find it, while at the same time holding an entire race ("*Afric's* sable race"—a blameless and beautiful race) in the bondage of servitude.

Wheatley also devised her development of a Black aesthetics in this period to highlight the *beauty from* Black humanity. This is especially significant given the historical context in which being Black was enough to remove any consideration for the possibility of producing knowledge. So, this ode that was featured in her work was radical, to say the least, because it was celebrating the genius and knowledge of beauty of another young African/Black slave. The lines of this poem are very instructive, as shown in the following excerpt:

> *To show the lab'ring bosom's deep intent,*
> *When first thy pencil did those beauties give,*
> *And breathing figures learnt from thee to live,*
> *How did those prospects give my soul delight,*
> *A new creation rushing on my sight.*[29]

There are deep meanings being communicated through the images painted by this young African/Black slave. The beauty that arose from the strokes of the pencil is striking and reveals the deep intent of the creator. The genius of the painter was also highlighted in the lines referencing how the painted image beheld by Wheatley can teach living beings, or breathing figures, how to live and create new meaning and a new world out of a truly ugly one. These painted figures were considered "a new creation" that proves the artist's ability to create a fictive world that mirrors the empirical world. This painter[30] is praised further by Wheatley:

> *Still, wond'rous youth! Each noble path pursue,*
> *On deathless glories fix thine ardent view:*
> *Still may the painter's and poet's fire*
> *To aid thy pencil, and thy verse conspire!*
> *And may the charms of each seraphic theme*
> *Conduct thy footsteps to immortal fame!*[31]

This particular poem has both philosophical and ontological implications for the status of Blackness in the anti-Black world of eighteenth-century America. Not only did Wheatley's literary productions and renditions expose the fabrications of the white intelligentsia, they also pointed to the existence of the Black intelligentsia, albeit unacknowledged during that period. The emphasis on the "painter's and poet's fire" reveals a metaphor for the creativity demonstrated and knowledge produced by Black people at that time. It is described as "fire" and filled with the charms of "seraphic" themes. Wheatley's words expressed in this poem are not mere words; they are words that signify an ontological understanding of the *beauty from* Black humanity as a gift to the world that is uplifting to the soul and to society. The ontological implications of Wheatley's poem, "To S.M. a young African Painter," also create a new epistemic understanding of Blackness, not just in relation to the body or somatic features but also in relation to the products of the mind, intellectual productions. This is crucially important because within the colonial context of her writing, the structure of knowledge and humanity was such that power was retained in the white male subject as the privileged knower and absolute mind that can produce beauty, knowledge, and understanding.[32] But through her writings, Wheatley released the Black body from the restraints of the structured idea of absolute objectivity found in the human biologic sciences of this period, which trap the Black body in an imaginary and empiricist world.

Wheatley's intellectual accomplishments in writing and publishing *Poems on Various Subjects* speak to the dimension of Black personal knowledge that was undermined by the hubris among whites during her lifetime. The attention she gives in her work to honor, validate, and celebrate other Black talented individuals such as S.M., the young African painter, shows her awareness of the social framework for knowledge construction and the importance of community in the process of knowledge acquisition and distribution. It also reveals her deep appreciation for the pursuit of knowledge as a virtue, which is aptly captured in her poem, "On Virtue."

> *O Thou bright jewel in my main aim I strive*
> *To comprehend thee. Thine own words declare*
> *Wisdom is higher than a fool can reach.*
> *I cease to wonder, and no more attempt*
> *Thine height t'explore, or fathom thy profound.*
> *But, O my soul, sink not into despair,*
> *Virtue is near thee, and with gentle hand*
> *Would now embrace thee, hoevers o'er thine head.*
> *Fain would the heav'n-born soul with her converse,*
> *Then seek, then court her for her promis'd bliss.*[33]

In this poem, she characterizes virtue as the insatiable quest for wisdom, a goal that is "higher than a fool can reach," which is one of the fundamental distinguishing features of a philosopher: to seek wisdom in life, above everything else. Wheatley's brilliant philosophical mind captures wisdom, the application of knowledge to the problems of human existence, as a "bright jewel" and the main aim of her existential strivings. In a newly published biography on Wheatley, David Waldstreicher's interpretation of this poem leans toward an eschatological understanding of virtue because Wheatley begins this poem with an admission of her immaturity with expressions such as "O thou bright jewel in my aim I strive / To comprehend thee. Thine own words declare / Wisdom is higher than a fool can reach."[34] It reflects the idea that "self-debasement" becomes a path to virtue as she reaches for the skies figuratively as well as literally. In this interpretation, "virtue" is seen as an abstraction that can be imagined as an angel, a guiding spirit "with gentle hand" who "hovers o'er thine head," with height imagined, immediately, as both a metaphor for achievement and a heaven above.[35] I interpret this poem as alluding to epistemic virtue—the pursuit of wisdom by Black subjects. In the lines quoted earlier, we also see her humility toward knowledge such that, even though she realized that she could not grasp fully the profundity of the wisdom for which she searches, she is able to contemplate and encourage her soul not to sink into despair but to be comforted by the realization that virtue—wisdom—is near and hovers over her head. It is remarkable that at such a young age, Wheatley described the main goal of her life as the search for wisdom; she considers this a very important virtue to succeed in life, especially in her youthful days. This was aptly depicted by the following lines in the second stanza of the poem: "attend me, *Virtue*, thro' my youthful years! But guide my steps to endless life and bliss."[36]

The fact that Phillis Wheatley was a Black genius cannot be overstated. Despite the many criticisms leveled against the scholarship of Wheatley, she became an accomplished and celebrated Black writer and orator who traveled between Great Britain and the United States delivering solicited speeches, poems, and oratory. In one of her speaking engagements in Britain, where she delivered some of her poems to the University of Cambridge, England (1767), she had this to say about America:

While an intrinsic ardor prompts to write,
The muses promise to assist my pen;
'Twas not long since I left my native shore
The land of errors, and Egyptian gloom[37]

In this poem, Wheatley recognizes the negative import of slavery on her sojourn in the New World (the land of errors), especially navigating the melancholic experiences she had as a Black woman demonstrating intellectual abilities that were believed to be a prerogative of white men. In this sense, she imagines her Blackness as something trapped in a metaphoric notion of "Egyptian gloom," which can also allude to the demonization of Blackness in eighteenth- and nineteenth-century ethnological theories on race.

Despite such inhibitions, Wheatley was able to display her genius through her many writings. In a sense, Wheatley's expressed literary and intellectual genius problematizes the virulent, racist, and sociological lens through which Blacks and Blackness were caricatured in eighteenth- and nineteenth-century ethnological science. The example of Wheatley further buttresses how the Black subject was excluded from the system of rationality. This exclusion later became valorized in modern philosophy, especially in the Enlightenment period, a context in which Black subjects would be increasingly framed in negative terms, in the encounter with nonwhites. It is such a framing where whiteness would be used to represent orderliness, rationality, and self-control, while nonwhiteness would be used to represent chaos, irrationality, violence, and the breakdown of self-regulation. Thus, Wheatley's rightful place within Black intellectual history is as a pioneering (albeit unlikely) Black female epistemologist who developed Black aesthetics as knowledge at a time when Blackness was not normally thought of in connection with positive values such as knowledge creation, intellectual gifts, life of the mind, enlightenment, or an aptitude for writing. This makes her contributions to the historical cataloging of knowledge during this period even more important.

4

Against Mental Darkness

Black Self-Knowledge in Frederick
Douglass's Anticolonial Epistemology

Frederick Douglass is one of the most revered thinkers within the Black intellectual tradition. The stories captured in *Life and Times of Frederick Douglass,* written by himself, and those written by his numerous biographers easily portray the magnitude of the impact and legacy that Douglass had on the racial uplift of the Black race and human civilization generally.[1] Undoubtedly, the history of the Black race in the United States cannot be completely articulated without acknowledging the place of significance that he occupies within such a genealogical narrative. Although Frederick Douglass has received a wide spectrum of consideration within and outside the corpus of Black intellectual history, no attempt has been made to consider him primarily as a social epistemologist.[2] This chapter engages in a philosophical analysis that considers Douglass's thoughts from the perspective of social epistemology. Even within his career as a slave, he understood the connection between social knowledge and social power.[3] Douglass is exemplary in terms of the resilience that his life represents for the Black race, especially in the face of the most violent, despicable, and dehumanizing institution ever established by humans: chattel slavery. This exemplarity is concretized by his exploits toward overcoming the terrible conditions of slavery and colonial exploitation, as well as dismantling the myth of Black inferiority that was developed within antebellum America to justify the despicable treatment of Blacks and their confinement to unbridled darkness, including moral, political, spiritual, and existential darkness. Yet, within the gloominess of such forms of darkness rose a giant and genius, Frederick Douglass, who explored the subtleties of his humanity and, through autodidactic means, struggled against the bondage of darkness and brought himself to the light.

The ideas of "darkness" and "light" are two important concepts that Douglass deployed in his numerous writings and reflections to share the vagaries, complexities, and difficulties of his lived experience from the time he was born into slavery until the time he escaped (as a fugitive slave) from the dehumanizing conditions of slavery. He deployed the concept of "darkness" to achieve both literal and metaphoric ends. On the one hand, he utilized this concept to denote the plethora of evil perpetrated by greedy white slave owners and extremely brutal overseers against Blacks as well as an exposition of the virulent nature of anti-Black racism prevalent in America during this period. In a different sense, he utilized the notion of darkness to metaphorically depict the asinine nature of the system of patriarchy and economic greed that undergirds the sense of "profit-making" that transmogrifies human beings into a commodity, especially emphasizing how Black bodies were transfigured into commodities to be bought and sold within the political economy of slavery in America. For example, in "The Heroic Slave," Douglass describes the immediate tragedy of slavery as consisting of the brutalization of men, women, and children, and generally objectifying Black souls as merely material components in a grand machine for economic gain.[4] In other instances, Douglass would deploy the concept of "darkness" to castigate and ridicule the hypocritical nature of the religious outlook portrayed by those who were actively engaged in and profiting from the enterprise of slavery. On the other hand, he deployed the notion of "light" to represent the ideals of truth that drove his ultimate quest for freedom. So, for Douglass, stepping away from "darkness" into the "light" signified the actual process of breaking free from the chains of slavery, both mental/psychological and physical chains, to attain the status of self-directed humanity.

This chapter explores the philosophical significance of Douglass's break away from the oppressive psychological and material conditions of slavery through certain subjective principles projected into the objective world while emphasizing the importance he placed on positive dispositions of mind as a catalyst for objective self-transformation in the world. Douglass's perspective, when considered from an epistemological perspective, is significant because it orients us toward a radical consideration of Black subjects as worthy, viable, reflective, and thriving epistemic agents within a social framework of knowledge that persistently fails to consider them as such. In other words, the example of Douglass reveals a unique perspective of the Black subject as a being that demonstrates reflective self-consciousness, which is a necessary condition for the avowal of knowledge claims in the first-person sense. The awareness of self-consciousness engenders the distinction between the subject and the object of existence in the material world, which Douglass clearly articulates in his tripartite autobiographies—*Narrative of the Life of Frederick Douglass, an American Slave, My Bondage and My Freedom,* and *The Life and Times of Frederick Douglass.*[5]

On the account of Douglass, the slave ceases to be a slave, physically and psychologically, when this distinction between the subject and object of existence is made through the power of knowledge or self-reflective awareness. In his autobiography, *Narrative of the Life of Frederick Douglass, an American Slave,* Douglass spoke of how he realized that slaves (including himself) were viewed as mere objects, just as any other form of material property, which explains why they were not expected to exhibit any forms of subjective qualities of existence. This awareness led him to "abhor and detest [his] enslavers."[6] In Douglass's view, the chains of bondage could only be broken by the sheer force of determination and intellectual strength, insofar as the light of freedom is embraced at the moment that the Black subject comes to such self-reflective awareness. In his "Address to the Colored People of the United States," Douglass describes this as a catalyst that makes it possible for Blacks (previously enslaved Blacks) to attain the very ideal of "human brotherhood."[7] It is how the Black slave is transformed from the category of nonhuman (material object) into the category of the human (capable of projecting one's subjective reality into the world).[8] Here, Douglass is emphasizing the idea of the existential struggle that elicits the awareness of the distinction between the subjective self and the objectified self and ultimately brings about the possibility of the understanding Black self-ownership.

It is this notion of the ownership of self that Douglass regarded as the authority of the Black subject to avow knowledge claims in the material world that was heavily conditioned by slavery. Although he was conceived in and born into a system of enslavement, nurtured within a framework of subversion and submission to the will of white slave owners and overseers, and groomed to embrace a life of servitude as the ultimate end or life goal of people of his kind, he dared to imagine himself to be something more. He strove to circumvent all of the expectations for which he was groomed and defied those expectations to become something else through his renewed sense of self-understanding. Although during the period of Douglass's life what was framed as "social episte-mology" was essentially forms of biological racism, he strove through his intellectual genius and wit to be categorized as human, thereby chal-lenging the false categories and general assumptions about the inferior-ity and the inhumanity of the Black race. In his critical reflections and writings, Douglass sought to make a case for Black humanity—one that could acquire knowledge both through engagement in intellectual activities such as reading and critical engagement with social reality to challenge what was being conveyed in nineteenth-century America as "truth" about the ethnological status of the Black race. Through such preoccupations, he laid the foundation for what would later be canon-ized as social epistemology, exploring how human social conditions impact the formulation of epistemological categories and how inter-personal and intrahuman communication reveal the extent to which humans rely on the self and others for knowledge attributions in the world. In "The Claims of the Negro Ethnologically Considered," Doug-lass debunks the idea that the negro [the Black subject] is not a human. This makes it possible for him to imagine the Black subject not only as a human but as a being capable of possessing and sharing knowledge and virtue within a social milieu.[9]

Two Social Epistemological Postulates of Frederick Douglass

There are two plausible social epistemological postulates that can be deduced from the philosophical thoughts of Frederick Douglass: first, the political nature of the epistemology of ignorance in a colonial con-text, and second, self-knowledge as the foundation of a Black anticolo-nial epistemology. But Douglass was very clear in his thinking that Black subjects could only gain an understanding of these notions through an appreciation of the value of education, which brings about genuine per-sonal and social transformation or reform. Douglass viewed education and knowledge as the paths to freedom. For this reason, he worked against all odds to teach himself how to read and write and continued to teach himself until he gained understanding. In 1831 he bought a copy of the *Columbian Orator*, an anthology of great speeches, which he studied closely.[10] As he writes in *My Bondage and My Freedom*:

> When I was about thirteen years old and had succeeded in learn-ing to read, every increase to knowledge, especially respecting

the FREE STATES, added something to the almost intolerable burden of the thought—"I AM A SLAVE FOR LIFE." To my bondage I saw no end. It was a terrible reality, and I shall never be able to tell how sadly that thought chafed my young spirit. Fortunately, or unfortunately, about this time in my life, I had made enough money to buy what was then a very popular school-book, viz: the "Columbian Orator."[11]

Here, Douglass is referencing his earliest struggles against both the physical and psychological warfare that the conditions of slavery imposed on Black folks. He was especially detailing how his acquisition of knowledge and his exposure to learning generated an awareness of the incongruence of the system of human slavery in the United States and his newfound enlightenment. In other words, a slave is destined to be a slave for life without developing the power to question the social hierarchies and systems that made the conditions of enslavement possible. Under this imaginary, the enslaved remain slaves because slavery is deemed and falsely categorized as their natural state.

Douglass emphasized the idea of ignorance as a "burden" in the American colonial context that was designed to keep Black folks perpetually enslaved within the political economy of slavery. Hence, he articulated that he "saw no end" to his bondage within this system because he was kept in ignorance. Although he described this as a spirit-breaking reality, he never allowed this to incapacitate or discourage him into inaction. He acted by investing almost all of his meager life's savings toward purchasing the *Columbian Orator*, which became one of the foundations for his psychological freedom and, eventually, his physical freedom. In *Frederick Douglass: Prophet of Freedom*, David Blight describes the *Columbian Orator* as a book that had a prophetic import in the life of Douglass because on page after page of this text he found the reality of his condition, as well as dreams and justifications for his escape.[12] To fully appreciate Douglass's genius and intellectual contributions to the social epistemological discourse, one must take into cognizance the context and conditions of his life, which began with the experience of slavery.

Frederick Douglass was a slave in antebellum America. One thing that was very clear during his early life as a slave was the knowledge that he was owned as "property." He was not the owner of himself. In many of his reflections, he clearly articulated a sense of the lack of self-ownership that undergirded the system of slavery through his sojourn in Colonel Lloyd's plantation, while under the ownership of Mr. Auld and his wife in Baltimore, and through the generational transference of owned slaves (considered as property) to the offspring of owners of slave plantations. For instance, in the letter he wrote on September 22, 1848, to Thomas Auld, his former slave owner, he decried the system of slavery that makes it possible for white slave owners to own Black bodies for economic gain. In a very confrontational tone, Douglass wrote directly to Auld, stating that "at this moment, you are probably the guilty holder of at least three of my dear sisters and my only brother in bondage. These you regard as your property. They are recorded on your ledger, or perhaps have been sold to human flesh mongers, with a view of filling your own ever-hungry purse."[13] Douglass considers this issue of lack of personhood status for his siblings (and other Black slaves) as one of the most devastating and pernicious aspects of the system of human slave trade developed in the United States. It is a system that utterly removed Black slaves from any consideration as human beings, reducing them to mere physical entities that existed for the cultivation and production of wealth for the greedy white "human flesh mongers." In *My Bondage and My Freedom*, Douglass goes on to state that "the grand aim of slavery . . . always and everywhere, is to reduce man to a level with the brute."[14] However, one of the functional ways that this process of reduction is achieved is by keeping Black slaves in a perpetual condition of ignorance.

Douglass's emphasis here speaks to the erosion of the self within America's slavery system. That is, slaves are only able to be owned when all their rights to self-ownership or self-authorship are relinquished or extinguished through all forms of repressive power systems, codes, edicts, laws, and social practices. It is essentially a description of the imposition of ignorance, as an epistemological category on the Black slave. In antebellum America, this imposition of ignorance was a form of legalized violence against Black slaves because it was used to achieve the naturalization of an unnatural state (of nonknowing) for Black slaves that is enforced through systematized, deliberate mechanisms put up by slave owners within the American institution of slavery to control and degrade millions of Black slave populations.[15] A powerful manifestation of this degradation was the prevention of all Blacks from gaining access to knowledge, systemized in the antiliteracy laws and slave codes. This was aimed at preventing Black slaves from developing any sense of self or self-worth that could signal forms of rebellion against the entire system of human enslavement. It explains why education/learning was primarily restricted to

humans, whereas slaves were considered nonhuman animals undeserving of such privileges. In the slave codes that were promulgated in the
mid-nineteenth century in the Southern United States, it was affirmed
that, due to the legal relation between master and slave, a relation which
confers the administration of rights on the master, the validity or law-
fulness of that relation is equivalent to a denial of the literary and religious rights of the slave.[16] That is, "the legal relation of slave ownership,
in America, as defined by the code that upholds it, is a relation that
cannot and does not coexist with the recognition (either in theory or
practice) of the intellectual and religious rights of the slave."[17] As written
in chapters 6 and 7, part 2 of *The American Slave Code*:

> The power to *permit* and to *confer* carries with it the power to
> *refuse* and to *withhold*. Both the master and the slave understand
> this, where permissions are most frequently given. It is injurious
> to confer, as it is degrading to accept as a boon, what belongs
> to every man as man, by absolute and inherent right. The rights
> of investigation, of free speech, of mental culture, of religious
> liberty, and conscience, are of this class.[18]

This shows how "ignorance" was codified as a legal-political tool to
keep Black slaves perpetually under servitude. In this instance, the "ignorance" of the slave was a way the slave master intended for him to know
the world. This was not a case of the absence of knowing; it was a phenomenon that is contingent on the denial of the right to the investigation
of mental culture, from which all slaves were barred. This means that if
any slave were to dabble in this sort of thing, that slave and the very pursuit of such an endeavor would be deemed as outlawed and abominable.

This also shows how ensuring that Black slaves were kept in mental
darkness not only functioned as a principal mechanism through which
white slave owners demonstrated their superiority in terms of social
hierarchies, but also served as a way of establishing and maintaining
the myths of their ontological and intellectual superiority. As a result,
in the sections of *The American Slave Code* cited earlier, the *powers*
to "confer" or "withhold" intellectual rights are restricted primarily
to the white slave owner. Yet, the phrase "both the master and the
slave understand this," suggests that the Black slave can demonstrate
some form of understanding of their altered and inferior place under
the law. If this is true, then it contradicts the very suppositions of the
inferiority of Black slaves, which was the predominant worldview during this period. It also reveals the arrogance of the framers of this code,

in their acknowledgment of the innate capacities possessed by Black slaves to pursue intellectual and religious concerns that could aptly be categorized as attributes of the investigation of mental culture. Douglass understands that the emphasis on mental culture would be one of the important grounds on which the Black struggle for freedom would have to be launched. The starting line in the battle for the liberation of Black people was to be drawn by Blacks themselves, and their resourcefulness toward this objective would have to be consistently demonstrated through the waging of psychological warfare and physical acts of resistance.[19]

Douglass on the Politics of Ignorance and Knowledge in a Colonial Context

Frederick Douglass understood mental darkness as the ultimate marker of colonial oppression. He perceived it as a racially imposed category of unknowing that restricts otherwise sentient beings to the realm of nonhuman property, especially in a colonial context. From the perspective of Douglass, ignorance as an epistemological category is not seen as the mere lack of knowledge or the absence of awareness of existent things on the part of Black subjects. Rather, he considers it as something deeper, including how "ignorance" was deployed in antebellum America as part of the political structures for determining who could aspire to the definitive characteristics of the "human" before the law, and who could not. He also considered how Black subjects (in this case, Black slaves) were prevented from being considered "knowledgeable" as the product of a constructed epistemological reality that restricted what any slave could become "knowledgeable about" to primarily learning to obey the master and accepting the conditions of servitude as normalized reality. Within this constructed epistemological reality, the good slave is deemed the one who knows about the breadth of servitude and subjugation and accepts this as a fact of life. Meanwhile, the bad slave is the one who refuses to accept this skewed sense of reality as a fact of life. The so-called "bad slave" is the one who challenges the false logic within the constructed epistemological reality that categorizes slaves as subhuman. By rejecting this racialized structure of reality, this slave (the bad slave) becomes knowledgeable of freedom and asserts their humanity.

For instance, in *Narrative of the Life of Frederick Douglass*, Douglass declares that one of the very first conditions for turning an individual into a slave is to condemn such an individual to mental darkness and make that person wallow in stark ignorance. He writes about this pointedly, stating, "I have found that to make a contented slave, it is necessary to make a thoughtless one. It is necessary to darken his moral and mental vision, and, as far as possible, to annihilate the power of reason. He must be able to detect no inconsistencies in slavery; he must be made to feel that slavery is right; and that he can be brought to that only when he ceases to be a man."[20] In other words, there must be a transformation from a rational human into something irrational. It is a calculated system that fundamentally denies the mental capacities of Black slaves to hasten and sustain the process of subjugation. Violent means were sometimes employed to ensure that Black slaves were contained or restricted to this realm of epistemic ignorance. Douglass writes about this succinctly in *Narrative*:

> Every moment they [slaves] spent in that school [Sabbath school], they were liable to be taken up and given thirty-nine lashes. They came because they wished to learn. Their minds have been starved by their cruel masters. They had been shut up in mental darkness. I taught them because it was the delight of my soul to be doing something that looked like bettering the condition of my race.[21]

From what Douglass recounts in the cited passage, the epistemology of ignorance under the political economy of slavery is exposed as profoundly political and nuanced. In particular, he notes the brutal ways in which the states of "unknowing" and "mental darkness" were enforced and carefully constructed to achieve dual functions—to help maintain white privilege and power as well as to ensure that Black slaves internalized such epistemic oppression as the norm.

In a reception speech he delivered at Finsbury Chapel, Moorfields, England, on May 12, 1846, he exposed the bound of ignorance within America's system of slavery as a brutal material and psychological warfare by avowing the following:

> This is American slavery; no marriage—no education—the light of the gospel shut out from the dark mind of the bondman—and he forbidden by law to learn to read. If a mother shall teach her children to read, the law in Louisiana proclaims that she may be hanged by the neck. If a father attempts to give his son a knowledge of letters, he may be punished by the whip in one instance

and another be killed, at the discretion of the court. Three millions of people shut out from the light of knowledge![22]

Here, we see Douglass's attestation to how the law under American slavery was utilized to mobilize ignorance as a violent political weapon to ensure that Black slaves were constrained to the realm of mental darkness, what he referred to as the "darkening of the mental vision." However, his reference to the "darkening of the mental vision" is crucial for unpacking the nuanced ways in which ignorance functioned within America's political economy of slavery to keep Black slaves outside of the domain of knowledge as *unrecognized embodied subjects*. This, for Douglass, is the political mission of the epistemological project of ignorance that undergirds the American colonial experience. Embodied subjectivity is denied to the Black slave because there was no ontological or biological basis for the recognition of the humanity of the Black slave. If embodied subjectivity were to be recognized, then it would nullify the legal, biological (scientific), anthropological, moral, and religious arguments developed to defend and sustain America's political economy of slavery.

In fact, from a critical reading of the autobiographical reflections of Douglass, the epistemological project of ignorance under this system is revealed as highly valuable not only for the sustenance of the myth of the superiority of the Caucasian race but also for the sustenance of the slave-master dialectic that was extremely crucial to maintaining the system of oppression. Douglass's exposition on this in *My Bondage and My Freedom* is quite interesting. He maintains that under the slavery system, "ignorance is a high virtue in a human-chattel; and as the master studies to keep the slave ignorant, the slave is cunning enough to make the master think he succeeds. The slave fully appreciates the saying, 'where ignorance is bliss, 'tis folly to be wise.'"[23] There are two important dimensions of the politics of ignorance within this system as characterized by Douglass. The first has to do with the designation of the Black slave as "ignorant" under the slave-master dialectic. Although this assumption is held by those who wielded the power to enslave Black bodies, Douglass reveals the superficial nature of such a belief based on a different kind of "ignorance"—the master's ignorance. This is the second dimension of ignorance that Douglass reveals here as the "real" ignorance happening within the slave-master dialectic, even though the master chooses to be oblivious of this truth. With this analysis, Douglass is also revealing the foolishness of the so-called master who thinks he is smart but cannot detect that "the slave is cunning enough" to make him think he succeeds. In other words, even though the idea of "knowledge" was politicized under America's political economy of slavery to project Black slaves as ignorant nonsubjects, they were not truly ignorant in the epistemic sense.

Douglass's struggle against the established and formalized systems designed to keep Black slaves eternally ignorant speaks to their superior intelligence. His desire to learn and break away from his condition of enslavement was borne out of this struggle and his recognition of the political and epistemic functions of "ignorance" within America's political economy of slavery. This is evident in the narration of his lived experiences at the house of his former slave master Hugh Auld, whose wife, Mrs. Auld, a somewhat religious woman, kindled his passion for learning. In *My Bondage and My Freedom*, Douglass describes a scenario in which Mrs. Auld frequently read the Bible aloud around the house, especially when her husband was away; this made him curious about how to acquire the skill to read and write, even though this was forbidden by law at that time. At some point, he summoned up the courage to ask his master's wife. He describes the experience in this manner: "Having no fear of my kind mistress before my eyes, (she had then given me no reason to fear), I frankly asked her to teach me to read; and, without hesitation, the dear woman began the task, and very soon, by her assistance, I was master of the alphabet, and could spell words of three of four letters."[24] He mastered not only the morphological formation of words in the American English language but also the art of thinking through a language that had been legally forbidden to all Black subjects. It was a monumental transgression of the structural systems put in place to constrain Black subjects to an endless dwelling in mental darkness.

The significance of this momentous foray into learning how to read and write in the language of the master was not lost on Douglass, especially after his master, Mr. Auld vigorously rebuked his wife for attempting to teach him, thereby potentially providing him with a pathway to break away from the realm of mental darkness that was reserved for Black slaves. Douglass recounts that his master, Hugh, "was amazed at the simplicity of his spouse, and, probably for the first time, he unfolded to her the true philosophy of slavery, and the peculiar rules necessary to be observed by masters and mistresses, in the management of their human chattels. Mr. Auld promptly forbade the continuance of her instruction; telling her, in the first place, that the thing itself was unlawful; that it was also unsafe and could only lead to mischief."[25]

In other words, it was through his quest to gain knowledge that Douglass became aware of the "true philosophy of slavery," which he describes as the political deployment of epistemic ignorance in antebellum America to ensure the enforcement of the rules and regulations that sustain the powers of white supremacy and the dehumanizing exploitation of Black bodies, including the destruction of Black souls. In this instance, Douglass's discovery of the true basis of the slave-master hierarchy served as the mechanism for his motivation to dismantle the burdens of ignorance placed upon him and his unyielding quest to break free from the shackles of slavery. He was particularly stricken by the philosophical sentiments that undergird the things his master, Mr. Auld, said while rebuking his wife for her racialized epistemic transgressions. In *Narrative*, Douglass memorializes his master's assertion that "a [Black slave] should know nothing but to obey his master—to do as he is told to do. Learning would *spoil* the best [Black slave] in the world."[26] Although this assertion may have had some negative impact on Douglass, knowing that his desire to gain knowledge was customarily denied and deemed summarily illegal, he did not allow this to dissuade him from his quest to transgress the realm of mental darkness. He had a positive response to this moment in his experience as a slave; it dawned on him that knowledge and learning must have some kind of liberatory potential or power, which is why they were forbidden by the slave masters. He describes both the negative and positive effects of the experience in this way:

These words sank deep into my heart, stirred up sentiments within that lay slumbering, and called into existence an entirely new train of thought. It was a new and special revelation, explaining dark and mysterious things, with which my youthful understanding had struggled, but struggled in vain. I now understood what had been to me a perplexing difficulty—to wit, the white man's power to enslave the black man [used in the generic sense]. It was a grand achievement, and I prized it highly. From that moment, I understood the pathway from slavery to freedom.[27]

Truly, the redemption of the mind from any process of mental colonization or oppression does not happen *ex nihilo*. It is a careful, thoughtful, and sometimes painful process (as in Douglass's case) that involves the conscious awareness of the schemes that enshroud the bounds of reason and the grounds for self-affirmation in the world. It is this painful process of self-conscious probing of the conditions of oppression, both material and epistemic, that Douglass references in his assertion that the pernicious words of his master "called into existence an entirely new train of thought." The allusion here is to something new—a new frame of thinking about the world that, when considered as an epistemic event, exposes the political character of the ignorance with which Black humans (in the context of colonial America) were projected as nonentities. It is this new frame of thinking that gave Douglass the understanding that "ignorance" was one of the most potent tools of colonial exploitation of Black people. Angela Davis alludes to this in her famous lecture series "Lectures on Liberation," delivered at UCLA in the early 1970s. In her opening lecture, Davis points out that looking at the American slavery system, through the eyes of Douglass, reveals that "keeping an oppressed class in ignorance is one of the principal instruments of that system of oppression."[28]

Douglass was very emphatic about his analysis of ignorance as a form of epistemic oppression in antebellum America. This is aptly captured in *My Bondage and My Freedom*, where he characterizes the American system of slavery as that which holds that "knowledge unfits a child to be a slave."[29] In other words, knowledge and slavery are considered as opposing values when it comes to Black slaves within this system of human flesh mongering and dehumanization. This revelation, because it came to Douglass at a critical moment in his life as a slave when he was pondering why he should be a slave for life, could be considered a grand achievement. That is, he was able to comprehend the fraudulent system of hierarchy, or caste system of power, and the knowledge schemes created within America's political economy of slavery as ostensibly designed to make Black people believe their subjugation or oppression as a given fact of life. The perfection of *ignorance* as a form of epistemic oppression was only achieved when the Black slave came to believe and accept such categories of unknowing as indubitable truths. It was an astonishing discovery for a young Black slave like Douglass, who never received any type of formal education. He describes his experience as such in *My Bondage and My Freedom*, maintaining that it was a new and special revelation for him. In particular, it dispelled a painful mystery against which his youthful understanding had struggled in vain, to wit: the white power structures aimed at perpetuating the enslavement of the Black man.[30]

Yet, he was relentless in his pursuit of freedom. Herein lies the overly positive project of Douglass. He was not satisfied with merely analyzing the structures of oppression designed to keep Black folks in perpetual conditions of enslavement. He was adamant that the awareness of these structures of oppression should be the very basis for negotiating the conditions of his freedom—a pathway from slavery to freedom. In his biographical work on Douglass, *Frederick Douglass: Prophet of Freedom,* David W. Blight correctly notes that it was through this awareness that "Douglass recollected himself and achieved an awakening for the first time to the white man's power to perpetuate the enslaving of the Black man. If 'knowledge unfits a child to be a slave,' Douglass later wrote, then he had found the motive power of his path out, or at least inward, to freedom."[31] What is being described here is the obstinate nature of a young Black slave whose eyes had been opened to the light of knowledge, and then proceeded to reject everything that the system of slavery stood for, even though he was still physically held in the condition of enslavement. This newly acquired sense of urgency and the pursuit of freedom through the liberation of his mind would largely contribute to one of the most consequential moments in Douglass's career as a slave—the fight with Edward Covey. Douglass himself describes his battle with Mr. Covey as the turning point in his career as a slave. He describes it as such because he believes it rekindled the few expiring embers of freedom and revived within him a sense of his manhood. It recalled the departed self-confidence to build a new foundation for self-knowledge and inspired him again with a determination to be free.[32]

Black Self-Knowledge as the Foundation of an Anticolonial Epistemology

It is important to consider Douglass's essay, "Self-Made Man," as a treatise on Black self-epistemology for two reasons. First, it is an essay that contained one of the most sustained, written reflections by Douglass on the subject of self-constitution, self-knowledge, and self-formation as a catalyst for transcending the epistemic and material oppression of colonial hegemony. Second, it is a reflection that exposes the role of the "self" (the liberated self) in exposing the contradictions and irrationalities of the slavery system as they pertain to the conditions of the Black slave. Through his reflections in "Self-Made Man," we see an articulation of the actual process of the Black slave transforming into a Black subject.[33] Under the system of coloniality instituted in America during the antebellum period, there was no such thing as a "Black subject." It was an unacknowledged apparition, a nonexistent thing. But the reality of Douglass's attainment of freedom from mental and physical enslavement through autodidactic means ruptures all of the categories that were held as the norm during this period. What is of interest in this discourse on self-epistemology in the philosophy of Douglass is the epistemic subversion of the colonial system of knowledge that originally excluded all Black slaves from attaining the status of a Black subject. Thus, for Douglass, self-knowledge, particularly Black self-knowledge, becomes the very foundation for building an anticolonial epistemology that is in opposition to the dominant frames of knowledge that concretized the conditions of slavery in the New World.

The grounding of the "self" as the foundation for building epistemic principles was very important in Douglass's reflections; through his investigation of his life-situations, he came to understand that recognition as a viable epistemic agent is possible through personal efforts and by building upon such personal efforts to attain a social agreement, especially in a world that perpetually refuses to consider Black people as being part of the human community. Douglass describes the self-made man as follows:

> By the term "self-made men," I mean especially what to the popular mind, the term itself imports. Self-made men are the men who, under peculiar difficulties and without the ordinary helps favoring circumstances, have attained knowledge, usefulness, power and position and have learned from themselves the best uses to which life can be put in this world, and in the exercises of these uses to build up worthy character.[34]

In Douglass's description of the nature of the self-made man we see an anticolonial turn, because he subverts what has been built as "established" notions of the "self" (subject) in dominant epistemological thinking, especially the racialized system of epistemologies that was prevalent between the early eighteenth and late nineteenth centuries in America. The peculiar difficulties he references in the passage cited earlier is reminiscent of his own condition under the circumstances, which have led commentators on Douglass to suggest that he was probably referring to himself as the epistemic exemplar in terms of the cultivation of the powers of self-knowledge toward achieving anticolonial ends. Even though the American system of slavery considered Black slaves merely as "ownable" properties, Douglass held a radical antislavery view in not only insisting that the Black slave is human, but also going a step further to avow that the Black slave is capable of developing a worthy character. In "Images of Frederick Douglass in the Afro-American Mind," Waldo E. Martin describes Douglass as "an archetypal black self-made man.

He was extremely and justly proud of his self-made success and saw himself as an example for his people to emulate."[35] This implies that Douglass functioned not only as a Black slave that undercuts America's political economy of slavery through an expression of epistemic freedom but also as an authoritative reference who simultaneously articulated and legitimized the Black quest for self-definition and autonomy.[36]

The interrelation of the notions of self-definition and autonomy are important aspects of the philosophy of Douglass that require further analysis. In examining "self-knowledge" as the foundation of anticolonial epistemology, there are two dimensions of the self that can be identified, namely, the cologenic self and the afrogenic self. The cologenic self refers to the colonized nonsubject possessing a mind that dwells in the mental darkness of ignorance created by the colonialists to enslave the colonized nonsubject within the hierarchy of being and knowledge of the dominant culture. This is the condition of the self under the circumstances of slavery as described by Douglass; it is a notion of self that cannot express any true sense of self-consciousness, self-authorship, or self-ownership—the absence of any references to human attributes of subjective experience. The genius and intellectual gifts within this dimension of the self are already prematurely assumed to be aborted due to the display of intellectual arrogance, stark violence, and other brutal schemes employed within the dominant culture to ensure that epistemic control belonged always to external forces rather than to internal forces of being. In this case, the world, as imagined, is already "othered" and racialized while the biological formations that are deemed to be outside of the dominant culture's terms of reference are considered as less formed and nonviable nonsubjects. In other words, the cologenic self cannot, under normal circumstances, express the logic of self-thinking that is necessary for a self-avowal because the self is already owned or "colonized" through material and psychological means of warfare, including the epistemology of ignorance.

However, the afrogenic self is the contradiction of the cologenic self. It is the self that can only exist through the absolute inversion of colonial logics and the transmutation of the subhuman categories of unbeing projected onto "othered" bodies (such as Black slaves) in the context of American slavery. The afrogenic self does not conform to the ethos of colonialism, which makes it an emerging anticolonial subject. The afrogenic self is the Black subject who can experience an epistemological awakening. When the afrogenic self fully emerges as the anticolonial subject, it demonstrates an awareness of a difference between the internalized world of the self and a world outside of the self (the colonial world) to which mental states are directed. This self is capable of constant self-remaking as a developed epistemic subject that avows knowledge claims and postulates epistemological categories in the world. This notion of the afrogenic self is consistent with what Douglass characterizes as the self-made human—specifically referring to the Black subject. Since Douglass understood mental darkness—the realm of the *unknowing being*—as a mark of colonial oppression, throughout his life he strove to develop a distinctive notion of Black self-epistemology that was directed at developing the political consciousness of Black folks and marshaling ideas toward the future of the Black race.

Douglass is an archetypal Black philosopher that embodies this notion of the afrogenic self. He painstakingly worked to establish himself as a worthy epistemic agent, even within a colonial system that ferociously prevented people like him from coming to such terms of self-discovery. This process of self-discovery requires conscientious, even humiliating, efforts. As Douglass describes in *Narrative*, "Though conscious of the difficulty of learning without a teacher, I set out with high hope, and a fixed purpose, at whatever cost of trouble, to learn how to read."[37] Douglass had to sometimes give away his derisory lunch to white boys who were his playmates, in order to learn from them. One can only imagine such difficulty in the condition of slavery where the rations apportioned to slaves were mostly inadequate. He had to devise various schemes and subterfuge to secretly learn to read and write without getting caught. He also risked being in contravention of the law, knowing the stiff consequences that might befall him if his secret efforts to acquire knowledge were discovered. Thus, he was conscious of the fact that this would be an arduous task to achieve for the individuals he describes as self-made men, "who owe little or nothing to birth, relationship, friendly surroundings; to wealth inherited or to early approved means of education; who are what they are, without the aid of many of the favoring conditions by which other men usually rise in the world and achieve great results."[38]

Douglass highlights the price that can be derived from the display of the fruits of self-knowledge even in conditions that are not all that favorable. It is an allusion to the courage to resist the structures of oppression even though there has to be some price to pay. Following Douglass, it is only when the Black subject achieves self-knowledge that the experience of genuine freedom can truly emerge. This notion of genuine freedom entails the ability of Black slaves to think for themselves while not appealing to standards of thinking that exclude them from the community of humans. It is important to also emphasize that he does not see Black self-knowledge as an immutable epistemic category that does not require further work on the part of the afrogenic self. He emphasizes the necessity of remaking oneself by affirming one's intellectual genius and epistemic authority to challenge such politicized and racialized categories that are designed to put Blackness outside of the limits of knowledge.

Self-knowledge in Frederick Douglass's philosophy is not merely about the constitution of the "abstract" self. Rather, it is a notion of self-understanding that is supposed to bring about transformational conditions or qualities in the world. It involves a sense of recognition that the self-in-the world is both a material entity and one that can display mental capabilities as human; it is a healthy sense of self-ownership that is devoid of the emptiness to which the self is described concerning Blackness under the colonial-hegemonic imaginary. For Douglass, the attainment of personhood (ownership of oneself), or the lack of attainment thereof, is what signifies the threshold between slavery and freedom. The slave is only able to continue in the career of slavery because there is an understanding that the self is owned by the other rather than by the self. In this case, the will of the slave will always be subject to the will of the other (master/overseer); that is, there is absolutely no trace of agential control over the processes of the mind or the evidence of thought. The only acceptable trajectory of action for the Black slave is primarily derived from the other; anything else apart from this is considered unacceptable and met with severe punishment. This was the case with the white overseer named Mr. Gore and the Black slave, Demby, that Douglass wrote about in chapter four of *Narrative*. He described Mr. Gore in this manner: "Overseers will sometimes indulge in a witty word, even with the slaves, not with Mr. Gore. He spoke to command, and commanded but to be obeyed; he dealt sparingly with his words, and bountifully with his whip, never using the former where the latter would answer as well."[39] What this suggests is that for the slave/caste system to be sustained, those who wield power must demonstrate absolute control, and its enforcement is necessary to maintain the evil and violence of the system of enslavement.

In one of the most grotesque representations to be found in Douglass's first autobiography, he memorializes the violent response that Mr. Gore put up against Demby, the Black slave, for attempting to express his own will or agency within the system of slavery. Douglass has this to say about Mr. Gore:

His savage barbarity was equaled only by the consummate coolness with which he committed the grossest and most savage deeds upon slaves under his charge. Mr. Gore once undertook to whip one of Colonel Lloyd's slaves, by the name of Demby. He had given Demby but few stripes, when, to get rid of the scourging, he ran and plunged himself into a creek, and stood there at the depth of his shoulders, refusing to come out. Mr. Gore told him that he would give him three calls, and that, if he did not come out at the third call, he would shoot him. The first call was given. Demby made no response but stood his ground. The second and third calls were given with the same result. Mr. Gore then, without consultation or deliberation with any one, not even giving Demby an additional call, raised his musket to his face, taking deadly aim at his standing victim, and in an instant poor Demby was no more. His mangled body sank out of sight, and blood and brains marked the water where he stood.[40]

In this passage, Demby was trying to exert his own will within a system that does not recognize such from a Black *unknowing being* or nonexistent subject. Within such a system, there is only one true will, and that is the will of the master. Thus, the Black slave lacks all sense of control over himself because he had been acquired and purchased as the "legal" property of the slave owner. It is interesting to note that in this extreme case concerning Mr. Gore and Demby, death is the ultimate consequence of a Black slave trying to display any form of consciousness or the control of the self under such a violent system of dehumanization. One can argue, philosophically, that for Blacks in debilitating conditions of dehumanization, death is sometimes seen as a form of "escape," the negation of unfreedom, and the final act to transcend all forms of anti-Black violence that seek to perpetually destroy Black lives. Even Douglass was aware that death was one of the possible consequences of his attempt to escape American slavery, yet he forged ahead courageously until he finally succeeded. We see a very vivid representation of how Black slaves had to struggle against death in his fictional representations of the travels of Madison Washington (one of Douglass's original slave names) in *The Heroic Slave*.

In *The Heroic Slave*, Douglass painted a picture displaying the interrelatedness of the question of freedom and the reality of the death of the Black slave. As he writes, the Black slave looks at the conditions of the birds in the air and contemplates his condition of unfreedom. This necessitates raising questions of this kind: "But what is freedom to me, or I to it? I am a *slave*,—born a slave, an abject slave,—even before I made part of this breathing world, the scourge was platted for my back; the fetters were forged for my limbs."[41] The bounding of the limbs with fetters, as practiced within America's political economy of slavery and reimagined here, highlights the condition of finality and absolute control that subjects the will of the self to that of the powerful other, which means it is the only condition for which Black slaves were "allowed" to be alive. Invariably, to make any negotiations or any attempt to go beyond this, would amount to inviting death. Douglass alluded to this in *The Heroic Slave* when he writes about the piteous cries of the Black slave, saying:

> I am galled with irons; but even these are more tolerable than the consciousness, the *galling* consciousness of cowardice and indecision. Can it be that I *dare* not run away? *Perish the thought*, I *dare* do any thing [sic] which may be done by another. When that young man struggled with the waves *for life*, and others stood back appalled in helpless horror, did I not plunge in, forgetful of life, to save his? The raging bull from whom all others fled, pale with fright, did I not keep at bay with a single pitchfork? Could a coward do that? *No, —no,* —I wrong myself, —I am no coward. *Liberty* I will have, or die in the attempt to gain it.[42]

When Douglass talks about doing things for oneself, "which may be done by another," he is referencing the courage to exhibit the elements of consciousness and self-hood, even if it means that one has to die to achieve it. Furthermore, the way in which he describes the heroic slave suggests that the inalienable rights of Black people are not self-evident but dependent on the acknowledgment of those rights from other governing structures. In short, rights are politically rather than naturally endowed, including the right to life.[43]

In the case(s) where the Black slave can escape death while striving toward freedom, Douglass emphasized the importance of self-affirmation and self-knowledge. In discussions about self-knowledge in contemporary epistemology, the concept is often associated with ideas such as an individual's awareness of their sensations, thoughts, beliefs, and other mental states.[44] But Douglass's allusion to the concept of self-knowledge is not restricted to the same abstract formulations of mental properties concerning knowledge of the self. His notion of self-knowledge includes a process of epistemic transformation (thoughts, dispositions, and beliefs) that leads to other practical ends—the achievement of freedom from the system of slavery and other forms of anti-Black oppression. It is a functional rather than an abstract sense of self-knowledge. This is demonstrated in Douglass's letter to his former slave master, Thomas Auld, on September 3, 1848, in which he tells Auld, "I am myself; you are yourself; we are two distinct persons, equal persons. What you are, I am. You are a man, and so am I. God created both and made us separate beings. I am not by nature bound to you, or you to me. Nature does not make your existence depend upon me, or mine to depend upon yours."[45] He is articulating a sense of self-ownership that necessitates a sense of self-knowledge that is unwarranted under the conditions of slavery.

Of course, it helps that Douglass is writing this to his slave master after he had successfully escaped from slavery and his freedom had been purchased by his supporters in England. This background also shapes how he made these demands from his former slave master. He goes further to say the following to his former master: "We are distinct persons, and are each equally provided with faculties necessary to our individual existence. In leaving you, I took nothing but what belonged to me, and in no way lessened your means for obtaining an *honest* living. Your faculties remained yours, and mine became useful to their rightful owner."[46] Here, Douglass is clear that he is now reclaiming his faculty/agency; he is reclaiming his previously subjugated self under slavery. He is now the absolute authority over the content (thinking) of his mind and he is, above all else, just like his master: *human.* This is an account of self-epistemology from a Black perspective that arrives at the concept of the Black human, which is a category that was denied to all Black subjects under the American system of slavery. Thus, for Douglass, the Black subject becomes a reformed "human" or "being." It is a thing that *is* and is constantly *becoming.* Through Douglass's reflections as articulated in this chapter, we see the development of a unique idea of Black self-epistemology that primarily conceives of the Black subject as a knower—a liberated epistemic agent that navigates the world through the strength of their knowledge. Herein lies the significance of Frederick Douglass as a social epistemologist within antebellum America.

5

Seeking Truth

Ida B. Wells-Barnett's
Pioneering Work in the
Sociology of Black Knowledge

Ida B. Wells-Barnett was an extraordinary Black woman who achieved great things by altering the social imagination and the reality held by many Americans in the twentieth century that was steeped in the violence of white supremacy. She relentlessly upheld the conviction that the use of racial violence as a mechanism for maintaining the structures of power, by the white vigilantes, mobs, and corrupted members of law enforcement in America, is antithetical to the principles of democracy that the nation claims as the cornerstone of its founding ideals. For Wells-Barnett, the ideals of freedom, equality, justice, and fairness could not be attained in America in a context where legal, social, and moral structures and a spiritual framework were all utilized to prevent the realization of the good life for African Americans and other oppressed peoples. Her work and ideas have received a great deal of attention from scholars across different fields of inquiry. She has been described, in many of the writings and works of literature that have been produced about her over the years, as an antilynching activist, radical educator, early leader in the civil rights movement in the 1870s, suffragist, and an unrelentless campaigner against racial terrorism. Perhaps she is most widely known for her work on the antilynching campaign at a time in America when the summary trial and execution ("jungle justice") of a presumed offender by white mobs superseded the administration of justice within the formal structures of the criminal justice system. In this chapter, I argue that there is more to her contributions to intellectual history than the mere classification as an antilynching activist. I examine her groundbreaking work in laying the foundation for Black knowledge in the twentieth century, especially highlighting her pioneering efforts in the creation of a new way of knowing, an epistemological framework that is grounded in the Black lived experience and aimed at understanding the existential problems that confronted Black folks in an anti-Black world.

I consider Ida B. Wells-Barnett as a remarkable Black female philosopher whose genius is all the more remarkable given that her groundbreaking ideas were fashioned at a time in America when women, and more so Black women, were thought of as second-class citizens unable to access the rights and privileges of a fully functioning citizenship.[1] Although Wells-Barnett is famous for her work on the antilynching campaign, what has not been highlighted in the scholarship about this remarkable Black intellectual is the unique and groundbreaking method of knowledge generation she established as a framework for understanding social phenomena in the late nineteenth and early twentieth centuries. She was one of the first Black thinkers to introduce empirical investigation and data collection into the cataloging of knowledge. Her intellectual contributions were remarkable because they emphasized how empirically generated data about human social conditions should inform the general understanding of social phenomena.

It is unsurprising that such a pioneering achievement by this brilliant Black female philosopher has not been acknowledged within the academic field of philosophy because the connection between empirical data and ideational categories is often disregarded as a viable method of "doing" philosophy. Philosophical ponderings, especially within the context of Western philosophy, are heavily grounded in abstract theorizations and thought processes that are ultra-disconnected from human reality and highly valued as marks of rational sophistication and epistemological achievement. This then becomes the ultimate standard for measuring what counts as philosophy or on whom the status of philosopher should be conferred. So, when such "measuring standards" are applied, a Black thinker such as Wells-Barnett would not be generally considered a philosopher because she offers a different method for looking at the world and the difficult problems that confront Black people within society. This is one of the endemic problems of method in Western philosophy: the idea that philosophical merit of creative thinking should be measured by its capacity to transcend empirical reality rather than be constitutive of it. I fundamentally believe that what a philosopher is or becomes is greatly shaped by the society or social context in which they live, and that philosophy is not disconnected from the material world. In fact, the empirical or material world offers valuable sets of data upon which philosophers build their theories. This perspective allows for the possibility of seeing Wells-Barnett as a recognized Black female philosopher.

One of the greatest problems concerning race relations in America, when Wells-Barnett became a prominent journalist, activist, and campaigner for civil rights, was the terrorist act of lynching that was perpetrated by white mobs and racist militia groups and supported by ordinary white individuals who had deep-seated hatred toward Black folks, under the guise of protecting the virtues of white women from the supposed sexual threat of African American men. This terrorist act was prevalent in post-Reconstruction America, when white communities developed Jim Crow laws to bypass the codified systems of law and order to create extrajudicial and illegal ways of enforcing white racial superiority by performing the dastardliest acts of man's inhumanity ever recorded. In her autobiography *Crusade for Justice*, Wells-Barnett described one particular incident of lynching as consequential for the trajectory of her life: the murder of her friend Thomas Moss through lynching, along with the co-owners of the People's grocery, Calvin McDowell and Will Stewart, in Memphis in 1892. As she describes it in her own words, "while I was thus carrying on the work of my newspaper, happy in the thought that our influence was helpful and that I was doing the work I loved and had proved that I could make a living out if it, there came the lynching in Memphis which changed the whole course of my life."[2] This incident impacted her so much that she focused a significant part of her life to advocate and campaign against lynching in both the United States and the United Kingdom. She desperately wanted to do something about the problem of lynching. For this to happen, she knew she had to approach the issue from a factual basis rather than from a purely emotional basis. It was important for her to, as she puts it, "get the facts for my people so that they know what to do."[3]

Thus, the pioneering work offered by Wells-Barnett in the sociology of Black knowledge centered primarily on using factual evidence to transform social perception and erroneously held opinions that were projected as accurate social knowledge. This sentiment was aptly captured by Eve L. Ewing, who wrote the foreword to the recent edition of her autobiography, describing her as "a woman who changed the world through meticulous fact-finding, who often established a record where there was none, using careful documentation when others were satisfied with hearsay or outright lies."[4] In order words, her meticulous approach not only entails the distinction between what is true and what is believed to be true but also, more importantly, exposes how the social construction of knowledge by whites with murderous intent toward African Americans had been used as propaganda to drive an evil agenda—to destroy their lives and property so they would never be able to pose any economic, social, or political rivalry. As Wells-Barnett studied the situation further, she became convinced that what is usually cited as the justification for lynching is really a subterfuge, and that the real reason was that the Southern whites who engaged in these acts had never gotten over their resentment that Black people were no longer their playthings, servants, and sources of income through exploited slave labor.[5] So, she directed her intervention toward attacking the oft-cited rationale of "protection" and turning it on its head in order to prevent such senseless killings. She understood that, given her status as a Black woman, her critique of this evil practice and the socially held beliefs and perceptions of this problem had to be achieved with the weight of something beyond mere words. This is what informed her emphasis on the empiricist knowledge generation methodology that is based on facts rather than opinions (even if widely held) and her insistence that this methodology, in turn, inform our social understanding or socially accepted knowledge.

The Empiricist Model of Knowledge Attribution and Social Change

In 1895, Wells-Barnett completed a monumental work, *A Red Record. Tabulated Statistics and Alleged Causes of Lynchings in the United States, 1892-1893-1894*, which emphasized the connection between statistical data and human understanding of social reality. It was the first work that would seriously study lynching as a form of white terrorism that was largely driven by falsehood rather than facts. What makes this work truly significant is her emphasis on the empiricist model of knowledge gathering and the dispelling of social myths in order to arrive at a more robust account of reality that would ultimately help improve racial relations in the post-Reconstruction era. Until Wells-Barnett brought forth this evidence-based approach in generating knowledge and applied it to the problem of lynching, this act was driven and reinforced purely by the false social perceptions generated by whites. But Wells-Barnett did not collect all the empirical evidence about lynching herself. That would have been an impossible task given the prevalence of its occurrence during this period, especially in Southern states. So, another stroke of genius that she employed was to investigate the statistical data collected and compiled by white men on lynching and use it to tell a different story, a counter-story to the one that was commonly told. She clearly articulates this in stating "the case" for writing *A Red Record*, affirming that "the statistics as gathered and preserved by white men, and which have not been questioned, show that during these years more than ten thousand negroes [Black folks] have been killed in cold blood, without the formality of judicial trial and legal execution."[6] She also believed that the dataset used in *A Red Record* was compiled by white men; it is only appropriate that "out of their own mouths shall the murderers [other white men] be condemned."[7]

The emphasis on "questioning" the statistical data depicts Wells-Barnett's interest in ascertaining what the data actually portrays, rather than merely reporting the data. In other words, she was focused on understanding how the empirical data that was collected and preserved can go beyond the surface of the extrajudicial killings to consider some of the excuses often cited as justificatory grounds for their prevalence and support by so many white people. She identified three main reasons in this work. The first excuse given for the mass murder of Black folks was to suppress and quell alleged race-riots. The second was to maintain white supremacy through racial violence with the objective of halting the Reconstruction Amendment (Fifteenth Amendment) that gave Black men the constitutional right to vote.[8] The third was the invented lie that Black folks had to be killed in large numbers in order to avenge the assault of white women and to remedy any form of "disrespect" against the white race. She contended that the collected data, when looked at critically, depicts a different reality altogether. In her view, the record "shows that a large portion of the American people [white people] avow anarchy, condone murder and defy the contempt of civilization."[9]

Put differently, Wells-Barnett is exposing the racist psychology of American society through the account she provides in her work, as it details the horrors and penchant for the grotesque destruction of Black bodies and provides the terrible statistics that amplify this national shame.[10] It also demonstrates the disposability of Black lives elicited by the assumption that they are less valuable than white lives. In the first chapter of *A Red Record*, Wells-Barnett writes that, as evidence of the absolute impunity with which white folks dare to kill Black folks, the same record shows that during the years under investigation, no white man had been lynched for the murder of colored people.[11] In his work, "The Fortune of Wells," Tommy J. Curry considers this as a consequence of racism in white society that determines, as a matter of necessity, the superior value of white life and the justification of violence against all other lives.[12]

A Red Record (1895), which listed all the known lynchings of Black Americans that took place between 1892 and 1894, is Wells-Barnett's longest antilynching work.[13] It utilized facts and figures from the Chicago Tribune's annual compilation of statistics on lynching across the United States. Wells-Barnett considered this a veritable resource to combat one of the most common excuses for this act, the assumption that Black men were lynched because of their assaults on women, by documenting that most of the accused rapists who fell victim to lynch mobs had been participants in illicit relationships that were kept secret rather than nonconsensual.[14] This fact-based conclusion, which she drew from the critical assessment of the empirical data, created considerable upheaval within the social fabric given the extreme volatility of the issue and the extent to which powerful whites worked so hard to maintain the white-Black color line through the trope of protecting the "virtue" of white women.

Wells-Barnett significantly challenged the trope that African American men pose a sexual threat to whites. Her investigations of the factual evidence showed that most of the so-called African American rapes were really affairs between consenting white females and African American males. This was also an indictment of the worthlessness of the antimiscegenation laws that were used to maintain the system of racial caste and white racial supremacy in antebellum America. A good example of this is the first anti-miscegenation law ratified by the Arkansas legislature in October 1837: "The statute declared all marriages between white people and [Blacks] Negroes or mulattos 'illegal and void.'"[15] These anti-miscegenation laws were instituted in order to enforce racial segregation by both preventing and criminalizing interracial marriages between white women and Black men. Thus, Wells-Barnett basically exposed the failure of white men to regulate or control the sexual and romantic choices of white women. In other words, instead of owning up to the reality that they could not police those whom white women decided to fall in love with, including Black men, they resulted to violence and the most horrible, despicable, and vile form of moral evil, lynching.

Some of the snapshots of the data that Wells-Barnett investigated support the view that this form of racial violence was reactionary rather than serving any progressive ends. She documents that "from 1865 to 1872, hundreds of colored men and women were mercilessly murdered and the almost invariable reason assigned was that they met their death by being alleged participants in an insurrection or riot."[16] But this claim that the victims were involved in insurrection is not supported by her investigation of the circumstances surrounding many of the cases that she carefully documents in her work. She also recounts that "during the year 1894, there were 132 persons executed in the United States by due form of law, while in this same year, 197 persons were put to death by [white] mobs who gave the victims no opportunity to make lawful defense."[17] These statistics showed the lack of respect for the rule of law by white Americans when dealing with colored people who were alleged to have committed crimes. They were intended to deal with instant outcomes of "jungle justice" because mob law, rather than positive law, was deemed to be most applicable to Black folks within a democratic society that was built on the structures of a white racial order. A few years after the publication of A Red Record, Wells-Barnett would pen an essay titled "Lynch Law in America," in which she regarded lynching as America's national crime because "it represents the cool, calculating deliberation of intelligent people who openly avow that there is an 'unwritten law' that justifies them in putting human beings to death without complaint under oath, without trial by jury, without opportunity to make defense, and without right of appeal."[18] It would not make much sense to try the accused under the law because they would most likely be acquitted, since most of them did not actually commit the crimes of which they were accused. So, rather than risk acquittal of the accused following the due process of the law, white Americans would rather engage in extralegal means, such as lynching, to achieve their nefarious ambitions.

Wells-Barnett was also able to use this data to ascertain that most of the victims of this form of white racial terrorism did not commit the crime of rape, thereby underscoring the hypocrisy and duplicity of the racism of Southern whites on this issue of protecting the "virtue" of womanhood.[19] She found that white men of the South practiced as acceptable for themselves what they assumed to be unthinkable for white women, in terms of interracial relationships. "They could and did fall in love with the pretty mulatto and quadroon girls as well as black ones, but they professed inability to imagine white women doing the same thing with Negro and mulatto men. Whenever they did so and were found out, the cry of rape was raised, and the lowest element of the white South was turned loose to wreak its fiendish cruelty on those too weak to help themselves."[20] In the antebellum and post-Reconstruction South, sexual liaisons between white women and Black men were generally considered taboo because they threatened the constitution of the racial order in a way that sex between white men and Black women did not.[21] In a very insightful section of her autobiography *Crusade for Justice*, Wells-Barnett emphasized another function that extralegal killing of Black folks served within the constructed white racial order: to eliminate any form of competition with whites in economic terms, that is, in the acquisition of property and wealth. She writes about how the pursuit of factual evidence helped transform her thinking about the fact of lynching:

> Like many other persons who had read of lynching in the South, I had accepted the idea meant to be conveyed—that although lynching was irregular and contrary to law and order, unreasoning anger over the terrible crime of rape led to the lynching; that perhaps the brute deserved death anyhow and the mob was justified in taking his life. But Thomas Moss, Calvin McDowell, and Lee Stewart had been lynched in Memphis, one of the leading cities of the South, in which no lynching had taken place before, with just as much brutality as other victim of the mob; and they had committed no crime against white women. This is what opened my eyes to what lynching really was. An excuse to get rid of the Negroes who were acquiring wealth and property and thus keep the race terrorized and keep [Black people] down. Then I began investigation of every lynching I read about. I stumbled on amazing record that every case of rape reported in that three months became such only when it became public.[22]

What she is hinting at is her motivation to ensure that prejudiced white people were not the ones defining and shaping social knowledge of the problems associated with white-Black relations within a segregated social context. She circumvented the status quo, in which white men were the ones who ultimately decided what reality is, to invent a new perspective grounded in the Black lived experience—the sociology of Black knowledge that is based on the empirical mode of knowledge generation. Thus, even before ethnographic research became a standard way of knowledge generation in sociology, Wells-Barnett laid the foundation in the twentieth century.

The method of knowledge generation highlighted here is what has been missing in the tomes of scholarship that have been produced about Wells-Barnett. Although she is popularly known as a militant antilynching activist that worked doggedly to confront the senseless killing of Black people by white racists, vigilantes, and bloodthirsty mobs, there is another important part of her intellectual legacy that has been glossed over in such scholarship—this fact-based approach to knowledge generation, meant to counter the lies that were purposefully paraded as truths and aimed at transforming society by building new perspectives and grounds for understanding. However, this method is focused on the production of knowledge not as an end in itself but as a means to an end—stemming the tide of racial violence motivated by anti-Black racism and creating social change. A fundamental characteristic of every human society is that the acceptability or condemnation of certain kinds of human actions is largely dependent on the norms, beliefs, and ideals that are held as social truths, or "common" knowledge or understanding insofar as they protect the way humans live and flourish. Unfortunately, during the lifetime of Wells-Barnett, white people in America held racist ideas about the myth of Black inferiority and beliefs about the devaluation and destruction of Black lives with impunity. Wells-Barnett's founding epistemological work strikes at the heart of this framework of social truths with the goal of transforming society and consequently improving racial relations. Once the fact-finding approach she pursued revealed a perspective that differed from the dominant systems of knowledge, it became obvious that something had to be done to achieve social change and prevent these senseless murders from happening.

While Wells-Barnett's use of statistics has been extensively praised as an important tool in her antilynching campaign and her unrelenting efforts to confront this racist practice, her methodic efforts to calculate, reframe, analyze, and represent the data have been glossed over or undervalued. Some of her inclination to inform and educate her readers and the many audiences she spoke to about this problem likely emerged out of her early years as a teacher.[23] She presented her work on the representation of this data as a source of enlightenment and transformation for many audiences in places where she had the opportunity to speak and for readers who had access to her journalistic writings. For instance, in one of her many lectures abroad, titled "Lectures in Bristol, England, on American Lynch Law," Wells reported that her audiences were shocked after they listened to her presentation of facts and statistics regarding the horrifying details of white lynchings. She recalled a certain "Dr. Miller Nicholson, the pastor of the largest and most influential Presbyterian Church in the city and . . . Mrs. Coote, president of the Women's Liberal Association of Bristol" who were both shocked on being told the actual condition of things regarding lynching and their facial expressions were painful to behold.[24] However, this does not mean that both of these highly influential individuals had never heard of lynchings in the American South until they met Wells-Barnett. She provided additional commentary on this, stating that "it is true they had read of lynchings, and while they thought them dreadful had accepted the general belief that it was for terrible crimes perpetrated by negro men upon white women."[25] Through the intervention of Wells-Barnett, these individuals became aware of the truth and would later work assiduously to support the antilynching campaign and argue for society's change from this evil.

In "Who Counts? Urgent Lessons from Ida B. Wells's Radical Statistics," Anne M. Brubaker emphasizes the significance of Wells-Barnett's use of statistical tabulations as a framework for changing people's minds as truly groundbreaking when we focus on the time period in which she lived. Brubaker notes that while numerical representation has a long history of dehumanizing, disenfranchising, and dividing people of color, Wells-Barnett showed its potential to restore dignity, expose injustice, and offer another perspective, one that is different from those constructed by the dominant group.[26] She relied on the weight of facts, evidence, and empirically verifiable truths to show the failures of the American legal system, especially its lack of protections for Black lives.[27] This was not a critique of the legal system based on mere words, but a clear demonstration of how the law failed to protect Black rights in public transportation and other public utilities.[28] She combated racism and structural injustice on many fronts, including exposing the hypocrisy of white Christians who supported lynchings; she was never afraid to speak up even when she was threatened with death and exiled from home by white mobs and vigilantes.[29]

Deborah L. Rhode describes Wells-Barnett's commitment to combating lynching in "Leadership Lessons from a Heroic, if 'Difficult' Woman: A Tribute to Ida B. Wells," as a response to the many aspects of racialization she was confronting, which led to the development of new strategies and a call for self-defense and civil disobedience, where appropriate.[30] For instance, she called for Black folks in Memphis to boycott the train, and trolley car boycotts were also necessary because the "appeal to the white man's pocket has ever been more effectual than all the appeals ever made to his conscience."[31] Undoubtedly, Wells-Barnett's work was a template for a more just approach to racial data collection and analysis, one that had the power to disrupt cycles of violence and dismantle entrenched narratives about race and ensure human progress.[32] This correlates with Christopher Waldrep's assessment in the "War of Words: The Controversy over the Definition of Lynching, 1899–1940," that although Wells-Barnett fought racial stereotyping with a variety of strategies, "her most effective weapon was statistics."[33] Her use of statistical data in building the case against lynching was distinctive and effective as it would have significant effects in changing the culture of the fetishization of Black death and was reflected in campaigns against lynching, even after the demise of Wells-Barnett.[34]

Wells-Barnett's Accomplishments in Epistemology

In the preface to *A Red Record*, Frederick Douglass had this to say about the achievement of Wells-Barnett, especially the transformative power of her use of evidence-based research to change people's minds about the real dangers of the problem of lynching and how it should be condemned by everyone in society in order to move toward social, political, economic, and racial progress:

> Let me give you thanks for your faithful paper on the lynch abomination now generally practiced against colored people in the South. There has been no word equal to it in convincing power. I have spoken, but my word is feeble in comparison. You give us what you know and testify from actual knowledge. You have dealt with the facts with cool, painstaking fidelity, and left those naked and uncontradicted facts to speak for themselves.[35]

What Douglass is stressing here is that Wells-Barnett's achievement deserves to be acknowledged because it approaches the phenomenon of human knowledge or counter-knowledge by testimony from actual experience. Today, discussions on the importance of testimony in knowledge generation are widely acknowledged, but Wells-Barnett was able to make this connection long before the epistemology of testimony became popularized within the context of Western philosophy. This is one of Wells-Barnett's greatest accomplishments in Black epistemology—the development, discovery, and utilization of testimonial knowledge to express the Black worldview about social reality and how it is significantly impacted by the problem of racialization.

She employed this testimonial knowledge framework in investigating lynchings, often risking her life by going to jails to interview those who were accused of committing crimes and returning with sworn statements from witnesses. It is through this method of knowledge gathering that she came to the conclusion that not all victims of mob violence charged with rape had committed the crime. Many of those charged were partners in interracial love affairs.[36] She understood that for testimonial knowledge to be reliable and successful in changing the minds of people within society, there had to be some established grounds for trust between the testifier and the inquirer/speaker. As a reputable member of the Black community, she was able to establish this foundation for trust, which allowed her method to be successful in advocating for Black folks. For instance, in the Arkansas riot of 1919, which resulted in the murder of scores of Black folks, twelve Black men were incarcerated for allegedly killing five white men. Wells-Barnett was asked by the National Association for the Advancement of Colored People (NAACP) and the National Equal Rights League to go to Arkansas to protest this unjust action and organize legal assistance. In *Crusade for Justice*, she wrote about using this method of gathering information through testimonial knowledge, stating that when she got to the prison where they were being held, she "talked to them about their experiences, asked them to write down everything they could recollect about the rioting, and what befell each one of them."[37] Expanding on this, she avows:

> I asked them also tell me the number of acres of land they had tilled during the year, how much cotton and corn they had raised, and how many heads [*sic*] of cattle and hogs they owned, and be sure to say what had become of it all. They told me that since they had been moved to Little Rock they had been treated with a good deal of fairness and consideration; but that while they were in jail in Helena they were in constant torment. First, a mob tried to get into the jail to lynch them. Then they were beaten, given electric shocks, and in every possible way terrorized in an effort to force them to confess that their organization was a conspiracy for the purpose of murdering white people and confiscating their property.[38]

This quote provides insights into how Wells-Barnett applied this method to real-life situations. Most of the victims of this misapplication of the law were often paralyzed by the fear of bodily and property destruction by the white mobs, and consequently were unable to speak about the truth of the conditions surrounding their arrest and impending deadly fate. But through the interventions of Wells-Barnett, they often found much-needed support to make a case for their innocence. In this particular instance regarding the Black folks imprisoned in Little Rock, she was able to make her findings public and created enough public pressure to get the authorities to release all twelve of the accused Black men.

This method of testimonial knowledge in the work of Ida B. Wells-Barnett was evident in her investigation of the race riot that occurred in St. Louis in 1917. In her account of this incident, she documents that a hundred and fifty Blacks were killed in the two days of rioting and nearly a million dollars' worth of property had been destroyed.[39] Even though Black people suffered such an enormous loss from the race riots, the white community put the blame on members of the Black community who were punished. Upon her investigation and testimony gathering, Wells-Barnett discovered that it was actually the white mobs that began the race riot and not members of the Black community. They drove a car through Black neighborhoods and began shooting into the homes of Black residents, who retaliated by firing back and killing two members of the white mobs. Through her fact-finding mission, Wells-Barnett concluded that the individuals under prosecution by the office of the Attorney General should not have been prosecuted because, going by the facts, it should have been seen that they "acted in self-defense and tried to protect their homes and their lives when refused protection elsewhere [by the state government]."[40]

She also used this method of testimonial knowledge to expose the hypocrisy of the United States government in the mistreatment of Black soldiers who fought to defend the country in World War I. In 1917, Black soldiers of the Third Battalion, Twenty-fourth Regiment, were accused of shooting up a police station in Houston, Texas; they were subsequently court-martialed for firing on the police and white citizens. About twelve of them were sentenced to be hanged, while the remaining members were sentenced to different terms of imprisonment. Wells-Barnett describes how "twelve were afterward hanged by the neck until they were dead and, according to the newspapers, their bodies were thrown into nameless graves. This was done to placate southern hatred."[41] She was able to show that the accusation that led to the killings of these Black soldiers did not reflect the fact that they were defending themselves from racist hatred because white citizens in Houston, Texas, were the first to attack the Black soldiers. When she protested this killing as a mark of the lack of regard for Black lives shown by the United States government, members of the Secret Service were sent to threaten her with the possibility of being arrested for treason, which she fiercely and bravely denounced.

Another important accomplishment by Wells-Barnett in Black epistemology is the modeling of epistemic authority, the epistemic authority of a Black woman to speak and write from the first-person standpoint about the plights of Black folks in the anti-Black context of the Victorian era. It was a period in America when women were seen as essentially belonging to the domestic domain, and this stereotype generally held that their primary responsibility was not to compete with men in the public domain, but to be home cleaners, child bearers, and caregivers. Wells-Barnett became responsible for taking care of her siblings at a very young age (fourteen years old) after she suddenly lost both of her parents in the 1878 yellow fever epidemic. However, she never allowed this extremely challenging life circumstance to define her or restrict her to the ideals of the Victorian era that relegated women to the sphere of domestication, all for the sake of aligning with the nineteenth-century idea of "true womanhood."[42] She made her thoughts known in an essay focused on this concept of "true womanhood," in which she criticized the nineteenth-century idea of *the ideal woman* who is expected to mirror or embrace the Victorian-era virtues of modesty, piety, purity, submissiveness, and domesticity. She particularly denounced this notion of the ideal woman because it was not extended to Black women; they were not considered to be capable of possessing such virtues during and after slavery. She writes pointedly in "Woman's Mission," asking, "What is, or should be, woman? Not merely a bundle of flesh and bones, nor fashion plate, a frivolous inanity, a soulless doll, a heartless coquette—but a strong, bright presence, thoroughly imbued with a sense of her mission on earth and a desire to fill it."[43]

Apart from the fact that this shows the inimitable courage and bravery of this incredible Black woman and intellectual, it also reveals her self-assurance, self-reliance, self-understanding, and her desire to not conform to limiting social expectations. She writes and speaks from a place of conviction of being a brilliant Black intellectual that possesses self-knowledge and the capacity to transform lives and society through the power of her work and words. Paula J. Giddings, in her very instructive book, *Ida: A Sword Among Lions*, describes Wells-Barnett as "a frank writer who leaves things out rather than tell an untruth, there is little to suggest what was at the core of a woman—a college-educated Black woman with Victorian values, no less—who had the imprudent courage to stand up to southern lynchers."[44] She was so courageous to transgress the boundaries of respectability that were mostly reserved for white men to speak in public spaces in the nineteenth century, and she claimed a place of importance in the public space, writing about and speaking against injustice and calling for an understanding of social reality that is fundamentally grounded in the Black experience.

During this period, the public space—the space of reason—was mostly reserved for white men.[45] Yet Ida B. Wells-Barnett courageously took on the male-dominated public sphere, arguing passionately and unapologetically for an end to lynching, emphasizing that those whites who engaged in it and supported it were barbarous while basking in the euphoria of being civilized.[46] She embraced writing and public life as paths to self-making and social change, which demanded critical, creative, and unrelenting engagement with a world that persistently associated Black women with the monstrous or unintelligible body.[47] It was an incredibly difficult thing to resist the norms and ideals of structured society and still try to find a place of acceptance within the larger society. Wells-Barnett suffered for her conviction and for daring to transgress the boundaries of gender roles and racial codes that were designed within society. Her challenge was essentially two-fold: questioning white women's purity—one of the central tenets and gender norm of white Southern society—and doing so as a young, Black woman, thereby transgressing racial norms.[48] At different points in her life, she was demonized as an "adulteress," "troublemaker," and "race-baiter," and she was attacked by Southern white men who attempted to silence her by destroying the newspaper she co-owned, the *Memphis Free Speech*. When this act of violence did not succeed in silencing her, these white men were mortally offended and vowed to brutally murder her for daring to stand up to them.

The examination of the contributions and accomplishments of Ida B. Wells-Barnett, as approached in this chapter, is not merely as a chronological account of the course of her life. This has been achieved in other excellent publications such as Naomi E. Jones, *Ida B. Wells-Barnett: Suffragette and Social Activist*; Mia Bay, *To Tell the Truth Freely: The Life of Ida B. Wells*; Pat McKissack and Fredrick McKissack, *Ida B. Wells-Barnett: A Voice Against Violence*; Alfreda Duster, *Crusade for Justice*; and Ida B. Wells, *The Light of Truth: Writings of an Anti-Lynching Crusader*, ed. Mia Bay, to mention a few. The aim of this chapter is to highlight Ida B. Wells-Barnett as an important Black female philosopher who accomplished great things as a creator of knowledge, as a Black epistemologist that understood, in a very in-depth manner, the connection between knowledge and power. She wielded knowledge like a sword to cut through the dark matter of racism and the white hateful practice of lynching, as well as the fetishization of the destruction of Black bodies for the amusement and enjoyment of white society at large, given the celebratory mood with which such lynching events were advertised, organized and actualized.

It was a ritual of death that was built on lies and unfounded notions that were held religiously as undoubtable truths. Wells understood that nothing cuts through lies and fabricated notions like the weapon of truth, hence, why she is regarded as the *seeker of truth* in this chapter. Her authority to speak the truth even at the risk of being killed by those who have perpetuated falsehoods to gain political, social, and economic power and by those who are brainwashed by the lies is particularly commendable. This is a lesson for the present moment in America, when many people seem to embrace and value lies and falsehoods even when there exists factual, experiential, or empirical evidence to the contrary. We need to take on the mantle of Wells-Barnett, to seek truth and refuse to be imprisoned by the threshold of lies. The truth ultimately leads to liberation.

6

W.E.B. Du Bois's Development of Positive Epistemology in the Twentieth Century

The idea of a person being Black and knowledgeable in America, in the twentieth century, was considered unrealistic because of the prevailing prejudiced and racialized *theories of the human*, which considered, discussed, and studied Blackness from the place of deficit or negation. When Blackness is considered in relation to negation, it evokes a negative epistemology that considers Black people generally from a place of intellectual, social, and psychological deficiency. In other words, the categories *to be Black* and *to know* were seen as diametrically opposed in a sense that undermines the agency, thinking faculty, and humanity of all individuals who identify as part of this racial group. The phenomenon of human knowledge is something so beautiful and vital to life that people can go to extreme lengths to acquire it, maintain it, and even deny others access to it. Whether or not a person, institution, or nation would rise above prevailing existential challenges and move toward prosperity, problem solving, and flourishing would largely depend not only on the quality of the knowledge base that is available to them, but also on the way that such accumulated knowledge can be applied to real-life issues.

To put it simply, knowledge is literally power because *to know*, or to have knowledge, is to be empowered, enlightened, and to gain awareness, which routinely leads to self-realization and social understanding and sets one on a path to achieving freedom and progress in all facets of life. So, the question to ask is this: if knowledge or *knowing* is so important and vital to human achievement and social progress, why then were Black people cut off from the categories of knowledge in twentieth-century America? The answer to this question lies in what W.E.B. Du Bois referred to in 1903 as the problem of the color-line, "the relation of the darker races to the lighter races of men,"[1] which imposes a "strange meaning of being Black . . . in the dawning of the twentieth century."[2]

This strange meaning of Blackness that Du Bois referred to was codified in the scientific racism inspired by the social Darwinist paradigm of this period. This paradigm was used to develop and promote the idea that Blacks were inferior beings and the view that their oppression in society was justified, given their natural status as "lower-grade" humans. The scientists of this time were unified in their perspective on this race theory, drawing from the Darwinian theory of evolution. Under the leadership of the respected philosopher and anthropologist Herbert Spencer, the Darwinian principle of natural selection was recommended as a palliative that, when applied to society, would resolve the problem of the color-line. It followed the logic that if biological organisms were known to evolve gradually by eliminating those that are least fit for survival, then social organisms must evolve at the same geologic rate and by the same process of elimination.

In other words, the Black race should be eliminated for the survival of the white race.[3] This eliminativist logic undergirded the racist assumptions that fueled the eugenics movement, which gained popularity from the 1800s to the 1920s. The movement propagated a biological determinist view that sought the improvement of the white race through selective breeding (considering genetics and hereditary factors) and the elimination of other races that were deemed as "threatening" to the survival of the white race. The movement's central precept was that scientific investigation can be used to delineate such traits as genius, feeblemindedness, criminal tendencies, and pauperism, which were part of the human germ plasm, and that the unfit must be reduced in numbers through social application of this scientific knowledge.[4] This racist theory provided fodder for the brutal treatment of Blacks in America at the turn of the century because many white people held the assumption that the moral failings of Black folks, especially Black men, were biologically determined through genetic and hereditary factors, and as such, they could not be remedied or rehabilitated. The only effective solution proffered was an obliteration or extermination that would wipe them off the face of the earth.[5] It was not a coincidence, therefore, that lynchings, criminalization, mass incarceration, and the lawless killings of Black people became a mainstay of American social life during this period.

One of the main aims of the scientific racism (racial "science") that was being developed at the time was to place Black people outside the domain of humanity using the stereotype or trope of "inferiority." As David Graeber and David Wengrow note in *The Dawn of Everything: A New History of Humanity,* one of the most pernicious aspects of such historical narratives is their aim to reduce people, actual human beings, to phony stereotypes.[6] The stereotype of Black inferiority was created in order to justify the extermination of all Black people from the face of the earth and, by implication, to erase any consideration of Blackness in regard to the precious, vital, and highly valuable human asset of knowledge. At that time, the general order of things was such that those who were not deemed to possess the full qualities of what it means to be considered human did not deserve all of the accolades, respect, prestige, and power that comes with knowledge acquisition.

The fact that Blacks were beginning to make racial progress in all areas of life, integrating into a sociopolitical economy that previously held them in captivity as owned property and exploited them as free laborers, was largely seen as a threat to the "normal" social order. In order to remove this threat, the racist myth of Black inferiority was introduced as both a racist trope and a fact, deduced from the scientific (pseudo-scientific) method of investigation of the mental capacities, intellectual acumen, and genius of members of the human race. Thus, the general conclusion held by those who espoused and supported such racist views was that since Blacks were not fit for the task of knowledge acquisition, there was no need to educate Black folks. In fact, the education of a Black person through formal academic learning was considered as "actually giving fools college diplomas."[7] Gains in Black education were described in this way because it was considered an impossible feat for Black folks to exhibit mental capacities, think critically, and demonstrate the qualities of brilliance associated with formal learning.

Certainly, these theories and mythological conceptions that definitively ascribed intellectual deficiency and moral depravation to Blackness and being Black were based on lies often disguised as "trusted scientific facts." Many white Americans believed these lies and even went to great lengths to enforce segregation laws, and they practiced misguided racist acts and evil forms of racialized violence against Blacks who they deemed subordinate to themselves. This belief and practice was motivated by a deficit-based view of Black humanity in particular and of the world in general. This epistemological view was driven by anti-Black racism, and its repudiation became one of the preoccupations of the scholarship of Du Bois at the turn of the century. This chapter focuses on Du Bois's epistemological project during this period, which concentrated on the development of a positive epistemology that would counter these negative attributions of Blackness and unveil a wholesome way to imagine Blackness unbound and flourishing in an anti-Black world. In his essay "The Conservation of Races," Du Bois directly responded to this claim for preservation of the white race by means of denigrating the Black race or reducing it to nothingness.

He argued that such claims were based on wrong and unfounded assumptions about the Black race, emphasizing that such discussions about the Black race in America have been centered on certain assumptions about natural abilities and political, intellectual, and moral status, which were not viewed as universal characteristics of all humans, regardless of the racial groups they belonged to.[8] He also attacked the idea that the weight of scientific evidence had been used to portray Black people as lacking in intelligence and as beings that were unable to acquire knowledge. He rejected this idea forcefully, writing in "Race Intelligence" that "for a century or more it has been the dream of those who do not believe Negroes [Blacks] are human that their wish should find some scientific basis."[9] He denounced the scientific racism used to undermine Black humanity and declared the idea that Black people cannot be educated as flawed. Du Bois knew he would have to utilize more than mere words to convince the world of the fault lines drawn by such scientific racist postulations. He understood that he would have to debunk the racist epistemology that informed the biological determinism propagated by the social Darwinists and eugenicists before he could develop a vision of knowledge and epistemological attainment that is centered on the Black individual or self.

Blackness Outside the Veil: The Humanizing Characteristic of Du Bois's Epistemology

The humanizing aspect of Du Bois's work regarding the phenomenon of human knowledge focused not only on critically responding to the flawed assumptions in scientific racism but also, and more importantly, on unveiling a discourse of the Black subject that went beyond the imagined lens of eternally deficient beings. It is an approach to knowledge that aims to answer the question of what it means to think of Black humanity in a context where race and epistemological categories are utilized to undermine the agency, subjectivity, and humanity of Blacks. In "The Burdened Individuality of Freedom," Saidiya Hartman seems to foreshadow this question when she inquires, "If race formerly determined who was 'man' and who was chattel, whose property rights were protected or recognized and who was property . . . with blackness as the mark of object status and whiteness licensing the propriety of self, then how did emancipation affect the status of race?"[10] This question highlights the deep roots of the erasure of Blackness from the realm of humanity propelled by a virulent version of biological racism, and the markers of race-based human differentiation, championed by early white anthropologists and ethnologists, which provided fodder for the heinous violence meted out to Blacks during slavery. It is a debased form of bifurcated logic between the *Self* and the *objected Other* that Black thinkers had to contend with in order to effectively formulate distinctive epistemologies of the self that could account for the undermined Black humanity—unbounding Blackness.

Du Bois fundamentally conceived of the ethnological assumptions and race-concept of the nineteenth century as flawed. He articulated this in many of his essays such as "The Propaganda of History," "On Being Ashamed of Oneself," and "The Concept of Race," to mention just a few. Du Bois believed that the faulty and hegemonic scientific imaginations contained in those systems of thought could be used to study the social or existential condition of Black folks in the real world. He was very clear about this in his numerous discussions of the problems of Black folks. According to him, "most persons have accepted that tacit but clear modern philosophy which assigns to the white race alone the hegemony of the world and assumes that other races, and particularly the [Black] race, will either be content to serve the interests of the whites or die out before their all-conquering march. This philosophy is the child of the African slave trade and the expansion of Europe during the nineteenth century."[11] Since this adapted epistemological system of modern philosophy is morally bankrupt and intellectually deficient, Du Bois constructed a new vision that "regards American [Blacks] as typical and human and the results of a study of his conditions as capable of being scientific."[12] What Du Bois advocates here is an epistemological paradigm that projects the Black human as a "Self" that is capable of logically structuring the phenomenal and nominal experience.[13] It orients us toward a world where Blackness is not thought of in relation to extraverted conditions of the human that are tangentially applied to the Black lived experience. In this context, Blackness occupies the epicenter of thought and how the world is lived. It is an epistemological posture that centers Blackness at its core, oblivious of the negative attenuations through which Blackness is reduced in the present order of knowledge.

Du Bois embarked on the project of creating Black knowledge as an important aspect of humanizing Blackness. For instance, in his essay on "The Training of Negroes for Social Power," Du Bois develops a Black socioepistemic perspective that focuses on the need for Blacks to eschew ignorance while providing insights on how Black people can achieve human progress with socioscientific knowledge of their material conditions within a repressive system and give the world a mass of truth worth knowing. He argues that the responsibility for their social regeneration ought to be placed largely upon the shoulders of Black people but such responsibility without power is a mockery and a farce. Therefore, if the American people are sincerely anxious for Blacks to put forth their best efforts to help themselves, they must see to it that they are not deprived of the freedom and power to strive. The responsibility for dispelling their ignorance implies that the power to overcome ignorance is to be placed in Black people's hands.[14] Du Bois's socioepistemic perspective largely focused on studying the Black problem; it encompassed the phenomena of social metamorphosis and Black people's place within society, and how to move this toward the project of racial uplift. He went beyond the stereotypical imagery of Blackness as an endemic manifestation of the pathologies of the human condition to avow the importance of creating knowledge about and for Black people through socioscientific inquiry, which demonstrates the epistemic authority associated with Blackness. Consequently, Du Bois argues in *Black Folk, Then and Now* that Blacks have long been the clown of history, the football of anthropology, and the slave of industry, emphasizing why these views can no longer be maintained.[15]

Du Bois fundamentally believed that the material conditions and the long years of discrimination that Black people have endured in the New World provides them with a unique insight into the world that is different from any Eurocentric epistemic analysis. Therefore, his sociological studies focused primarily on the *Souls* and conditions of Black folks. For Du Bois, sociological investigations of existential phenomena should aim to study those finer manifestations of social life, which statistics cannot count, such as the expression of Black life in all its manifestations. This includes expressions in literature, music, folklore and the wellspring of aesthetic life that demonstrates the manifestation of a distinct social mind.[16] This idea of a distinct social mind would become important in Du Bois's discussion of social power for Blacks. He refers to social power as the growth of initiative among Blacks, the spread of independent thought, the expanding consciousness of mankind, which is conceived of as the inevitable corollary of the fixing of social responsibility.[17] This notion of "social power" for Blacks developed by Du Bois is a cardinal feature of his thought on the epistemology of the Black self.

Du Bois's view on the epistemology of the Black "Self" emphasizes the creation of Black knowledge without recourse to alien accretions. As he argues, "to know all about Blacks, it is certain that we can know vastly more than we do, and that we can have our knowledge in more systematic and intelligible form."[18] Thus, in the discourse of knowledge, the Black "Self" is seen as a self-legislating being with epistemic authority to make knowledge claims. By advocating a new system of Black self-epistemological thinking, Du Bois was presenting a living alternative to the Western idea of positivism and scientific objectivism. In this new system of thinking, Black knowledge production in this Du Boisean construal is an active process whereby the researcher, scientist, or practitioner actively engages the object of knowledge. Hence, an unbreakable dialectical relationship emerges between the Black subject and the object of knowledge. In this line of thinking, knowledge for its own sake, as a reified object of science is rejected. For Du Bois, what is important is that the active subject engage with objects that themselves are active and ever-changing. Knowledge is, therefore, a living product of the intellectual engagement of the active Black subject with the living objects of knowledge.[19]

He utilized this notion to emphasize the link between personal and political epistemologies through education and social organization because he believed that experience and knowledge constitute the genuine wealth that can truly make Black people rich. As Du Bois reasons:

> There must surely be among Negro [Black] leaders the philanthropic impulse, the uprightness of character and strength of purpose; but there must be more than these; philanthropy and purpose among black as well as among whites must be guided and curbed by knowledge and mental discipline—knowledge of forces of civilization that make for survival, ability to organize and guide those forces, and realization of the true meaning of those broader ideals of human betterment which may in time bring heaven and earth a little nearer. This is social power—it is gotten in many ways by experience, by social contact, by what we loosely call the chances of life. But the systematic method of acquiring and imparting it is by training of youth to thought, power, and knowledge in the school and college.[20]

Here, Du Bois is fashioning a philosophy of education that takes the project of Black acquisition of knowledge for personal and social transformation seriously. This vision is one that seeks to humanize Blackness. In this regard, he believes that a rationally arranged college course of study for men and women who are able to pursue it is the best and only method of putting into the world Blacks who have the ability to use the social forces of their race to stamp out crime, strengthen the home, eliminate degenerates, and inspire and encourage the higher tendencies of the race not only in thought and aspiration but in everyday toil.[21]

Du Bois's project of humanizing Blackness entails the celebration of the achievements of Black people in various areas of human endeavor including commerce, literature, industry, political life, and learned professions to show that there were actual black inventors and pioneers in these areas who created great ideas and businesses without any recourse to white/Eurocentric frames. Du Bois's referencing of Black genius here ruptures the pretentious hegemony of colonial narratives that consider knowledge production in all fields of human endeavor as a prerogative or privilege of white subjectivity. He recognizes the Black epistemic authority that Black subjects possess as a function of why they had so many achievements and distinctions, both material and spiritual, to contribute to human civilization.[22] It is exemplified in his belief that "the gift of the spirit" is one of the areas where Blacks have contributed to American life and human civilization, even though this is hard to define or characterize. It is the beautiful spirit of a people (Black people), imbued with "a slow and dreamful conception of the universe, a drawling and slurring of speech, an intense sensitiveness to spiritual values—all these things and others like to them, tell of the imprint of Africa on Europe in America."[23]

Du Bois is both a transformative and transgressive Black epistemologist who used his philosophical genius to unbound Blackness from the shackles of liminality and triggered epistemic ruptures in the hegemonic order of Western knowledge and epistemological categories. Such epistemic rupturing, in the end, changed not only the way we think about the world and ourselves but also the way we exist in the world. Du Bois, from theoretical and epistemological standpoints, was a revolutionary thinker. His innovations occurred from the margins of white academic and intellectual practices and from within the veil. Yet, he emerges organically from the lived experience of Blacks outside the veil while asserting, in the most transgressive civilizational sense, the centrality of Blackness to humanity's knowledge of itself.[24]

This view of epistemologies of the Black "Self," which emphasizes Black knowledge as a living knowledge, is featured in many of the writings of Du Bois. For instance, in "My Evolving Program for Negro Freedom" he writes, "Up to this time, I had been absorbing a general view of human knowledge: in ancient and modern literatures; in mathematics, physics and chemistry and history. It was all in vague and general terms—interpretations of what men who knew the facts at first hand, thought they might mean; I was in possession of the average educated man's concept of this world and its meaning. But now I wanted to go further: to know what man could know and how to collect and interpret facts face to face. And what facts were."[25] This existential approach was very pivotal to his many groundbreaking studies that resulted in monumental works like *The Study of the Negro Problems* (1898), *The Philadelphia Negro* (1899), *The Negro in Business* (1899), *The Souls of Black Folk* (1903), numerous publications from his *Atlanta Sociological Studies* (1897–1910), and so many more.

W.E.B. Du Bois did not leave anyone in doubt about the fact that his work was primarily centered on Black people. As he clearly states: "[T]he scope of my program of life [is] to center it in a group of educated Negroes [Blacks], who from their knowledge and experience would lead the mass."[26] This indicates that Du Bois did not rely on Western systems of knowledge or epistemic authority to create knowledge. Thus, he centered Blackness in many of his accomplishments in the sociology of Black knowledge in the Atlanta Sociological Laboratory.[27] As Du Bois articulated himself: "Thus in my quest for basic knowledge with which to help guide the American Negro [Black], I came to the study of sociology."[28] One of the most definitive studies regarding Du Bois's founding role in the birth of American sociology is *The Scholar Denied: W.E.B. Du Bois and the Birth of Sociology*, by Aldon Morris. In this work, Morris argues that although Du Bois and his collaborators did indeed build a sociological school (The Atlanta Sociological Laboratory) that challenged scientific racism by generating findings that suggested races were socially constructed and that social conditions largely determined racial inequality, his research was suppressed by white sociologists.[29] There were obvious reasons why white sociologists suppressed Du Bois's scholarship. To embrace Du Bois's sociology, they would need to acknowledge that their theories proclaiming the biological and cultural inferiority of Blacks could not be supported scientifically.[30] Additionally, there were deeply personal and cultural reasons why white social scientists suppressed Du Bois's scholarship. Early in the twentieth century, whites viewed all African Americans as inferior, even Black intellectuals such as Du Bois. White social scientists could not embrace Black excellence in science, let alone the superiority of a Black scientist.[31] Based on his findings, Morris argued that "the Du Bois-Atlanta school deserves credit for founding scientific sociology in America."[32] What is crucially important to stress here, beyond this debate, is the significance of the work produced within the Atlanta Sociological Laboratory for the sociology of Black knowledge.

Sociology of Black Knowledge and the Atlanta Sociological Laboratory

The sociology of knowledge involves the study of the relationship between human thought and the social context in which such thoughts are generated. In other words, the phenomenon of human knowledge is considered as that which is socially grounded because factors such as human relations, place in society, identity categories, and power dynamics within society play a prominent role in knowledge attribution. The work of Du Bois at the Atlanta Sociological Laboratory constructed a foundation for the sociology of Black knowledge during a period in history when Black people were largely considered thoughtless and incapable of demonstrating the features of human knowledge. In order to achieve such a massive feat, Du Bois turned to science to develop a positive epistemological account of Blackness in the world, which informed the breadth of the work he did at the Atlanta Sociological Laboratory. Before Du Bois began the Atlanta studies in 1897, he had already completed a novel sociological study of Black folks in the Seventh Ward of Philadelphia, commissioned by the University of Pennsylvania in 1896.[33] During this period, the Seventh Ward had the largest population of Blacks in the city of Philadelphia. The report from this commissioned study would later be published as the *Philadelphia Negro*, published in 1899. Du Bois's *Philadelphia Negro* was one of the earliest scientific studies on race produced by a Black thinker that specifically used empirical data to connect structural racism to the poor health and social conditions, and high mortality rates among Blacks in the Seventh Ward.[34] Making the study of the condition of Black folks his lifelong project, Du Bois went on to compile two centuries of history of the Negro in Philadelphia and the Seventh Ward and a breadth of work that touches on almost every aspect of Black life in that period.

In fact, Du Bois described the work he did at the Atlanta Sociological Laboratory as one of the most important accomplishments of his lifetime:

My real-life work has begun at Atlanta for 13 years, from my 29th to my 42nd birthday. They were years of great spiritual upturning, of the making and unmaking of ideals, of hard work and hard play. Here I found myself. I lost most of my mannerisms. I grew more broadly human . . . and studied human beings. I became widely acquainted with the real condition of my people. . . . The main significance of my work at Atlanta University, during the years 1897 to 1910, was the development at an American institution of learning, of a program of study on the problems affecting the American Negroes, covering a progressively widening and deepening effort designed to stretch over the span of a century.[35]

Here, Du Bois's reference to becoming more broadly human speaks to his separation from the denigrating sociological view about Blackness that was prominent at that time, which claimed that a universal racial order of inequality emerged from natural or biological causes. Rather than agreeing to be lost in such theoretical formulations, Du Bois "found himself" and used such critical self-awareness to interrogate the universal color lines that had been drawn, and their production of worldwide race stratification, which led him to conclude that dominant whites constructed the racial stratification hypothesis to ensure global white supremacy.[36] As an alternative to this mischaracterization of Blackness, Du Bois constructed a Black-centered view of the world through a scientifically rigorous and emancipatory sociology of knowledge. It was scientifically rigorous because, in contrast to dominant white sociology, Du Bois pioneered multiple methods that relied on both quantitative and qualitative methods to provide empirical evidence for his analyses.[37]

Du Bois's work at the Atlanta Sociological Laboratory is important because it was the first time that Black people would be studied seriously, over two centuries (278 years, to be precise) after the slavery system began in the United States. This explains why Du Bois is often considered as the scholar who pioneered the use of the empirical method of validating knowledge and the study of the condition of Blacks through scientific or empirical evidence.[38] However, this is not an accurate representation of the facts in the chronicling of ideas within Black intellectual history. As examined in the previous chapter,

Ida B. Wells-Barnett was the thinker and philosopher who pioneered this empirical method, which Du Bois would further develop, concretize, and popularize at the turn of the century, especially in the formal setting of the Atlanta Sociological Laboratory. This does not in any way undermine the significance of the groundbreaking nature of the work Du Bois achieved through the laboratory.

In the studies conducted within the Atlanta Sociological Laboratory, Du Bois emphasized an empirical approach to study the relationship between Black thought and how it arises in the social context, while stressing the importance of empirical evidence and scientific fact in achieving these goals. He describes the principal focus of the Atlanta study in *Efforts for Social Betterment Among Negro Americans*, one of the many reports of this study, noting that "this study is, therefore, a further carrying out of the Atlanta University plan of social study of the Negro American, by means of an annual series of decennially recurring subjects covering, so far as is practicable, every phase of human life. The object of these studies is primarily scientific—a careful research for truth, conducted as thoroughly, broadly and honestly as the material resources and mental equipment at command will allow."[39] What this shows is an emphasis on data collection and the use of the inductive method, which emphasizes the collection of facts as the basis for generating true beliefs. In other words, Du Bois was using the method of science to construct a concept of Blackness in the world that brings all Black people into the conversation about humanity.

Du Bois underscored the need to utilize the method of scientific investigation to transcend the practice whereby the opinions of intellectuals who were deeply prejudiced against Black folks were rated as the final word on their agency, subjectivity, and social viability. He advocated a different methodology in order to achieve the higher purpose of Black racial uplift and racial freedom. As he states in "My Evolving Program for the Negro," "scientific investigation and organized action among the Negroes, needs to be in close cooperation, so as to secure the survival of the Negro race, until the cultural development of America and the world is willing to recognize Negro freedom."[40] The emphasis on centering Blackness in scientific investigation highlights the notion that racism had made neutrality in the pre-existing theoretical approaches in studying Black Americans an impossibility. This is due to the overwhelming reliance on the prejudiced opinions of so-called scientists and not on actual facts. Du Bois was advancing a framework that would make an objective assessment of the true nature of Black folks and their actual condition in society. Hence, he did not subscribe to a positivist fetishization of data collection as an end in itself but as a means to an end.[41]

He diagnosed the central problem with pre-existing theoretical approaches as immersed in thought systems that "degenerate into bad metaphysics and false psychology," all for the sake of demonizing and defining Black people as what they are not.[42] Thus, Du Bois hoped that the context of his research at Atlanta University, being in the midst of the Negro problems, would "become a centre of such a systematic and thoroughgoing study of those problems as would gradually raise many of the questions above the realm of opinion and guess into that of scientific knowledge." This implies that Du Bois deeply understood that knowledge production is very much influenced by a people's social condition, and in order to offer a truthful assessment of a people's condition, there has to be some form of empirical investigation to determine the authenticity of the beliefs and opinions formed about them.

By establishing this program at Atlanta University, Du Bois envisioned the employment of the most advanced practices in research methods and scholarly inquiry as a means of producing objective scientific studies on the social, economic, and physical condition of Blacks in America.[43] Such scientific evidence, he believes, would be the only way to effectively dispel the myth of Black intellectual inferiority and the fairytale that was widely spread at the turn of the century that college-educated Blacks were as good as being uneducated and were not a useful human resource for gainful employment. Du Bois's ultimate objective was to upgrade the investigations from a purely descriptive analysis of human behavior and the collection of empirical data to facilitate opinions that are grounded in rigorous scientific truths and systematic inquiry.[44] For instance, at the American Negro Exhibit, organized as part of the 1900 World Fair in Paris, which focused on the representations of achievements and the racial and social progress of different social groups in the world, Du Bois created a collection of graphs, charts, maps, and tables that were generated from a mix of existing records and empirical data that had been collected at Atlanta University by his sociological laboratory to showcase the achievements of Black folks in the past century while looking toward their contributions in the next century.[45] Du Bois utilized the exhibit to refute the notion that Black people were intellectually inferior, uninterested, and incapable of learning.[46]

The work at the Atlanta Sociological Laboratory provided Du Bois with an opportunity to solidify his innovative empirical methodology and deepen his dedication to understanding the Black condition. This dedication deeply influenced the Atlanta University Publications series that ran from 1896 to 1914 and the numerous works that were produced about Black folks within this period. These include *Morality among Negroes in Cities* (1896), *Social and Physical Conditions of Negroes in Cities* (1897), *The Negro in Business* (1899), *The College-Bred Negro American* (1900), *The Negro Common School* (1901), *The Negro Artisan* (1902), *Health and Physique of the Negro American* (1906), *Economic Cooperation Among Negro Americans* (1907). They were among the first attempts to study scientifically the problems of Black people in America using factual, empirical evidence as the source of epistemic authority.[47] Through a factual approach to the sociology of Black knowledge, Du Bois was able to unveil and highlight many of the achievements of Black people in different areas of human life. For instance, in Atlanta University Publications no. 15, *The College-Bred Negro American*, Black intellectual achievements were highlighted in education, employment, professional practice, and general learning. In this report, it was stated that Black college graduates were gainfully employed. Data collected by Atlanta University researchers indicated that 85 percent of the 800 respondents were employed. Out of that number, 54 percent worked in education, while 20 percent were preachers, 7 percent practiced medicine, and 4 percent practiced law.[48] This fact, according to Atlanta University officials, affirmed that Negro graduates were, at that time and with few exceptions, usefully and creditably employed, and it dispelled the myth that college-educated Blacks would be unable to find employment because of racial prejudice.[49]

The numerous reports and findings from the research conducted at the Sociological Library would in turn help build self-understanding among Black people that they are an enlightened race and an extremely gifted and knowledgeable people, even though they were previously misrepresented and mischaracterized in white sociological theories as incapable of rational thought and as a people that would eventually cause the extinction of the human race. Du Bois would later describe such approaches to studying Black people in the white imagination as mainly drawing "metaphysical lines" instead of "seeking men as the natural unit of associated men."[50] On this account, Du Bois indicts the disciplines of philosophy and sociology, and human sciences generally, as engaging in fictive ruminations for failing to focus on the conditions and life-situation of Black folks as humans in society, instead preferring to focus on abstractions drawn from prejudiced, myopic views of the real world. This was one of the primary concerns raised in his essay, "Sociology Hesitant." Despite years of misrepresentation of Black people by white philosophers, historians, and sociologists, this was not enough to totally erase Black contributions to human civilization and social progress in the world. Rather, it became a propelling force for Black people to continue to demonstrate the beauty of their humanity and their unquenchable thirst for both personal growth and the social advancement of the race.

Thus, Du Bois utilized his development of a Black sociology of knowledge to expand on the view that the many contributions that Black people have made to social progress in America have been de-emphasized and diminished in order to maintain a false worldview of white power, achievement, and intellectual development as a peculiar feature of those who belong to that race. However, the social, empirical reality and measurable truth is that Black people have not just been mere footnotes to history and have surely not remained on the sidelines when it comes to the contributions to human progress within society. Du Bois's contributions to the development of a positive epistemology in the twentieth century provided a different view of Black people, one that focused particularly on the persistent quest of Blacks for knowledge and self-understanding.

Du Bois contended that amid all the difficulties of Jim Crow dis-crimination and racist oppression, Black people lifted themselves up and made significant contributions to America, which should be seen as a positive achievement. He asserts that some of these accomplishments were easily recognizable in three areas, namely, in democratic govern-ment, free public schools, and new social legislation. All of these were made possible by the tireless pursuit of knowledge by Black people for individual and social advancement. This led Du Bois to conclude that Black people's thirst for knowledge, one that has been too persistent and durable to be mere curiosity or whim, gave birth to the public school system of the South. It was this achievement that Black con-stituents and legislators insisted on more than anything else during this period. Although it was possible to find vestiges of free schools in some Southern states before the war, a universal, well-established system of free schools began the day that Black people got political power.[51] This system of education (free public education) established by Black folks was beneficial for both Blacks and whites in the Southern states. They were deeply convinced that education is a fundamental right of all citi-zens within a constitutional democracy. The upshot of this is that Black knowledge has been, is still, and will continue to be a gift to America.

7

Frantz Fanon on Black Knowledge and the New Foundation for Black Humanity

Frantz Fanon, the critical anticolonial thinker, continued the philosophical tradition advanced by W.E.B. Du Bois that offered a humanizing view of Blackness that was not captured in the Western view of modernity and its modal language of dehumanization. However, he took a radical departure from Du Bois by arguing that the task of creating a humanizing view of Blackness must be developed using a *new concept,* or language. This language is one that must remain untainted by the flawed assumptions of Blackness in the white imagination, which constrains it to a mirage or a *nonentity* in the world. To put this differently, while Du Bois diagnosed the color-line as the problem of the twentieth century, evident in the classification of racial difference among human groups based on the color-line, Fanon's objective in fashioning an anticolonial epistemological critique of the current order of knowledge, was geared toward rupturing this color-line.

The color-line, in the historical framing of difference along ethnic, racial, phenotypical, and gender lines, was used as marker of power differentials, but ultimately as a principal prism for determining the boundaries of humanism. It was used to define groups of people who qualified to be regarded as humans and those who were deemed unqualified. In this world, and within this imaginary of the colonial empires of the mind and space, Black people were constructed and located outside of humanity. This is what Fanon means when he describes the life of a Black person within this context, as a "life caught in the noose of existence,"[1] a life that exists but whose mortality is asphyxiated and is constantly being challenged and called into question for being different. This is the logic of the color-line: that there are "humans" existing in two dialectically opposing worlds—the zone of being and nonbeing. In this dialectical and colorist ideation of the world, Black people are generally adjudged to exist in the zone of nonbeing. As Fanon describes it, it is "an extraordinarily sterile and arid region, an incline stripped bare of every essential from which a genuine new departure can emerge."[2]

In his writings, Fanon fiercely rejects the boundaries of the color-line as a way of looking at the world because this leads to alienation and inflicts psychological harm on Black people. He used the Creole term *comparaison*[3] to reference this phenomenon of the color-line, which creates a system of alienation in which the Black person's worth, merit, and value is measured on the grounds of its comparison to members of other races. As he writes in *Black Skin, White Masks*, "The black man is *comparaison*. That is the first truth. He is *comparaison* in the sense that he is constantly preoccupied with self-assertion and the ego ideal. Whenever he is in the presence of someone else, there is always the question of worth and merit."[4] This is similar to what W.E.B. Du Bois describes in *The Souls of Black Folk* as the estrangement caused by racism and colonialism, which leads to a situation where the Black individual feels a sense of "two-ness, two souls, two thoughts, two unreconciled strivings; two warring ideals in one dark body, whose dogged strength alone keeps it from being torn asunder."[5] As a trained clinical psychologist, Fanon understood the deep psychological and existential implications of this bifurcation, in terms of its potential for creating an existential crisis and the problem of estrangement for Black subjects. It lends itself to living in the world not for *oneself* but for the *other*, which implies that the Black subject is living in the world, immersed in a web of pathology of many subjectivities and abject sublimation. Fanon sees this color-line as a problem that creates a crisis of existence for the Black subject, given that the value and merit of subjectivity and the way in which the human experience is measured comes not from within but from without. This has significant implications for the concept of "universal humanism" as it pertains to the work and thought of Fanon.

In recent scholarship on Fanon, it has been assumed that a logical consequence of Fanon's rejection of the color-line, under the present order of colonial structures of knowledge, was that he subscribed to the idea of "universal humanism."[6] This characterization is evident in the works of scholars such as Gili Kliger, Lewis Gordon, Karen Ng, and Stefan Kipfer. Although this is a somewhat popular view attributed to Fanon, a more careful analysis of his thoughts and writings reveals that this notion claiming that Fanon embraced the idea of universal humanism is not consistent with his actual writings and critiques of the hegemony of ideological constructions. In "Humanism and the End of Empire," Gili Kliger argues that Fanon's analysis in *Black Skin, White Masks* stating that "both the black man, slave to his inferiority, and the white man, slave to his superiority, behave along neurotic lines thus exposed the apparently universal 'human' in its particularity as both white and situated among 'the arsenal of complexes that germinated in the colonial situation.'"[7] He argues that this is what necessitated Fanon's attempt to "reclaim humanism" in its universal form.[8] Similarly, in his work *What Fanon Said*, Lewis Gordon claims that Fanon's inquest into what would happen to white French women in the struggle for liberation in Algeria—particularly what would happen to them if, instead of defending colonialism as the liberator, they joined the anticolonial struggle—presupposes or suggests that Fanon "had faith in universal humanism."[9] Both Karen Ng and Stefan Kipfer in their work on the defense of humanism portrayed Fanon as an advocate of universal humanism since he exposed the intellectual bankruptcy of the idea of humanism espoused by European colonists and their supporters, while at the same time defending the normative importance of a true version of humanism.[10] These views are not consistent with those of Fanon.

For Fanon, the imaginary of the idea of "universal humanism" under the present order of knowledge is already tainted because it was developed in the colonial situation and not with all of humanity in mind. As he directly puts it in *Black Skin, White Masks*, "I am not a prisoner of history. I must not look for the meaning of my destiny in that direction. I must constantly remind myself that the real leap consists of introducing invention into life. In the world I am heading for, I am endlessly creating myself."[11] He understood that the epistemological struggle is not really about rehabilitating the moral bankruptcy of Western ideas concerning the human but about moving toward a more positive project of "inventing" new ways of looking at the world especially for Black subjects. He believes such a task (rehabilitation) would be a waste of time and valuable resources, involving material and intellectual resources, to concentrate on such a project because it does not allow for an interpretation of a reality that is detached from the apron strings or the vestige of colonialism and its alienating language and axioms. As he writes in *Black Skin, White Masks*, "by appealing, therefore, to our humanity—our feeling of dignity, love, and charity—it would be easy to prove and have acknowledged that the Black man is equal to the white man.

But that is not our purpose. What we are striving for is to liberate the black man from the arsenal of complexes that germinated in a colonial situation."[12] Fanon is clear in his thinking about the cunning of the Western view of the equality of humanity or humanism as generating psychological trauma (arsenal of complexes) for the Black subject that needs to be examined and rejected in order for the true liberation of the Black subject to be accomplished. This is the upshot of the anticolonial move in the thoughts of Fanon.[13]

Fanon's anticolonial critiques do not accommodate the puritanical understanding of humanism as conceptualized in its exclusionary sense as constituted within Western hegemony. In "Frantz Fanon and the Ethical Justification of Anti-Colonial Violence," Oladipo Fashina argues that "each human being is similar to every other respect of certain capacities, for example, the capacity to feel pain and pleasure, to love and to hate, and to have moral relations." Similarly, the assumption of an intrinsic moral worth of all human beings is not consistent with the work of Fanon.[14] I agree with Fashina's description of Fanon's view of the ideological imposition of the Western framing of the concept of humanity that is devoid of any of the qualities or characteristics of humanity, especially for those in the liminal axis of existence. He contends that "Fanon seems to have rejected [the] appeal to [common] humanity."[15] It will be contradictory to claim otherwise because Fanon's argument for anticolonial violence is a direct confrontation against a previously designed colonial world order that prevents the mutual recognition of humanity between the oppressed and the oppressor.

Put differently, Fanon believed that an appeal to humanity will not work in this way, at least because the colonized and the settler do not share a concern of humanity.[16] Rather than make a case for those who have been violently placed outside of the categories of humanity to be brought back (through the back door), Fanon essentially makes a defense of the demolition of both the ideological and material structures that have been put in place to undermine the humanity of those who are deemed as "non-human" through the evolution of a new way of thinking and the reimagining of a new human.

To this end, David Marriot, in "Inventions of Existence: Sylvia Wynter, Frantz Fanon, Sociogeny, and 'the Damned,'" was correct in describing Fanon's project as an "invention of existence," the invention of Black existence that was basically exterminated under the Western imaginary of humanism.[17] Fanon fundamentally believed and worked primarily to create a theoretical and practical vision for the emergence of Black subjectivity, Black agency, and Black humanity from within the dehumanizing categories created for the Black being within the veil of Western humanism and the historicization of human civilization. This historicization and ideals such as humanism have been corrupted by colonial and racist constructions of hierarchies that have mostly favored those who have designated themselves and their social kinds with nomenclatures of power such as "dominant," "enlightened," "intelligent," "knowledgeable," and so on. Fanon reinforced this in his critique of what he regarded as "a racism of contempt" in *Wretched of the Earth*, inveighing that "the bourgeois ideology that proclaims all men to be essentially equal, manages to remain consistent with itself by urging the subhuman to rise to the level of Western humanity that it embodies."[18] Through his anticolonial critiques, Fanon was able to unveil the violence of the epistemological framework that is embedded in the politics of Western modernity and ideals of humanism and demonstrate how this has been used historically and contemporaneously to justify the subjugation, exploitation, and dehumanization of Black people in the world.

Frantz Fanon on the Violence of Epistemology and the Epistemology of Violence

The anticolonial epistemological project in Fanon's thought exposes the violence of epistemology in Western constructions of the nature of human knowledge and the advocacy of an epistemology of violence that is necessary to rupture this framework of constructed violence. In other words, Fanon was clear about the fact that the question of violence is always a present reality, even if it is unacknowledged, in all of its facets in the created world where the dialectics of being are already formed or deformed by the axes of power and hierarchies of being penned into it. In this context, knowledge as power and archeology of achievement become a site of contest and the ultimate marker of the distance between existential dread and existential solace—such that to be is either to be *known* or *unknown*. Fanon contends that Black subjects or Black people generally were constructed and restricted to the unknown axis of reality, which constitutes one of the most gruesome forms of violence embedded within the colonial systems of the world. As he laments in *Wretched of the Earth*, "the colonized subject is . . . starved of anything that humanizes him."[19] In other words, Fanon views the manner in which the world was constructed as projecting violence toward Black people because they were located outside of humanity. Consequently, Fanon regards the tools of epistemic thinking developed within the Western framework (the Manichean world) such as "dialectics," "relationality," or "recognition" to be outmoded, useless, and irrational because of their inherent violence. He resolves that "challenging the colonial world is not a rational confrontation of viewpoints. It is not a discourse on the universal, but the impassioned claim by the colonized that their world is fundamentally different. The colonial world is a Manichean world."[20] Manicheanism is a form of epistemic violence because it is designed to maintain the dehumanization and damnation of Black people.

The violence of epistemology consists of its usage within Western categories of thought to demarcate between beings that are considered to exist in the zone of being and those, like the Black subject, that are restricted to the zone of nonbeing. In other words, Fanon provided a global lens to consider the problem of the color-line as fundamentally an epistemological problem nested in the contraries of being (*to be, to exist, to be real*) and nonbeing (*to not be, to be unreal, not to exist*). With such analyses, Fanon asks his readers "to feel" with him "the open dimension of every consciousness" before directing this call back to himself and to his own body, thereby recognizing embodiment as an essential source of knowledge for those in need of a guiding light in a world stricken by the imposed systems of violence and alienation.[21] Fanon talks about this form of violence as unraveling with the intent to shame and "unveil" the colonial subject and all that is within its grasp of power, just as the French colonialists sought to violently and inhumanly unveil the Algerian woman. Fanon describes this in *A Dying Colonialism*, stating, "There is also in the European the crystallization of an aggressiveness, the strain of a kind of violence before the Algerian woman. Unveiling this woman is revealing her beauty; it is baring her secret, breaking her resistance, making her available for adventure."[22] Whereas the European colonialist thinks this is adventurous, it is actually imposing violence to violate the humanity and freedom of the Algerian woman, just as it is for other Black subjects. Thus, Blackness within the framework of imperialist and colonial domination of the world is nothing but a contradiction created by the imposition of colonial structures and epistemic schemes on spaces occupied by those who are categorized as being outside of the domain of existence.

For Fanon, colonialism was an exceptionally violent phenomenon because it dehumanized the colonized, divided and exploited them, deformed their culture, and transformed them into a lesser people. It was premised on force not political consensus, and it resulted in the denial of people's fundamental rights.[23] He describes this as a system that imposed a "bleating paternalism towards blacks and the obscene idea drawn from Western culture that the black race is impermeable to logic and science reign in all its nakedness."[24] It is a system that seeks to unilaterally project an entire group of people as inferior only from the strength of a comparative analysis with Western culture and modes of living. It is primarily a system of domination and oppression that is designed to keep them down and one that prescribes mental disability as the norm of Black experience. Fanon diagnosed Western/colonial epistemes and accretions as the prime causative of mental disorder and the psychological feeling of inferiority among colonized Black folks, including all forms of self-estrangement, in the same manner that Du Bois divined the color-line to be the problem in the twentieth century that generates the phenomenon of double consciousness as well as self-estrangement. As Fanon asserts in Black Skin, White Masks, "inferiorization is the native correlative to the European's feeling of superiority. Let us have the courage to say: *It is the racist who creates the inferiorized.*"[25] Fanon's critique has something to do with the convergence of the problematic of colonialism with that of subject formation, especially the absence of recognition for Blacks within colonial systems of thought. As a psychoanalyst of culture, and as a champion of the wretched of the earth, he is an almost irresistible figure for a criticism that sees itself as both oppositional and postmodern.[26]

In his psychiatric writings, Fanon makes the connection between European colonialism and its effects on Black patients such as mental alterations, character deformation, and psychic disorders. Fanon's dissertation, which he defended in Lyon in November 1951, explored some of these themes.[27] Prior to his pioneering work in this area, clinical psychologists typically considered mental illnesses as natural entities that are onto-generative. But in his dissertation, Fanon maintained that "mental illnesses are not natural 'entities' while recognizing the possibility of their organic origin, which was an important novel stance to take in the medical debates of the time."[28] He would go on to establish groundbreaking findings that would upend the foundations of colonial ethnopsychiatry. He was preoccupied by the connections between the ills of organized society and mental health, just as he was passionate about the linkages between history and alienation.[29] He would later elaborate on the links between colonial categories of cataloguing human experience such as "dialectics" as a source of psychological illness or neurosis that results from the failures of the colonized subject to achieve "recognition" that is so much desired. In Black Skin, White Masks, Fanon describes the psychological trauma that the Antillean experiences as something that is not naturally constituted or occurring but something that is imposed through the dialectics of oppression, imposed by the colonial system such that the "Antillean does not possess a personal value of his own and is always dependent on the presence of 'the Other'"[30]

Thus, what Fanon describes as colonial recognition will often provoke within the oppressed a desire to "escape" their particularity, to negate the differences that marked them as morally deficient and inferior in the eyes of the colonizer, codified in *Black Skin, White Masks* through such expressions as "The [Black] is an animal, the [Black] is bad, the [Black] is wicked, the [Black] is ugly."[31] Once internalized, these derogatory images often produce a pathological yearning to "be recognized not as *Black*, but as *White*."[32] Fanon uses several terms to describe the result of this process: "inferiority complex," "psycho-existential complex," "neurosis," and "alienation" are the most common. All of these designations were used by Fanon to describe the subjectifying hold that colonial power can have on those within its reach. What this reveals is the fact that there is nothing "inherent" about the perceived "inferiority" attributed to colonized subjects by the colonial or oppressive society, nor is there anything "natural" about the so-called "complexes" they suffer as a result. Both are the product of colonial social relations: "If there is a flaw, it lies not in the 'soul' of the [colonized] individual, but his environment,"[33] which necessitates the dismantling of this colonial system of thought and its knowledge categories, even if it means that an epistemology of violence needs to be imagined to counter the violence of Eurocentric, colonial epistemology.

In the *Wretched of the Earth*, Fanon talks about three stages of development through which the colonized intellectual or writer can disrupt the schemes of the colonizer. The first has to do with possible dreams of "assimilation" within the colonizer's culture, which makes any achievement of freedom from alienation practically impossible. The second phase is where doubt is cast in the minds of the colonized intellectual while engaging with harmful Western ideas. The third phase is the stage of combat—where a true epistemology of violence is fashioned to resist and reject the colonial schemes often projected as the axiomatic and normative view of the world.[34] It would involve the evolution of a new register, language, and a new mind-set in thinking about being in the world because the colonizers have not left behind a state of things that can be used to build a new future.

In fact, it is not in the best interest of the colonizer for this to happen. The devastation is such that nothing less than a resolute and forceful disengagement from its aftermath is required—a struggle for liberation and freedom.[35] Fanon's concern here is to reveal where the colonized subject's counter-violence originates and why the epistemology of violence is necessary. In fact, because of colonialism, Black subjects point fingers at the European colonialists for the creation of racism, discrimination, and ontogenetic categories such as "Blackness," "whiteness," and dehumanization. In order to disrupt this order of things, Fanon imagines the epistemology of violence as a mechanism that can recover, restore, repair, and re-honor those who have been seriously affected by colonial violence.[36] It is through this means that the birth of a new human and a new account of civilization emerges, which is essentially grounded in a philosophy of life, a methodology for development, and a defense of Black dignity.[37]

Fanon's Anticolonial Epistemology and the Re-emergence of Black Humanity

Toward the end of *Black Skin, White Masks*, Fanon raises some deeply probing questions regarding how the oppressed, in this case, the Black subject, can engage with the world from this place of subjugation or damnation. He advocates that "it is through self-consciousness and renunciation, through a permanent tension of his freedom, that man can create the ideal conditions of existence for a human world."[38] He emphasized the anticolonial reimagining of Black self-consciousness that is grounded within the Black subject rather than within the categories of being derived in alien philosophical, metaphysical, and phenomenological thinking about the human experience. Fanon insists that an inquiry into metaphysics as a pathway to engage with Black humanity is often highly destructive.[39] Rather, he insists on a conceptualization of Black humanity outside of the chains and restrictions of coloniality and the negative ascriptions that are projected onto "the Other." This is a radical vision of a world in which the emergence of Black humanity is regarded as self-constituted with authorial musings and first-person (contrasted with third-person) accretions about things in the world. Fanon understood that the question of "what it is like to be Black" in the world has been conditioned, for too long, by the assumptions of the normativity of whiteness, and this trend has to be interrupted by a different or new way of thinking—an anticolonial epistemological framework of thinking—in order to get to the beauty of Black humanity. As he writes in *Black Skin, White Masks*, in the process of trying to discover the true meaning of Black identity, one would discover that

"White civilization and European culture have imposed an existential deviation on the Black man."[40] He argues that for this search for meaning to be positive, one has to arrive at an "incomprehension and discord" that will eventually lead to the discovery of the true meaning of Black humanity.[41]

I consider Sylvia Wynter's perspective on this point to be very insightful. In "Towards the Sociogenic Principle: Fanon, Identity, the Puzzle of Conscious Experience, and What It is Like to Be 'Black,'" Wynter argues that Fanon's dually third-person and first-person exploration of the lived experience of being Black in his book *Black Skin, White Masks* was both to develop the earlier insights of Black American thinkers such as W.E.B. Du Bois concerning the conflicted "double consciousness" in Blacks in Western civilization and to put forward, as the explanatory cause of his "double consciousness," a new theoretical object of knowledge—sociogeny.[42] What Wynter is suggesting here is that since Fanon was able to diagnose that the present/dominant order of knowledge undermines or erases Black humanity, it was important for him to develop a new concept of Black knowledge or the science of knowledge—sociogeny—that upholds a new conception of the human that humanizes the Black subject.

As Fanon writes, "the alienation of the Black man is not an individual question. Alongside phylogeny and ontogeny, there is also sociogeny . . . [which] unlike biochemical processes, does not escape human influence. Man is what brings society into being."[43] So, Fanon imagines sociogeny as a new science for understanding the condition of the Black subject in the world that will take into consideration the robustness of its reality or "sociodiagnostics," unlike under previous scientific imaginations. It is a new beginning for history, science, knowledge, and essentially the creation of a new world. In "The Impossible Life of Frantz Fanon," Albert Memmi, Thomas Cassirer, and G. Michael Twomey raised the question concerning why Fanon would propose a vision of a totally unprecedented man, in a totally reconstructed world.[44] But Fanon provides the answer in the conclusion of *The Wretched of the Earth*, stating that "For Europe, for ourselves and for humanity, comrades, we must make a new beginning, develop new thought, try to create a new man."[45]

For Fanon, though, the history of the human starts from and ultimately returns to historical Blackness as his own autoethnographic locus and, more importantly, as the living record inscribed with the inverted projection of the instincts that have shaped the modern global landscape, characterized, as it is, by racialized imperial capitalism and (neo-) colonialism. That is to say, Blackness, as Fanon observes, bears the sociogeny of its own being and that of its Other in a way that its Other does not and cannot possibly reciprocate; it tells the sociogenetic story of Blackness.[46]

As imagined by Fanon, sociogeny is a comprehensive interpretive scientific lens of engaging with the historicity of Blackness in the world, and this approach is focused on a positive interpretation of the Black lived experience. For Wynter, "such a new science would, invariably have to be (as already suggested by Fanon's exploration of the lived experience of the Black subject) one able to harness the findings of the natural sciences (including the neurosciences)."[47] It will also transform the structure of knowledge in other humanistic disciplines in the social sciences, propelled by a new system of thinking that will ultimately lead to the reimagining of modes of being, and the development of a new human identity. What Wynter identifies in Fanon, in "Towards the Sociogenic Principle," is the dire need to transcend hegemonic ascriptions of knowledge that cast Blackness in a negative light and move toward a new conception of the "Black" human. To create a new Black epistemology that accounts for Blackness or the Black lived experience, Fanon makes it clear that such a project will have to struggle with *reason* as unreason.

To put it more succinctly, Fanon acknowledges that because the normative principle, including the moral ethos of viewing the world through a colonial-hegemonic lens, is adjudged and consecrated as that which is derived out of "reason" or reasonable grounds of judgment, any attempt to stray away from or challenge such colonial logics or schemes of rationality will always be seen as "irrational." This is what Fanon highlights when he maintains in *Toward the African Revolution* that "the unilaterally decreed normative value of certain cultures deserves our careful attention. One of the paradoxes immediately encountered is the rebound of egocentric, sociocentric definitions."[48] That is, insights into the laws that govern the realm of the subjective experience, human and nonhuman, and the interrelated phenomena of identity, mind, and/ or consciousness are founded on precepts that are codified as the normative way of viewing the world.[49] Fanon understood that colonial exploitation was not just about the imperial practices of pillaging the land and human persons as sources of odious material gain, but was also a form of psychological warfare with the purpose of forcibly making Blacks believe themselves to be inferior under the Western or colonial ethos and a calculated attempt to create a fictive being out of the colonized.

Fanon argues that "the colonial subject is a man [human] penned in; apartheid is but one method of compartmentalizing the colonial world. The first thing the colonial subject learns is to remain in his place and not overstep its limits."[50] Here, Fanon is signifying one of the ultimate objectives of the colonial project, which is to demarcate a horizon of control that includes the control of markers of being such as agency, subjective articulation of experience, and the freedom to challenge imposed systems of thought and norms. The "human penned in" is a powerful metaphor for the colonized subject that has been captured under this system of control and is now exhibiting characteristics of pathology as the "normalized state," while staying within the boundaries of humanity—as the nonhuman. This dichotomy is maintained because, as Fanon says, the colonial world, including the colonial logic of rationality, is already imposed through the bifurcated logic of segregation (self and other), in all its political, economic, social, material, and metaphysical manifestations. It is interesting to note that Fanon's diagnosis of this pathological condition of the colonized/Black subject penned in was necessary for him to imagine its contrary—"the human penned out."

The idea of the "human penned out" is a powerful idea from Fanonian meditations that focuses on the creative epistemic power of the authorial being (Black subject) toward "penning" an alternative sociogenic reality where Blackness demonstrates a form of agential control that is not merely geospatial but also controls its own mental or psychological states. As Fanon himself puts it, "deep down the colonized subject acknowledges no authority. He is dominated but not domesticated. He is made to feel inferior, but by no means convinced of his inferiority." With this, Fanon challenges the colonial epistemological categories that erase Blackness from the space of "reason" and unleashes a new vision for Blackness in the "space of reason." This is a state of awareness where the Black subject exhibits its epistemic authority by "acknowledging no [other] authority" for cataloging the lived experience. Fanon imagines a different kind of agential control that consists of affirming the epistemic power of the Black subject in refusing to be caricaturized and relegated to the realm of liminality.

Whereas the colonial epistemological system of understanding the world is one that operates on an "irrational" logic because it obeys a system of thought that normalizes race-prejudice, for Fanon, such a system of "race prejudice obeys a flawless logic. A country that lives, draws its substance from the exploitation of other peoples, makes those peoples inferior. Race prejudice applied to those people is normal."[51] Fanon opposes the normalization of raced and prejudiced logic that thrives and derives its validity from the inferiorization of Blackness. This necessitates a struggle for reason—reasonable grounds for putting Blackness back into the human world—which is a subversion of "reason" in colonial logic. Thus, Fanon's rationalization of the irrational world is in itself a new conception of anticolonial epistemology, one that is primarily focused on rupturing the order of knowledge and colonial impulses that perpetually pursue a categorization of Blackness as a conceptual impossibility—a nothing or nonexistent entity. Fanon, therefore, begins his anticolonial epistemology with an affirmation of Blackness in the present tense and reclaims Blackness from the so-called normative imaginary that castigates the *itself*, a mythic configuration of that which is not.

In Fanon's words, "my blackness was there, dense and undeniable. And it tormented me, pursued me, made me uneasy, and exasperated me. [Blacks] are savages, morons, and illiterates. But I knew personally that in my case these assertions were wrong. There was this myth of [Blacks] that had to be destroyed at all costs."[52] Fanon's torment is a description of the internal conflicts and struggles that Black subjects experience as they are coated with negated categories of being. Fanon is also describing how the psychological residue of the affliction of the colonial mythic constructions and negations, accentuate the goal of undermining Blackness, even when it is undeniably present, as he asserts. The only way for the Black subject to be free from this mythic categorization is to dismantle it or "destroy it at all costs." This passage from *Black Skin, White Masks* also suggests that Fanon's existence raises the question of the relationship between humanity and reason, and the problems posed by what he calls "the fact of blackness." If even reason or understanding is infected with racism, where unreason stands on the opposite pole as a Manichaean abyss of Blackness, then a Black person who reasons finds themself in the absurdity of the very construction of self as a human *who reasons*. Such a Black person, just like Fanon, is deemed to be irrational. Thus, for Fanon, the Black subject that was previously categorized as "irrational" now becomes "rational" under a new regime of epistemology—Black epistemology. The orientation of knowledge under Black epistemology elevates Black subjectivity/humanity, and it is constantly opposing and moving away from the Western logic of rationality, given its epistemic deficiency. As Fanon powerfully declares in *Black Skin, White Masks*, "I had rationalized the world, and the world had rejected me in the name of color prejudice. Since there was no way, we could agree based on reason, I resorted to irrationality."[53]

Like Du Bois, what Fanon is articulating here is the need to subvert the hegemony of Western logic and initiate a new kind of logic for viewing the Black lived experience in the world—an anticolonial logic of the self that captures the changing dynamics for ordering and othering the world. This is what he means when he asserts further that "for the sake of the cause, I had adopted the process of regression, but the fact remained that it was an unfamiliar weapon; here I am at home; I am made of the irrational; I wade in the irrational. Irrational up to my neck."[54] Taking on the persona of the "irrational" for Fanon is in itself a weapon of liberation and the weapon of power: the power to construct a new world where Blackness is not inferiorized but humanized. Fanon is also laying the foundation for characterizing Black epistemic authority to construct a new vision of the world that is devoid of anti-Black racist impulses; this is a vision of existence that displaces and discountenances the hegemonic logics in the Western epistemological framing of the world, including all bifurcated regimes of meaning that catalog Blackness in alternate categories of being. For Fanon, "the irrational" is not irrational, it is the new form of "rational," primarily, a Black expression of rationality. This is how the Black subject can make sense of the world replete with the colorized prejudice that informs the colonial codification of reason. Thus, a Black expression of rationality under a different scheme, such as the sociogenic understanding of knowledge, *à la* Fanon, is at the same time an expression of the ontogeny of Black humanity.

The exposition in this chapter aims to show that the critical and philosophical reflections of Fanon orient us toward a vision and a regime of knowledge where Blackness is not erased, but affirmed. It is an intellectual space where the Black subject or "Self," in *itself*, is conceived as an epistemic agent that constructs knowledges from the vantage point of the Black experience. Thus, the significance of this discourse on epistemic authority, in relation to Blackness, is that Black subjectivity becomes a symbol of power—the power to avow knowledge concerning Black existence and the validation of Black intellect, brilliance, and genius—it is a project of humanizing Blackness. This project is important not only to the preservation of Black intellectual heritage but also in the affirmation of the necessity of Black existence in a world where the pathologization of Blackness is regarded as an acceptable social reality.

8

In the Spirit of Biko

Black Consciousness as
Anticolonial Epistemology

This chapter focuses on the formation of Black epistemologies in the African diaspora in the later parts of the twentieth century. It specifically examines the philosophy of Black Consciousness, as espoused by Steve Bantu Biko, the antiapartheid revolutionary thinker, community organizer, philosopher, and inspirational leader whose political relevance transcends the South African geospatial polity. This particular engagement with the philosophy of Black Consciousness, as pursued in this chapter, aims to unravel the subtleties of the epistemological constructs that informed the formation of this ideology and political movement and the way of life that this philosophical system was predicated upon. It is a survey of the principles of the psychological and social principles of knowledge that are contained in Biko's notion of Black Consciousness and how such principles were employed to confront the repressive existential conditions experienced by Black subjects in the context of extreme anti-Black oppression. Thus, the thrust of Biko's anticolonial epistemology was mainly directed at confronting the belief systems, political ethos, and knowledge categories of white colonial hegemony that constructed Black subjects as inferior in the domain of knowledge and as "outsiders" even within their own territorial and epistemic space.

Biko's anticolonial epistemology was aimed at evolving a system of knowledge that primarily considers Black people as subjects, not merely as objects of knowledge. In one of his autobiographical reflections titled "We Blacks," Biko describes a sense of Black agency that makes this anticolonial epistemological move possible. It rests on the fact that Black subjects are forced to engage in a dialectical assessment of the present conditions of life imposed upon them by external hegemonic systems of power, and that this process can unravel and reject their condition of epistemic dislocation. As he poignantly articulates, "My thinking and every other facet of my life has been carved and shaped within the context of separate development."[1] This kind of awareness is necessary for the Black subject to be able to confront and transcend the systems of white colonial hegemony. As Biko articulates further, "In stages during my life I have managed to outgrow some of the things the system taught me."[2] This form of awareness is at the epicenter of Biko's notion of Black Consciousness. He succinctly makes this case when he avows that "what I propose to do now is to take a look at those who participate in opposition to the system—not from a detached point of view but from the point of view of a Black man, conscious of the urgent need for an understanding of what is involved in the new approach—'Black Consciousness.'"[3]

The anticolonial epistemology that undergirds Biko's notion of Black Consciousness sees knowledge as a product of an existential contradiction in a colonial context—on the one hand, it is used to construct the basis of being in the world, while on the other hand, it is used to invent evidence of those who are considered to be "in the world" but not "of the world." That is, within the material world that is constructed through a colonial-hegemonic vision, two forms of consciousness are in existence but only one is unacknowledged: Black consciousness. So, Biko's attempt to tackle the problem of lack of self-consciousness for Blacks within apartheid-era South Africa takes on an epistemological character. This consists of his insistence that Black subjects avow themselves as "knowledgeable beings" in the face of virulent racist characterizations of Blacks as incapable of demonstrating the attributes of the mind or consciousness. This informed his view that Blacks needed to reclaim their agency as a phenomenon that is functional and separate from the fixed ascriptions apportioned to them within the illogic of white colonial domination. Since Biko was already well aware of the fact that "the [il]logic behind white domination is to prepare the Black man for the subservient role in [his] country."[4] It is this [il]logic of domination that has reduced the Black subject, in Biko's words, to an "obliging shell" that looks with awe at the white power structure and accepts what he/she regards as the "inevitable position," completely defeated, drowning in misery while bearing the yoke of oppression with sheepish timidity.[5] Biko was adamant that the process of changing this subversive position that most Black people find themselves in has to start with changing the Black mindset to perceive reality differently. This was aimed at achieving freedom for the mass of the South African Black population that had been bound under the shadows of colonial hegemony.

It is important to briefly acknowledge the overarching political context in which Biko developed and propagated his idea and ideal of Black Consciousness. In this regard, Biko's reflections in *I Write What I Like* are pertinent:

> Born shortly before 1948 [the year in which the Nationalist Party came to power], I have lived all my conscious life in the framework of institutionalized separate development. My friendships, my love, my education, my thinking, and every other facet of my life have been carved and shaped within the context of separate development. In stages, during my life, I have managed to outgrow some of the things the system taught me. Hopefully what I propose to do now is to take a look at those who participate in opposition to the system—not from a detached point of view but from the point of view of a black man, conscious of the urgent need for an understanding of what is involved in the new approach—"black consciousness."[6]

The references Biko makes here regarding institutionalized separation were aimed at highlighting the brutality of the apartheid regime in South Africa, driven by the white minority rule that established a system of colonial hegemony and a system of white domination that denied basic human rights to Black South Africans. Black South Africa in the 1960s (referred to as Azania by Black nationalists during this period) was ripe for an ideology of liberation informed by a distinctive epistemological apparatus. Since the oppression of apartheid society took place overtly and blatantly, with all opposition silenced and institutionalized racism triumphant, Blacks were portrayed stereotypically as innately inferior, accustomed to dehumanized living, sexually promiscuous, intellectually limited, and prone to violence. Such portrayals draw from the mythos of Blackness as symbolizing evil, demise, and uncleanliness, in contrast to whiteness, which equaled order, wealth, purity, goodness, cleanliness, and the epitome of beauty. Exclusionary practices over centuries led to what can be described as the "inferiorization of blacks," inevitably internalized by the victims themselves.[7]

In this context of "inferiorization," Blacks could not come to think of themselves as worthy epistemic agents capable of claiming distinctive knowledge about their world and how they perceive reality. In other words, the colonial imposition of categories of negation upon Blacks in such hegemonic contexts undermines the very basic conditions of epistemic agency. This is why it is crucial to read Biko's Black Consciousness as an anticolonial epistemology that embodies a form of Black resistance aimed at demolishing the structures of colonial hegemony and psychopathologies, including epistemological axioms that antagonize Black people's livity in an anti-Black world.

Biko reveals that white colonial repression has only one ultimate objective, which is to conquer the Black mind. This is why he affirms that "the greatest potent weapon in the hands of the oppressor is the mind of the oppressed."[8] The profound implication of this diagnosis is that, for Black people to imagine freedom, they must free their minds (a metaphor for being and becoming, self-identity, and autonomy) from colonial domination and resist the hegemonic systems that categorize Black existence as a subaltern. The emphasis here is on the demonstration of an attitude of the mind that unleashes the autonomous self (the Black self) as the primary apparatus for living in a world that is already anti-Black in its ontological formations. Thus, Biko's Black Consciousness, when considered as an anticolonial epistemological structure, reverses the epistemic status of Black subjects from "non-thinking things" to "thinking subjects" who are in control of their stream of consciousness and are aware of the contradictions that are socially imposed by external forces to deny them the reality of subjective experiences. Black Consciousness philosophy as imagined by Biko is focused on developing a notion of the Black conscious experience, untainted by the false categories imposed upon it by the dialectics of being that have gained currency under the Western (foreign) imaginary. Biko argued that such imaginary constructions, a product of the Western culture, should be vehemently rejected. He argues thus:

> In rejecting Western values, therefore, we are rejecting those things that are not only foreign to us but that seek to destroy the most cherished of our beliefs—that the corner-stone of society is man himself—not just his welfare, not his material wellbeing but just man himself with all his ramifications.[9]

In other words, the Western imaginary that equates the natural category of being ("man") with non-Blacks has to be rejected as a phenomenological nonreality and an epistemological foundationalism that is deeply flawed. Its deep flaw consists of its inability to capture the subjective experience, belief systems, and stream of consciousness of Black subjects as the phenomenological and intellectual production of "man himself." The idea of "man himself" that Biko alludes to rescues Black agency from the Western dialectic of being that denies the Black subjective experience as the evidence of nonthinking things. He frames Black Consciousness as both an existential act and a philosophical system that look at the cognitive life of the Black subject as a phenomenological experience that signifies freedom—epistemic freedom.

Biko expands further on this idea of Black Consciousness as a mechanism designed to achieve epistemic freedom for the Black subject when he maintains that "Black Consciousness seeks to talk to the Black man in a language that is his own. It is only by recognizing the basic set-up in the black world that one will come to realize the urgent need for a re-awakening of the sleeping masses."[10] This action of re-awakening is a metaphor for epistemic freedom. This is evident in how Biko defines his philosophy of Black Consciousness:

> Briefly defined, therefore, Black Consciousness is, in essence, the realization by the black man [Black folks generally] of the need to rally together with his brothers around the cause of their operation—the blackness of their skin—and to operate as a group in order to rid themselves of the shackles that bind them to perpetual servitude. It seeks to demonstrate the lie that black is an aberration from the "normal" which is white. It is a manifestation of a new realization that by seeking to run away from themselves and to emulate the white man, blacks are insulting the intelligence of whoever created them black. Black Consciousness, therefore, takes cognizance of the deliberateness of God's plan in creating black people black. It seeks to infuse the black community with a new-found pride in themselves, their efforts, their value systems, their culture, their religion, and their outlook on life.[11]

Here, Biko emphasizes the need to achieve freedom from the kind of mental slavery that white colonial values have imposed on Blacks, which invariably has generated a deep sense of alienation from the Black self as something liminal compared to that of the colonialists. The upshot of such self-alienation is self-hate, which Biko addresses as a phenomenon that evolved as a logical consequence of the colonial invasion of Black existential territories. To combat against this problem of existence, he advocates a new but radical philosophical system of thought—Black Consciousness—that aims to engage with this problem from its very ontological and epistemological foundations: by making sure that Black people living in this context develop a healthy sense of self through an emphasis on group pride as well as on building new epistemic categories that center African/Black culture as the core for being in the world with an emancipated self-consciousness. Biko goes further to assert that:

> The interrelationship between the consciousness of the self and the emancipatory program is of paramount importance. Blacks no longer seek to reform the system because so doing implies acceptance of the major points around which the system revolves. Blacks are out to completely transform the system and to make of it what they wish. Such a major undertaking can only be realized in an atmosphere where people are convinced of the truth inherent in their stand. Liberation, therefore, is of paramount importance in the concept of Black Consciousness.[12]

It is apparent from this assertion that Biko is expressing a radical anti-colonial sentiment that calls for the submerging of the colonial system, its logic, and knowledge schemes because it does not cater to the Black experience. He argues that a reformist agenda should not be accommodated in any guise because it would amount to replicating the hegemonic system of a false sense of intellectual superiority that informs colonial practices in Africa and the so-called colonies. So, he insisted that the goal of evolving a new system of thinking (Black Consciousness) is to "completely transform the system" and reconstruct it into what Blacks want it to be. In other words, the Black experience should be the very basis upon which Black folks should construct the ideas and systems they live by and not through extraverted or alienating systems.

The emergence of the Black Consciousness philosophy in the late 1960s is one of the most important philosophical developments ever to take place in the evolution of African political thought in Azania. This philosophy surfaced at a time when above-ground black political activities were virtually nonexistent in Azania following the banning of the African National Congress (ANC) and the Pan Africanist Congress (PAC) by the white racist government in 1960. It was at this critical historical juncture that the alienation of Black youth from the dominant

Black society found concrete expression in the categorical rejection of white liberal leadership by the newly formed all-black South African Students Organization (SASO), which laid the foundation for and became the cradle of the Black Consciousness Movement (BCM) of Azania. The founders of SASO advocated the adoption of a radical political ideology that, in addition to its deep roots in orthodox African nationalism, borrowed major elements from the revolutionary writings of Black thinkers like Malcolm X, Frantz Fanon, and pan-Africanists like Sékou Touré, Kenneth Kaunda, Kwame Nkrumah, and Thomas Sankara.[13] The philosophy of Black Consciousness as propounded and effectively articulated by Steve Biko, the Black militant who was known as the father of Black Consciousness in Azania, drew breath from some of these anticolonial political views that were prominent during this period in the African diaspora.[14] Although the objectives of Black Consciousness were political from the start, in the interests of their survival, its propagators chose to mute its political thrust and publicly emphasized its more cultural and intellectual side.[15] It is this intellectual side that is of principal interest in this work.

Two Epistemological Dimensions in Biko's Black Consciousness Philosophy

The epistemological underpinnings of Black Consciousness as construed by Steve Biko symbolize the assertive power or agential control of the Black subject to advance knowledge ascriptions about the self in the face of brutal epistemic and violent political oppression within systems of coloniality. Black consciousness is intended by Biko as a corrective to the damage that coloniality and oppression have caused Black people, especially Black South Africans. It aims to repudiate the negative categories and existential pathologies created by the colonial mentality seeking to negate Black humanity, render Black existence meaningless, and restrict Black lives to an abyss of absurdity. This attempt to negate Black humanity is exposed as a concretization of fictitious or false entities and imaginary Black objects that are deemed to be inferior. This is a casting of white ignorance and racism, devised to maintain false dialectics of superiority and inferiority. The anticolonial epistemological underpinnings of Biko's Black Consciousness show that these are false taxonomies that do not apply to the Black experience.

At a fundamental level, Black Consciousness deals primarily with the question of the human that emerges as an epistemological project:

the epistemological project (anticolonial epistemology) that unravels the dehumanizing attributions of nonepistemic schemes and the nonattribution of knowledge attributes to Black subjects. It also simultaneously focuses on bringing Black subjects closer to their existential horror by making them recognize the fact that they are not wholly at fault for being in this existential hell. Rather, it is the hubris of coloniality that has been projected to undermine their minds and the materiality of their existence. What this shows is that Biko was preoccupied with the existential condition of Blackness in the anti-Black world, and the fundamental questions he posed center on the existential struggles that haunt Blackness: what it means to exist in an anti-Black world.[16] Therefore, Biko avers that the project of achieving liberation through Black Consciousness must begin with a resistant notion of Black subjectivity— making Black individuals come to terms with their self-identity and having a full appreciation of their Blackness. In his magnum opus *I Write What I Like,* Biko writes thus:

> The first step [toward liberation] therefore is to make the black man come to himself; to pump back life into his empty shell; to infuse him with pride and dignity, to remind him of his complicity in the crime of allowing himself to be misused and therefore letting evil reign supreme in the country of his birth. This is what we mean by an inward-looking process. This is the definition of "Black Consciousness."[17]

It is clear from this assertion that Biko believes that if Black people are to break away from the cycle of oppression that holds them bound, they must develop a new mental attitude, a resistant mental attitude that renounces the categories of alterity projected onto their being by the system of coloniality, and cultivate a sense of self-affirmation, a self-description that celebrates the beauty in Black existence.

Black Consciousness thus views humanity as implicit to an awareness that fundamentally constituted the self as much as it was realized outside the self.[18] In this regard, the title of the compilation of Biko's writings, "I Write What I Like," depicts a powerful metaphor that emphasizes a sense of liberation that focuses on the avowal of Black knowledge— avowing knowledge claims to affirm Black subjectivity and the condition of Black existence in the context of white oppression and, more importantly, writing to affirm Black intellect in a world where Black people are thought to be intellectually handicapped.[19] When Biko maintains that Black Consciousness is an inward-looking process, he is affirming that both the agency and community that inform Blackness are a rallying point for the imagination of Black liberation. It is contingent on the belief that the agency and shared commitment of Black people should constitute the basis of consciousness-raising. There are two important aspects of anticolonial epistemological formation in Biko's Black Consciousness philosophy that warrant serious philosophical consideration. The first aspect deals with *cognitive-affective epistemology*, while the second is concerned with *political epistemology*. Both epistemological aspects are mutually inclusive in that they are geared toward achieving one goal: Black liberation.

Cognitive-affective epistemology considers the mind as the epicenter of knowledge acquisition, formation, and internalization. The cognitive epistemological dimension of Black Consciousness deals primarily with the mind of Black folks—ensuring the development of some kind of mental resistance to the damage that colonization has done to the Black psyche. Through his emphasis on the mind as a site of struggle for meaning-making and self-realization, Biko provides another way of mobilizing the politics of the psyche. He exemplifies a line of psycho-politics that utilizes the terms of psychological experience as a means of consolidating resistances to power.[20] Biko understands that colonial domination has done a great deal of damage to the mentality of Black folks, particularly Black folks in apartheid-era South Africa, which has led to their negative conception of the self that makes it difficult to fight back against such false categories that are projected as categorical truths. As Hashi Tafira observes, "Colonial ontological difference and exteriority of the Other as racially marked, as different, like the scum of the earth, as the wretched who is imbricated in the hegemonic epistemic and structures of domination, is a very prominent feature of South African colonial modernity."[21]

However, for Biko, knowing this situation, showing epistemological awareness of this reality is crucial to imagining freedom for Black people. Essentially, he sees colonial domination and exploitation as a battle of the mind—especially the link between colonial hegemonic knowledge construction and domination. He sees the hegemonic schemes of white civilization as constructed to ensure white dominance of the world. This is why his notion of Black Consciousness calls for the psychological and cultural liberation of the oppressed as a necessary prerequisite for political freedom; in his view, mental emancipation is a precondition of political emancipation.[22] In this case, the mind is conceived not as an abstract or disembodied entity but as an embodied subjectivity that actively guides affairs in the material world. It is an actionable view of the Black mind, both as an end in itself and as a means to an end. Biko makes references to the cognitive-affective state of the Black subject as the fundamental location for the reimagining of a different future and a different world where Blackness is not condemned to the realms of dehumanization. In other words, the imagining of Blackness through a humanizing lens has to begin with an attitude of the mind that is not trapped in the colonial projection of subpar psychological traits or categories onto Black bodies. Biko's anticolonial epistemology, therefore, takes root in this insistence that conative states and agency are human traits that Black subjects embody and should display to bring about a new conception of humanity—Black humanity.

It is in a bid to counter such hegemonic posture of coloniality that Biko conceives of Black Consciousness as emblematic of a liberation movement of the mind to counter the faulty and false patterns of thinking imposed on Black people as colonial subjects. In opposition to self-negating ways of thinking, Biko called for solidarity among those whom apartheid labeled "nonwhite," emphasizing the need for oppressed groups to identify themselves as an autonomous, creative, and potentially powerful solidarity, and to advance the liberation struggle based on the expression of freedom of the mind.[23] This is what Biko means when he referred to being Black as a mental attitude. In his words, "being black is not a matter of pigmentation—being black is a reflection of a mental attitude. Merely by describing yourself as black, you have started on a road to fight towards emancipation, you have committed yourself to fight against all forces that seek to use your blackness as a stamp that marks you out as a subservient being."[24]

What this implies is that the road toward freedom must entail a dimension of an epistemology of opposition that focuses on the repair of the Black subject's psyche that has been brutally damaged by colonialization. From Biko's perspective, then, Black Consciousness meant an understanding that the emancipation of Blacks and the liberation of society as a whole required a mental renaissance of the Black intellect.[25] The ultimate goal of this cognitive/affective dimension of Biko's Black Consciousness is to make Black people overcome this negative sense of self and psychological paranoia that stem from a systematic manipulation of the Black mind by the white race, a race that had long recognized the value of thought control devised to uphold the conditioning of Black existence at the subliminal level. Biko's Black Consciousness philosophy emphasizes several aspects such as African humanism, an affirmation of Black identity, and Black solidarity, but one of its most important aspects has to do with psychological emancipation.[26]

This idea of self-reliance that Biko emphasized in his Black Consciousness philosophy is what Daniel Magaziner refers to in "Black Man, You Are on Your Own!" as the politics of the personal geared toward achieving a proper existential condition for Black folks. According to Magaziner, "The politics of the personal and the challenges of the intellectual had long resonated in Black South African history. Although student thinkers appropriated symbols and language from their global moment—afros, clenched fists, concerns with 'authenticity' and '[B]eingness'—they were also engaged in a deep-rooted local struggle."[27] Thinking of the Black Consciousness struggle in this way shows that Biko was interested in ensuring that Black people generally internalize or localize the struggle at the level of the individual and that the negotiations for freedom have to be personalized first before any form of social cohesion or community solidarity can be formed. Part of the power of Black Consciousness lay in its rhetorical force and its sophisticated analysis, which emphasized the psychological dimension of oppression and personal agency, that the oppressed should liberate themselves through a style or way of life.[28] Biko was interested in making sure that Black subjects personally assess their condition as socially situated subjects within a system that does not recognize them as such, while working out what that means for their process of rediscovery.

Although Biko provided structural frameworks for making such individual negotiations, he was aware that individual circumstances and experiences of Black South Africans under apartheid were not univocal, even though they shared certain similarities in general outlook. So, Biko's philosophy of Black Consciousness must be seen as a fluid anticolonial epistemological framework that made it possible for Black South Africans to see themselves in the process of imagining a life independent of colonial impositions. This anticolonial framework was used to shape the ideas about the proper way of life in the anticolonial movements that were starting to take shape around this time:

> From the founding of SASO through 1972, in the pages of the *SASO Newsletter* and other media, student activists defined a new approach to political experience. As they interrogated the category of blackness and demands of consciousness, they developed ideas about what constituted a historically appropriate "attitude of mind," which would, in turn, generate a proper way of life.[29]

Biko's Black Consciousness can be regarded as a protean movement—it drew from diverse trajectories of ideas constituted in distinct spaces, ideas molded to fit a purpose—to resuscitate Black pride and to generate a renewed project of political empowerment. This notion of Black Consciousness emphasized a "way of life," which those oppressed by apartheid should adopt to embody a liberated mind.[30] However, this emphasis on the construction of a way of life, through a historically appropriate attitude of mind, resonated with the victims of apartheid. It aided them in the development of a critical disposition to stand against the categories of coloniality and the forceful rejection of any philosophical system that seeks to relegate Blackness to the realm of subalternity.

Thus, for Biko, coloniality is first an empire of the mind before it materializes into an empire on the land. Therefore, the battle against it must begin at the cognitive-affective level by transforming how Blacks think of themselves and about the world as it is. Black Consciousness entails the centering of Black agency as the grounds for all knowledge that should inform how Black people live their lives. It is a bold conception of the Black subject as an epistemic agent with the intellectual ability or power of the mind to construct knowledge categories as well as existential precepts in the world. It also orients us toward the appreciation of an epistemological worldview that eschews the forms of epistemological precepts that have nothing to do with the Black experience, especially those that are psychologically and materially harmful to the conditions of Black folks in an anti-Black society.

Biko and the advocates of Black Consciousness practiced a politics of psychological empowerment that woke Black people from their dogmatic slumber. It gave Black people a sense of awakening that unraveled the structures of domination that violently excluded them from the domain of reason and also prevented them from having any meaningful political participation in the affairs of their homeland. Thus, the essential political project of Black Consciousness was to overthrow the yoke of colonialism in its manifested form of apartheid. In this, it shared a deep historical connection with the anticolonial struggles of the world.[31] As a leader, Steve Biko challenged Black people to confront their inner fears head-on, including the fear of death. His unique contribution lay in his vision of the interrelationship between consciousness and culture on the one hand, and developmental and political action on the other.[32] This brings us to the second epistemological dimension in his philosophy of Black Consciousness—political epistemology.

The second epistemological dimension of Biko's Black Consciousness philosophy has to do with the domain of political epistemology.

It is a political epistemological scheme that is crucial to the project of sociopolitical transformation primarily driven by Black people. Broadly construed, political epistemology ascribes sociopolitical power to political actors as epistemic agents, authorial knowers, and change agents. In conditions of sociopolitical repression, this agential act is often driven by a set of unique political ideas that are formulated in the hope of bringing about positive social change to oppressed groups within society. This understanding of political epistemology takes seriously the epistemic life of groups by exploring collective agency within such groups as collective power and as an outlet to effect sociopolitical transformation. It is at this impersonal level where the changes that happen to the Black mind, through cognitive epistemological restructuring, are affected in praxis to initiate political change or transformation. This, for Biko, includes Blacks taking back their country and political destiny from the hands of the white minority rule. Political epistemology entails the belief that ideas do influence political behavior heavily, if not entirely. It involves an understanding of the nature of knowledge and beliefs as they are shaped by political actors and institutions.[33] In the movement for Black liberation in South Africa and even in the diaspora, Steve Biko is a notable political actor who understood and worked tirelessly to ensure that Black people understood the connection between political ideas and their influence in bringing about sociopolitical change.

Looking at Biko's Black Consciousness philosophy through this lens reveals a form of political epistemology that affirms the shared experience of Black people as the basis for political action. Therefore, he states that "Black Consciousness is, in essence, the realization by the black man [Black folks] of the need to rally together with his brothers around the cause of their oppression—the blackness of their skin—and to operate as a group in order to rid themselves of the shackles that bind them to perpetual servitude."[34] In other words, Biko tapped into notions of solidarity and communal associations that were highly appreciated values within African diasporic communities to build a political epistemology that takes on an anticolonial character, in terms of the collective rejection of the group denigration that is predominantly espoused in colonial systems of knowledge and practices. As Biko insists in "Black Consciousness and the Quest for a True Humanity":

We [Blacks] must reject, as we have been doing, the individualistic cold approach to life that is the cornerstone of Anglo-Boer culture. We must seek to restore to the black man [Black folks in general] the great importance we used to give to human relations, the high regard for people and their property and life in general. . . . These are essential features of our black culture to which we must cling. Black culture above all implies freedom on our part to innovate without recourse to white values.[35]

Here, Biko emphasizes the need for the display or demonstration of intellectual independence in terms of value judgment and its influence in shaping the trajectory of life. He also stresses the importance of construing the communalistic elements of "Black culture" as a rallying point for the formation of group coalitions in the struggle against the impositions by the colonial powers. Biko's published essays and speeches strongly suggest that we are, indeed, dealing with a humanist philosophy born in struggle and sustained by faith.[36] As a political epistemology, Biko theorizes Black Consciousness as a scheme that humanizes Blackness through the emphasis on group associations as a kind of epistemic circle, where revolutionary ideas are workshopped, critiqued, and propagated to foster a liberatory consciousness and build chords of solidarity among Black oppressed peoples in South Africa.

Biko's Black Consciousness is a radical humanist politics of solidarity that operationalizes Blackness and concomitant notions of identity and culture around the political objective of liberation rather than viewing them simply as psychological ends in and of themselves. It is not an operation that was primarily focused on improving human thinking for its own sake, but one aimed at directing human thinking toward tackling and resolving social problems. We need to bear in mind that apartheid's dominance was, in many ways, due to its divide-and-conquer approach, which systematically cultivated in-group violence within Black communities (often along ethnic lines), preventing, as an absolute strategic imperative, the forging of any overarching unity and solidarity among the oppressed. It is for this reason that antiapartheid Black Consciousness maintained the priority of a robust and unifying group identity of resistance.[37] In other words, Biko was very clear that the liberation struggle had to begin with providing knowledge to Blacks about who their true oppressors were as well as the true sources of such oppression. It was a strategy that was deployed to prevent the internalization of oppression that leads to ethnic group violence. This is why Biko largely emphasized the importance of group associations and solidarity in the fight against colonial oppression.

This power of group associations became crucial in generating episodes of civil disobedience and group protests that constituted serious problems, both locally and internationally, for the white minority government in South Africa. As a political epistemology, Black Consciousness emphasized the social, political, and epistemic power that is contained in collective associations, especially when such associations are motivated as a force for socially situated knowledge that could be harnessed to achieve social transformation for Blacks. Biko and other advocates of Black Consciousness in South Africa understood the role that those small Black communities in South Africa, and the Black community in diaspora, played in the broader goals of achieving liberation and self-government within a repressive state ruled by a white minority.

Biko's philosophy of Black Consciousness as an epistemology of resistance is not limited to the African context. It also displays some important similarities with the black struggles against the forces of oppression in the African diaspora. This is what Biko conceives as the last step in Black Consciousness:

> The last step in Black Consciousness is to broaden the base of our operation. *One of the basic tenets of Black Consciousness is the totality of involvement.* This means that all Blacks must sit as one big unit, and no fragmentation and distraction from the mainstream of events to be allowed.[38]

It is a call for an epistemological look at Blackness as a force for ideological and political alliances based on shared human experiences regardless of geospatial peculiarities. Biko's allusion to Blackness as "one big unit" also speaks to the Black intellectual lineage from which he draws his idea of Black Consciousness. The concept of Black Consciousness drew intellectual and political inspiration and dialogue from the civil rights and Black Power movements in the United States, as well as from various forms of postcolonial thinking in Africa, including Negritude.[39] Most scholarship on the life and work of Steve Biko locate his thought within the politics of the 1960s, particularly the rise of Black Consciousness in the United States and decolonization movements in Africa.[40] However, Biko's thoughts deserve to be considered from an epistemological standpoint as well. In what follows, I explore the epistemological affinities in the revolutionary ideas of Steve Biko and Huey Newton, a cofounder of the Black Panther Party for Self-Defense, an American revolutionary party founded in the United States in 1966.

Anticolonial Epistemological Affinities in Black Diaspora: The Case of Biko and Newton

A historical look at anti-Black oppression through a diasporic lens reveals that within the framework Black people have devised to imagine freedom from archetypes of race-based injustice, including racialized epistemic oppression, there has always existed some form of epistemic affinity or interaction depicting shared grounds for resistant coalitions. The ideas of Biko and Newton are an archetype of such grounds for epistemological affinities. Biko's development of the philosophy of Black Consciousness to counter the problem of Black inferiority in South Africa connects with Huey P. Newton's analysis of reactionary suicide as a heuristic to directly address the inferiority complex that renders Black subjects powerless in the face of virulent anti-Black racism in the United States. This is especially apparent when examining the manner in which Biko focused his critiques of white racism on the problem of the inferiority complex as a product of the psychological warfare waged against Black subjects by white power structures in apartheid South Africa and the way in which Newton developed similar critiques against the structures of white power in the United States as a mechanism that resulted in reactionary suicide, a condition of deep psychological paralysis or spiritual death.

Worthy of note is the fact that these ideas were not developed out of thin air; they were largely influenced by the struggles against white colonial policies, practices, and legal doctrines that sought to keep Black people within and outside the African diaspora in a perpetual state of existential comatose. Influences beyond South Africa helped Biko and others formulate the Black Consciousness philosophy, as it was not a new phenomenon on the global map. The advocates of Black Consciousness, especially in the South African context, were avid readers, and they attentively followed political developments in Africa and beyond. For example, Biko read extensively the works of the advocates of American Black Power ideology such as Kwame Ture (a.k.a. Stokely Carmichael), Charles Hamilton, Frantz Fanon, Martin Luther King Jr., and Elijah Muhammad as well as works by Brazilian scholar Paulo Freire.[41] The development of the Black Consciousness philosophy also coincided with a period in which many colonized countries in Africa gained their independence (South Africa would follow much later in 1994).[42] The American Black Power ideology provided a theoretical source for the renewal of Black South African thinking (psychological subjectivity). It accelerated the development of the movement, helping to transform existential feelings into ethical-political conceptions of the world.[43]

Both Biko and Newton were relentless in their advocacy of a framework for Black freedom, both individually and corporately, from the oppressive white systems of power in their specific contexts of struggle. However, they understood that such freedom can never be achieved if the problem of the inferiority complex created by the colonial experience, is not first addressed. For instance, in his paper, "White Racism and Black Consciousness," Biko argues that Black consciousness is about ridding the Black "minds of imprisoning notions (such as the idea that Blacks are inferior beings) which are the legacy of the control of their attitude by whites."[44] He was vehemently against the totality of white racist takeover of Black lives, so much so that Blacks living in South Africa in the mid-sixties could not even formulate any coherent, cogent, and meaningful perspective on their livity and political destiny within a society they called "home." For Biko, the strategy to overcome this problem of white supremacy should include:

> A program worked out by black people . . . to defeat the one main element in politics which was working against them: a psychological feeling of inferiority which was deliberately cultivated by the system.[45]

This emphasis on the psychological subjectivity of struggle is evident in the different descriptions of Black Consciousness as a tool for dismantling the ultimate consequence of white oppression—the Black inferiority complex. As Biko succinctly puts it, "From this [conditions on anti-Black oppression] it becomes clear that as long as blacks are suffering from inferiority complex—a result of 300 years of deliberate oppression, denigration, and derision—they will be useless as co-architects of a normal society where man is nothing else but man for his own sake."[46]

Similarly, Newton developed the concept of reactionary suicide as an incapacitating psychological disposition that is triggered in Blacks by their experience of extreme anti-Black racist oppression in the United States. He picks up the same concerns that Biko raised in his philosophy of Black Consciousness regarding the problem of Black inferiority, which he described as reactionary suicide—the reaction of Black subjects who take their own life in response to negative social conditions that overwhelm them and condemn them to existential helplessness, especially those who have been deprived of their right to live as proud and free human beings.[47] In Newton's view:

> Connected to reactionary suicide, although even more painful and degrading, is a spiritual death that has been the experience of millions of Black people in the United States. This death is found everywhere today in the Black community. Its victims have ceased to fight the forms of oppression that drink their blood.[48]

Here, Newton is emphasizing that social rather than personal factors are the principal cause of suicidal behavior among Blacks. This struck a chord with him because he observed that, as a young Black individual, he was living at a time when suicides among his contemporaries had doubled. Also, Newton observed, among many Blacks, varying attitudes of hopelessness, demoralization, and the disposition of apparent acceptance of their oppression, which he termed "reactionary suicide."[49]

Like Newton, Biko always centered the possibility for change within the subjectivity of the oppressed person, not within the hierarchy of the South African hegemonic system (an inversion of power).[50] Biko viewed Black Consciousness as the essence of Black individuals' efforts to elevate their position by positively looking at those value systems that make them distinctively human in society.[51] It is under this new vision of Black individuality that they can arrive at the concept of being human in society. Since Newton imagines reactionary suicide as a function of a false notion of inferiority that is sold to Blacks by the antics of oppressive white power structures, he makes a case for revolutionary suicide as a way for Blacks to rupture these oppressive structures and gain psychological freedom from the imprisonment of the imposed colonial logics through self-assertion and the revamping of the Black mindset. Newton fundamentally believes that man ultimately makes himself, which is why "man attempts to define phenomena in such a way that they reflect the interests of his class or group. He gives titles or values to phenomena according to what he sees as beneficial."[52] In this vein, Blacks need to define themselves not in the language of psychological dependency but of self-authorship, a language that is driven by an authentic expression of their intellectual capabilities and psychological dispositions as functional elements of their existence, rather than as a collection of encapsulated abstract entities that are eternally shut out from the material world. This shows how Newton directly responded to the problem of the inferiority complex as a fundamental tool of white oppression, directed at Black folks in the United States, comparable to the terrible experiences of Blacks in apartheid-era South Africa.

Discussion of the epistemological affinities that Black Consciousness philosophy shares with the concept of Blackness in the American Black

Power movement can be narrowed down to the thoughts of Biko and Newton because their perspectives on the mobilization of Black intellect against white hegemonic empiric impulses overlap in many areas. The ideological affinities between these two Black thinkers of the Black radical tradition further reinforce the idea that Black Consciousness, as a philosophy for Black social mobilization against the white racial empire, is not a static formation but rather a fluid system that can be adapted to different geospatial territories where Blacks experience the negative impacts of colonial hegemony and racialized treatment. In other words, the connections between Biko's and Newton's revolutionary thoughts on resistance codify Black anticolonial epistemologies as a product of a living philosophical thought process capable of standing against anti-Black oppression on many fronts. This is especially evident in light of the fact that the developments in the 1960s and 1970s in the United States and anticolonial movements in the African diaspora were also importantly and intricately connected, especially with the Black Consciousness movement in Azania, South Africa.[53]

The 1960s and 1970s were two momentous decades in the twentieth century, a period when white repression and anti-Black oppression took on a forceful, cataclysmic, and violent global character. In the United States, the agitations of civil rights for Black folks, inspired by the movement for the Black revolution, gained momentum, reaching its legislative and judicial summit. However, this did not lead to material gains as there were record-high numbers of unemployment, social exclusion from assistance programs, relatively low income, and predominant police brutality against members of the Black community. This snowballed into violent responses such as race riots, guerrilla warfare against the United States government, and massive conflagrations that were witnessed in many American cities. It was also in this period that the Black Panther Party, led by Huey P. Newton and Bobby Seale, mobilized Black communities across the United States to fight against police brutality and the repression of members of the Black community. Meanwhile, in the African diaspora, a wave of political independence from years of colonial rule in Africa by European countries like Britain, France, Belgium, Spain, and Portugal was sweeping through the continent, inspired by the vociferous critiques by scholars such as Leopold Senghor, Kwame Nkrumah, Obafemi Awolowo, and Julius Nyerere. They focused their critiques on the models of European modernity, their mechanism of capitalist exploitation, and the arrogance of Western colonial power structures.[54] Yet, it was during this same period that Dutch colonialists, who constituted the white minority government in South Africa, were consolidating their colonial power on occupied African territories through the institution-alization of apartheid, a racist system of government that conceives of Black people as animals rather than as humans. This was a period when Blackness was entangled in the drama of existence occasioned by the perpetual struggle against colonial systems.

Both Newton and Biko understood that the drama of existence for Black folks under any colonial regime, institution, or system is fraught with psychopathologies created by the colonialists to destroy the Black subject's lived experience. They both saw the ultimate goal of coloniza-tion as a scheme to make Black people internalize and accept episte-mologies of oppression as a fact of life. They both worked tirelessly to develop anticolonial epistemologies focused on rupturing such systems of coloniality. According to Hashi Tafira, "Stolen land and inferioriza-tion of Black people provoked the rise of Black Consciousness move-ments of which Biko is known as its most able articulator in South Africa. But genealogically speaking, Black Consciousness is traceable to the Diaspora."[55] This intersection of the philosophy of Black Con-sciousness is propelled by the similarity of the schemes of white oppres-sion against Black people in African and African diasporic contexts. In South Africa, as in the United States, coloniality was not only the arrival of an economic system of labor and capital and extraction of surplus value but also a hodgepodge power structure that included cultural, spiritual, religious, and cosmological aspects. Thus, we see a colonial power matrix that is multidimensional and multitudinous, with race being the primary criterion for structural individuation.[56] This is why attempts to combat the colonial matrix of power also take on a multi-dimensional outlook based on the specificity of regional experiences by Black oppressed subjects.

The imaginations of Biko and Newton also intersect at the view that both psychological disposition and physical struggle are necessary to ensure Black liberation. Newton, like Biko, emphasized the role of cognitive-affective epistemology in achieving mental emancipation or psychological freedom from colonial schemes. For instance, when speaking to the Black Panther movement in 1968, he asserted, "We have a mind of our own. We've regained our mind that was taken from us and we will decide the political as well as the practical stand that we'll take against white domination."[57] Newton further noted that the historical relationship between Blacks and whites in America can be compared to the slave-master relationship. What is unique about Newton's view of this historical relationship is that, in such social imagination, the slave is reduced to a subdued material entity—*the body*, while the master regards himself as *the mind*—the intellectual, powerful, and higher force that ultimately controls the slave. As such, "the slave would carry out the orders that the mind demanded him to carry out. By doing this, the master took the manhood from the slave because he stripped him of a mind. He stripped Black people of their mind."[58] This implies that Black subjects were stripped of agency and rendered politically impotent. Thus, Newton, like Biko, believes that Black liberation should begin with liberating the minds of Black people from the shackles of white domination and oppression. The idea that Black people have a mind of their own, as expressed by Newton, is an affirmation of an anticolonial epistemology of the cognitive-affective variant grounded in the notion of an authentic expression of embodied Black subjectivity that assumes the positionality of a self-authorial epistemic and political agent in the world. Therefore, to change the environment (the material conditions of Blacks) is to change the mind at a phenomenal level.[59]

Both Biko and Newton were revolutionaries in the true sense of the word. They held similar worldviews about the fact that the movement for Black liberation must begin with the construction of an anticolonial epistemology—political and cognitive-affective epistemological systems that are fortified with the power of Black agency and motivated by the imaginations of freedom. In this case, a true revolutionary is conceived as someone who recognizes the importance of Blacks exercising agency in the quest for liberation or freedom. This centrality of the place of Black agency in the process of liberation is highlighted by the distinction that Newton draws between reactionary and revolutionary suicide. For Newton, reactionary suicide is the reaction of a person who takes his own life in response to social conditions that overwhelm him and condemn him to helplessness.[60] This form of reaction lacks the exercise of agency because a person whose self is dead, or who allows the self to die vainly, is a victim of what Newton calls reactionary suicide and has engaged in murdering the self or self-murdering. He diagnosed that, connected to this notion of reactionary suicide, although even more painful and degrading, is a spiritual death that has been the experience of millions of Black people in the United States. As Newton sees it, this death is found everywhere today in the Black community. Its victims have ceased to fight the forms of oppression that hold them bound.[61]

This implies that no condition of oppression will give way to freedom except some form of assault that is wielded against the hegemonic epistemologies upon which such oppressive systems are constructed.

This is why Newton advocates revolutionary suicide over and above reactionary suicide. In his own words:

> I do not think that life will change for the better without an assault on the Establishment, which goes on exploiting the wretched of the earth. This belief is at the heart of the concept of revolutionary suicide. Thus, it is better to oppose the forces that would drive me to self-murder than to endure them. Although I risk the likelihood of death, there is at least the possibility, if not the probability, of changing intolerable conditions. This possibility is important because much in human existence is based upon hope without any real understanding of the odds.[62]

Newton speaks of revolutionary/liberatory consciousness as a psychological disposition that is crucial for raising (Black) consciousness.[63] It is constructed on a framework of resistance that advocates the exercise of Black agency, as well as a radical (anticolonial) epistemology, in a manner that directly confronts systems of oppression; even if ultimately, this results in death. For Newton, such death has a meaning that reactionary suicide can never have. It is the price of self-respect.[64] Steve Biko expressed similar revolutionary thoughts about Black Consciousness in an interview given three months before his final imprisonment. It was published in *New Republic* magazine in January 1978. In this piece, Biko states that:

> You are either alive and proud or you are dead, and when you are dead, you can't care anyway. And your method of death can itself be a politicizing thing. So you die in the riots. For a hell of a lot of them, there's nothing to lose—almost literally, given the kind of situations that they come from. So if you can overcome the personal fear for death, which is a highly irrational thing, you know, then you're on the way to liberation.[65]

This revolutionary thinking exhibited by Biko and Newton is conceived as a vehicle that will transform the attitudes and thinking of Black people for generations to come. It is revolutionary because it rejects the old approaches to liberation, including slogans, protests, and meaningless rhetoric previously used in the struggle against white domination and oppression.

There is also a manifest connection between Biko and Newton on the relevance of collective Black agency in the quest for Black liberation.

Biko calls this "group pride," and Newton refers to a similar phenomenon as "revolutionary intercommunalism." In "Black Consciousness and the Quest for True Humanity," Biko asserts that "the philosophy of Black consciousness, therefore expresses group pride and the determination by blacks to rise and attain the envisaged self. Freedom is the ability to define one's self, possibilities, and limitations held back, not by the power of people over you."[66] This draws on the philosophy of peoplehood, embracing the shared experiences of Black people, including their shared commitments, as a source for envisioning and actualizing freedom. To break the chains of oppression asphyxiating Black existence, Biko advocated solidarity among Black people. Black solidarity is a solid commitment to the resistance to white domination and oppression.[67] The lived experience of Blacks demands that they engage in a Black solidarity strategy, with the aim of liberating themselves.[68] In a similar fashion, Newton affirms in "War Against the Panthers" that "the Black Panther Party (BPP) was formed in the United States in 1966 as an organization of Black and poor persons embracing a common ideology, identified by its proponents as 'revolutionary intercommunalism.'"[69] He clarifies further:

> A central tenet of revolutionary intercommunalism, for example, is that "contradiction is the ruling principle of the universe," that everything is in a constant state of transformation. Recognition of these principles gave Party leaders an ability to grow through a self-criticism that many other radical political organizations seemed to lack.[70]

These concepts of Black solidarity and revolutionary intercommunalism are not merely theoretical; they had a significant, positive impact on the materiality of Black existence in African and African diasporic struggles against the forces of colonial domination. It is this idea of group pride or solidarity that led to the numerous survival programs initiated by the Black Consciousness Movement (BCM) in South Africa and the Black Panther Party (BPP) under the respective leadership of Biko and Newton. As Newton notes, "a second distinguished characteristic of the Party has been its specific strategy to achieve revolutionary intercommunalism: the building of 'survival' or community service programs. The purpose of these programs is to enable people to meet their daily needs by developing positive institutions within their communities and to organize the communities politically around these programs."[71]

David Hilliard describes the objective of the Black Panther community programs succinctly by avowing that, to achieve its goals of organizing and serving Black and oppressed communities, the Black Panther Party developed a wide variety of survival programs (the Ten-Point Program) after the party's founding in October 1966. The Ten-Point Program, covered such diverse areas as health care and food services, a model school, decent housing, and freedom from police brutality. These were designed to meet the needs of the community until such a time when Black people could feel safe in their own communities and could afford the things they needed and desired.[72] Similarly, through the SASO and BCM movements, Biko was able to provide welfare community programs to poor Black people in South Africa such as free health care, education, and a food program through what he named the Black Community Programs. The link between the Black Consciousness Movement's Black Community Programs and the Black Panther Party's Ten-Point Program is striking. It represents the intersectionality of Black resistant epistemologies toward achieving freedom from colonial domination and racial oppression within African and African diasporic contexts. Thus, Hashi Tafira is right to point out that the Black Consciousness Movement (BCM) in particular borrowed from anticolonial struggles in Africa and the diaspora. The meaning of Black Consciousness for BCM draws from the militancy of Huey P. Newton, Bobby Seale, Eldridge Cleaver, Stokely Carmichael (Kwame Ture), and Paulo Freire.[73]

One point that deserves to be further fleshed out is how these concepts of Black solidarity and group pride connect to the Black Power movement—the idea of collective epistemology as the basis for Black resistance. This idea of collective epistemology was evident in Stokely Carmichael's liberatory project, which advocates a movement from Black Power to Pan-Africanism. In *Stokely Speaks: Black Power Back to Pan-Africanism*, Stokely Carmichael, made this clear by asserting that "we [Blacks] must organize the Black community power to end these abuses, and to give the Negro community a chance to have its needs expressed."[74] Carmichael also taught lessons in Black Consciousness at the "Free Huey" rally in Oakland, California, in February 1968, where he began to advocate the concept that "all persons of African descent, regardless of where they were born or lived, are Africans, and that we [Black revolutionaries] must develop the concept of 'undying love' for our [Black] people, and the necessity of joining the nine hundred million Africans scattered around the globe."[75] Carmichael also considers the concept of Black Power as that which entails seeing the Black struggle for freedom as a global phenomenon. As he puts it, "Black power, to us, means that black people see themselves as a part of a new force, sometimes called the Third World; that we see our struggle as closely related to liberation struggles around the world."[76]

This reveals the transnational relevance of the anticolonial epistemology of Black Consciousness to Black struggles against oppression, especially in the African and African diasporic contexts. What is of utmost significance is how the framework of these anticolonial epistemologies was deployed to challenge the hegemonic constructions of the Black existence in the Black diasporic contexts. Thus, Black Consciousness is all about repositioning the epistemological worldviews of Black people in a positive direction—toward achieving both personal and collective liberation. This is why Biko's thoughts about the positivity of the notion of Black Consciousness are apposite. According to Biko, the call for Black Consciousness is the most positive call to come from any group in the Black world in a long time. It is more than just a reactionary rejection of whites or white schemes by Blacks. Its quintessence rests on the realization by Black people that to do well in the game of power politics, they must use the concept of group power to build a strong foundation for survival. As a historically, politically, socially, and economically disinherited and dispossessed group, they have the strongest foundation from which to operate. Thus, the philosophy of Black Consciousness expresses group pride and the determination by Blacks to rise and attain the envisaged self.[77] The envisaged self that Biko refers to here is the liberated Black self—a *being* with infinite possibilities.

In sum, this chapter advocates a reading of Biko's Black Consciousness philosophy as a form of anticolonial epistemology that demonstrates its influence as a framework for achieving liberation from mental and political oppression. Since racism and colonial domination target the mind and the sociopolitical circumstances of Black people, Black Consciousness—as conceived by Biko—seeks to combat these as a two-pronged struggle focusing on mental emancipation and political freedom. Black Consciousness conscientizes Black people regarding the conditions in which they live so that they can grapple with their problems; equipped with a mental and physical awareness of their situation to find solutions, they can provide for themselves and not look toward externally generated solutions.[78] When considered from African and African diasporic frameworks, Black Consciousness reveals the interrelation of Black anticolonial epistemologies for combating epistemic oppression, colonial impulses, and hegemonic political and epistemic systems that facilitate the alienation of Black subjects from themselves. Through the two epistemological dimensions emphasized in this work, these revolutionary exemplars brought about a paradigm shift in the philosophical, cultural, and revolutionary thinking of Black people, not just about being in the world but about a *being* thriving in the world, and they also gave voice to what it means to find meaning as a Black subject in an anti-Black world.

9

I Am We

Huey P. Newton's Revolutionary
Intercommunalism as
Political Epistemology

In the gamut of scholarship that has explored the relevance of the Black Panther Party (BPP) to the Black civil rights movements in the United States from the early 1960s to the late 1980s, Huey P. (Pierce) Newton is characterized as many things, such as a radical revolutionary, a brilliant legal mind, a debater, and a theoretician, among many others. However, the genius of Newton, as exemplified by his numerous theoretical formulations that served as a guide for the practice of radical resistance by the Party, as well as his intellectual and practical engagement with the Black community during his lifetime and his uncompromising stance while dealing with the repressive organ and force of the "imperial state," points to the fact that he is more than any of these characterizations alone. In other words, to fit Newton into any of these single categories is to undermine the prodigy of one of the greatest Black thinkers that ever lived. Furthermore, to plug him into such a narrow frame of reference would largely undermine the fluidity and flexibility with which Newton thought about his anti-imperialist and anticolonial ideas in real time.

As the chief ideologue, theoretician, and leader of the Party, he developed critical and analytical systems, from Marxist dialectical materialist systems to grassroots mobilization schemes, and structural critiques to determine the various ways by which the economic and political aspirations of the United States (the "imperial state"), aimed at achieving global expansion to fulfill its consumptive capitalist interests, necessarily generated conditions of Black repression at home and the exploitation of nonwhite populations abroad. The genius of Newton is quite remarkable in this regard because he made his critical ideas adaptive and pertinent to the changing patterns of the forces of repression created by the repressive imperial state. His focus was to liberate oppressed communities across the world, at intervals in the unfolding of history. This capacity for the adaptation of political ideas to changing social realities may have been responsible for the Party's longevity, particularly his progressive commitment to adapt Black Panther ideology to changing times, especially as these changes pertained to world affairs.[1] One can see evidence of this genius in his articulation of how he arrived at his idea of revolutionary intercommunalism. He recounts, "I woke up one morning with this concept of intercommunalism, and it was like a vision: it didn't seem as coldly calculated when you work out a mathematical problem, which is how I usually handle things intellectually. I just woke up one morning and I had solved the contradiction in my sleep. And I was excited to get it out."[2]

In this chapter, I consider Huey P. Newton as a Black political epistemologist whose evolving political ideas about countering oppressive systems of power revolve around the methodical organization of the Black community into a collective or unified force striving against the repressive forces of the imperial state. The central concern of a political epistemologist is to investigate knowledge as a phenomenon and consider how this can be applied to politically relevant aspects of human lives. So, this takes into consideration the historical realities that shape human lives while giving credence to certain subjective principles or epistemic-political formulations that will be preferred when dealing with the multifarious problems that arise from such situations. In this sense, one can consider the valuation of subjectivity as a form of expression of humanism that is demonstrated through the deployment of cognitive capacities of the mind and the avowal of political ideas to challenge structural problems in the world.

Using the history and politics of the BPP and its exploration of anticolonial epistemologies as an analytical framework, in a specific historical context, this chapter explores the role of ideas in influencing human behavior and achieving some degree of social transformation. In particular, it considers the process of putting into practice the BPP's basic revolutionary principles that are acquired through the rigorous analysis of how historical and present social conditions impact Black lives. These principles are not only related to economic and social evils, but they are also caught up in the economic and social evils of this system that oppresses Black people.[3] It also entails the ideological formations that guide Black social mobilization, the intellectual grounding of constructive human affiliations, and the conquest of domineering systems of thought or social arrangement that prevent Black folks from attaining a meaningful existence.

Newton's notion of political epistemology emanates from an acute historical exegesis of the Black condition in the diaspora, including how oppressed peoples around the world are exploited by structures of power in society. It generally constructs knowledge schemes in a manner that unearths the Black subject both as a gifted social and political epistemic agent, and as a human, capable of proffering solutions to the problems that confront Black people in the world. This is a vision of Black epistemology that centers Blackness in its discussion of how epistemological categories can be deployed to bring about individual and social transformation. The example of Newton's revolutionary intercommunalism highlights the fact that Black thinkers have created unique ideas and political epistemological categories and thought systems merely by focusing on ways to improve the Black condition.

Although Newton was influenced by various intellectual, political, and ideological streams such as existentialism, psychoanalysis, communism, guerilla warfare, Marxism, the revolutionary thoughts of Frantz Fanon and Malcolm X, and Pan-Africanism, he was clear about the fact that no single ideological position could resolve the complexities and the problems that confront the Black community (or the Black colony within the American empire). Although the violent/militant ideas of Malcolm X and Fanon largely influenced Newton and other leaders of the BPP, they came to consider global white supremacy and the forces of imperialism as the most basic forms of genocidal/violent warfare against oppressed communities across the world. It is in a bid to overcome these negative attributions of political knowledge embedded in America's ideal of democracy that Newton developed a new conception of political epistemology from the Black perspective, which he referred to as "revolutionary intercommunalism."

Revolutionary Intercommunalism: The Core of Newton's Political Epistemology

Revolutionary intercommunalism is one of the most important aspects of Newton's political epistemology. Newton conceived revolutionary intercommunalism as a philosophical stream of thought that maintains a progressive orientation about how Black subjects both in the United States and across the world should be viewed based on shared group affiliations as a common epistemological denominator of social power. He utilized radical ideas to challenge the structures of power that propel white dominance in the global sphere. For instance, in his essay, "Dialectics of Nature," Newton describes revolutionary intercommunalism as "founded on the basic concept of the unity of nature underlying and transcending all arbitrary national and geographic divisions."[4] In other words, revolutionary intercommunalism upholds an epistemological vision of the world order as deconstructed, destructuralized, and imagined from the place of subjugation. It is an imagination that unsettles the colonial hegemonic ways in which imperialist powers have constructed nonwhite peoples of the world as captives within "colonies." Within the imperialist structures and psychology of colonial domination, such peoples are typically not regarded as capable of exhibiting the capacity for independent thought, which makes it impossible to imagine ways by which such oppressed groups could ever find common ground to form anti-imperial and anticolonial alliances.

In *Revolutionary Intercommunalism and the Right of Nations to Self-Determination*, Newton argues that:

> If colonies cannot decolonize and return to their original existence as nations, then nations no longer exist. Nor, we believe, will they ever exist again. And since there must be nations for revolutionary nationalism or internationalism to make sense, we decided that we would have to call ourselves something new. We say that the world today is a dispersed collection of communities. A community is different from a nation. A community is a small unit with a comprehensive collection of institutions that exist to serve a small group of people. And we say further that the struggle in the world today is between the small circle that administers and profits from the empire of the United States and the peoples of the world who want to determine their destinies.[5]

Here, Newton's emphasis is on the necessity of creating a global alliance between oppressed communities across the world (based on a destructuralized conception of the nature of reality) through his idea of revolutionary intercommunalism. It is an affront to an empire such as the United States that seeks to consolidate its power through divide-and-conquer tactics; it is also a testament to Black intellectual strengths that could be harnessed to fight against colonial hegemony when Black political epistemologies are fashioned through a united front. This emphasis on a global alliance of thinking of oppressed groups as a "dispersed collection of communities" is based on the idea that there are differences in degree between what is happening to the Blacks in the United States and what is happening to all other oppressed peoples in the world. Their needs are the same and their energies are the same. Furthermore, the contradictions they suffer will only be resolved when the people can establish a revolutionary intercommunalism where they share all the wealth that they produce and live in one world.[6]

In "War Against the Panthers," Newton speaks of these contradictions as the very reason why the struggle against imperialism and colonial-capitalist exploitation began in the first place. He writes thus:

> The ultimate form of struggle [was] born of this contrived contradiction, a contradiction which is as old as the life of the American republic itself. The contradiction which provides much of the source material for [Black resistance] would doubtless have never existed nor reached such dastardly and volatile proportions if it were not for the societal wide ingestion of a class—and racially-biased social philosophy, which stemmed from the original premise of American social organization, a deeply ingrained belief that society [is] by nature divided into superior and inferior classes and races of people. This vision of the "natural order" of society, rationalized by those who have a vested interest in its maintenance, has kept Americans of different classes and races either directly engaged in social warfare, or forever poised in a position of battle.[7]

At this point in the development of his political epistemology, Newton had begun to depart from his earliest framing of the revolutionary politics of the BPP in Black nationalist terms. His nationalist stance was based on the development of a political epistemological system focused on improving the condition of Black folks living within the American colony (internal colonialism). As he moved toward the revolutionary intercommunalist phase, Newton became aware of the oddity of imagining a nationalist framework of revolution without ownership of a clearly defined physical or geographical space—a nation. At this point, he realized the global nature of capitalist exploitation/greed and the systems of oppression that sustain the racial, economic, political, and social dominance upheld by Anglo-American empires, in particular how these colonial/hegemonic empires oppress communities of color across the globe.

Newton utilized his idea of revolutionary intercommunalism to expose the illogic and moral bankruptcy of colonial and imperialist exploitation embarked upon by European states and the United States in the global sphere. One of the dominant traits of political mobilization in the twentieth century among industrialized European nations and the United States was the adoption of the colonial model of nation-state building. It was constructed on the logic of insulated territorial systems of demarcating national interests, which encapsulated the desires to create a homogenous "national culture" based on particular markers of codification and belongingness such as language, racial, and ethnic affiliations, among other salient features and categories considered vital for determining those who are either insiders or outsiders.[8] One salient category that was utilized to make such demarcations possible is the category of the *human*. Racial/ethnic affiliations became crucial in determining who qualifies to be named *human* in relation to whether one belonged to the dominant group or the subdominant group. In this instance, the appellation "national interests" became what categorized the dominant group projects as salient. So, these imperial states continue to seek exploitative/capitalist expansion within and beyond their border's framework in an unrestricted fashion, while at the same time espousing nationalist ideologies in highly narrow terms to exclude members adjudged to be part of subdominant communities (outgroups).

These categorical distinctions between dominant and subdominant groups, Newton argues, were how a state/empire like the United States was able to develop highly sophisticated machinery of exploitation and a capitalist wealth system that condemns Black folks to the social condition of the underclass. In this regard, Blacks in America cannot participate in the so-called "national interest" of the imperial state. Rather, Blacks, especially Black revolutionaries, are considered as posing threats to the "national security" of the state for demanding that Black lives matter in the face of trenchant antiblack oppression. For Newton, oppressed communities need to form a global alliance—a global community of reformed/radical subjects—to have the clout to be able to free themselves from both the psychological and physical shackles of imperial exploitation. As he affirmed, "We saw that it was not only beneficial for us to be revolutionary nationalists but to express our solidarity with those friends who suffered many of the same kind of pressures we suffered."[9] This strategy was aimed at consolidating power that comes from group association, which necessitated new definitions to capture such realities, as depicted in Newton's expression: "We changed our self-definitions. We said that we are not only revolutionary nationalists—that is nationalists who want revolutionary changes in everything, including the economic system the oppressor inflicts upon us—but we are also individuals deeply concerned with the other people of the world and their desires for revolution. To show this solidarity, we decided to call ourselves internationalists."[10] Newton's emphasis on forging deep connections with other oppressed people of the world was based on his conviction that due to the imperial state's historical accumulation of power, imperial expansionism, and political influence in the global polity, regional mobilizations alone would not suffice to engage with it. This represents an important pillar of Newton's notion of revolutionary intercommunalism.

He proceeded from this position to argue that revolutionary intercommunalism should be conceived as a world culture to be actualized through the revolutionary politics of oppressed peoples across the world. It is a revolutionary politics that is driven by the radical epistemological goal of transposing Black subjects into the realm of the human within; that is, it challenges the hegemonic concept of the human as deficient because Black subjects are not recognized as such. In this light, Newton contends that revolutionary intercommunalism must begin with the realization that the material conditions exist that would allow the people of the world to develop a culture that is essentially human—negating all forms of ascriptions that undermine this reality while nurturing those things that would allow the people to resolve contradictions in a way that would not cause their mutual slaughter. The development of such a culture would be revolutionary intercommunalism.[11] Elaine Brown, one of the women in the leadership of the BPP, describes Newton's philosophy of intercommunalism as one of the earliest recorded premonitions of present-day "globalism," which became the guiding intellectual current of the Party, infusing the Panthers with a global perspective that flew in the face of nationalism.[12]

It is pertinent to note that Newton's development of revolutionary intercommunalism as a political epistemology went through different stages of metamorphosis. In this sense, one might consider Newton as a thinker who was deeply interested in the epistemology of change as well as changing epistemologies to suit social realities. For him, political epistemology should be considered as a phenomenon that is in a perpetual state of flux—always changing. As he asserts:

The struggle of mutually exclusive opposing tendencies within everything that exists explains the observable fact that all things have motion and are in a constant state of transformation. Things transform themselves because while one tendency or force is more dominating than another, change is nonetheless a constant, and at some point, the balance will alter and there will be a new qualitative development. New properties will come into existence, qualities that did not altogether exist before.[13]

This concretizes Newton's thinking that sociopolitical ideas should be made consistent with the changing nature of reality. He may have arrived at this diagnosis from his in-depth study of the dialectical material analysis of history in the works of Marx and Lenin, especially the emphasis on the conflict of social forces in the movement of history. However, he differs from Marx on the perspective of analysis of dialectical materialism concerning the "present" struggles of the people. He thought that Marx's dialectical historical materialism specifically utilized the past conditions of working-class Europeans and used that to develop a theory of capitalist and class-based exploitation.

Newton did not think that this should be the proper approach to combating the forces of capitalist exploitation. For him, the "present" should be the groundwork for understanding the unforeseen ways by which the imperial state reinvents itself and expands its consumptive appetite to exploit globally oppressed communities. This necessitated a broader vision of resistance than mere class-to-class analysis of the nature of the existential struggle faced by oppressed people in the world. Thus, in his role as the BPP's foremost philosopher, he took the Party through ideological metamorphoses, experimenting and wrestling with many theories aimed at finding solutions to problems such as poverty, racism, classism, and sexism. Openness to change was a characteristic that enabled Newton to continually redefine and reevaluate conditions and situations.[14] This is evident in how he continued to revamp the Party's ideological and epistemological positions at different periods in the life of the Party.[15] Through their community survival programs, the Panthers laid the foundation for self-actualization (providing Black subjects with the motivation to recognize their full capabilities). Internally, the Panthers also reached higher levels of awareness as their ideology advanced across four stages: Black nationalism (1966–1968), revolutionary socialism (1969–1970), internationalism (1970–1971), and finally, intercommunalism (1971 to 1982, when the Party ceased operations).[16]

The development of the Panthers' revolutionary ideology is a testament to their ability to adapt and grow with the changing political landscape within the United States and throughout the world. As Newton notes in *Revolutionary Suicide*, "Revolution is not an action; it is a process. Times change and policies of the past are not necessarily effective in the present. Our military strategies were not frozen. As conditions changed, so did our tactics."[17] What Newton is communicating here is the philosophy of change at the heart of his political epistemology: always changing the sociopolitical epistemes developed to guide the Party and the movement in ways that would allow them to stay relevant to the needs of the Black community in the United States while also taking into consideration the interests of oppressed peoples in the global community.

Having such a disposition toward changing philosophies made it possible for Newton to rework his ideas in real time to determine the areas of strength and areas of weakness that required further work. He was able to determine the effectiveness of any political epistemology based on the extent to which it contributes to changing the nature of social reality. For instance, in describing the move from Black nationalism to revolutionary nationalism, Newton talked about how rigorous analysis was a crucial part of this process, especially in determining how oppressed communities in the world can transform themselves into a dominant force that has the clout to confront the dehumanizing practices of the imperial state. For this reason, the Black Panther Party developed their political epistemologies from a plain nationalist or separatist nationalist orientation into a revolutionary nationalist orientation. They held that social mobilization against the forces of imperialism and colonialism must be a product of an alliance with all of the other people in the world struggling for decolonization and nationhood who called themselves a "dispersed colony" because they did not have the geographical concentration that the other so-called colonies had.[18]

Collective Agency and the Foundation of Newton's Revolutionary Intercommunalism

In *Revolutionary Suicide*, Newton articulates the collective epistemological framework that is at the heart of his anticolonial/anti-imperialist epistemological system known as revolutionary intercommunalism. He

draws this from the African philosophy of collectivism, which empha-
sizes the power of social association toward achieving existential goals.
As he notes, "There is an old African saying, 'I am we.' If you met an
African in ancient times and asked him who he was, he would reply,
'I am we.' This is revolutionary suicide: I, we, all of us are the one and
the multitude."[19] What is of philosophical interest to Newton from this
African aphorism is the idea of the strength in Black collectivism. He
then projects this as the paramount ideal that undergirds revolutionary intercommunalism as a collective epistemology. Here, we see an
affirmation of group solidarity and group pride as important matrices
for building coalitions that could generate enough political strength to
combat the imperial and colonial exploitation by the imperial state. In
other words, when oppressed communities across the world organize
to form social coalitions, as Newton imagined, they come to form a
united front for social change. That unity in itself becomes a fundamental source of power—the power of the multitude—directed toward
breaking the material and ideological chains that hold them bound.
From this standpoint, the BPP engaged not just with the materiality
of racialized Black oppression in the United States but also with the
plight of oppressed communities across the world suffering under the
weight of global white supremacy. The Party insisted that an understanding of the geographies of white supremacy requires an understanding of how white supremacy organizes itself across space and through
time. It also requires an understanding of racialization and the process
through which abstract notions of difference and subalterity are made
material in various oppressed communities across the world.[20]

When the BPP was formed in 1966, it held a vision of racialized and
socialized progress that was grounded in the idea of community. The
original vision of the Party was to develop a lifeline to the people within
the community by serving their needs and defending them against their
oppressors, from the armed police force to the capitalists. They knew
that this strategy would raise the consciousness of the people and also
garner their support.[21] As Newton himself articulates, "The primary
concern of the Black Panther Party is to lift the level of consciousness
of the people through theory and practice to the point where they will
see exactly what is controlling them and what is oppressing them, and
therefore see exactly what has to be done."[22] This assertion shows Newton's understanding that for any revolutionary system to be successful,
it must begin by changing the thinking of the oppressed people through
the raising of their consciousness to enable them to ascertain the conditions and sources of their oppression.

This is why Newton maintained that the BPP served as the vanguard in helping people bring about intercommunalism. As he saw it, part of the role of the Party was to expose imperialist antagonisms, contradictions, and motives and to raise the people's consciousness in a way that would compel them to undertake revolutionary social action.[23] For Newton, all oppressed people within the bounds of the American empire are in some sense colonized. This is what A. J. Williams-Myers describes in *Destructive Impulses* as the consequence of "the African American intrusion (socioeconomic and political) into the community of whiteness."[24] This is similar to Kenneth B. Clark's observation in *Dark Ghetto: Dilemmas of Social Power* that the colonization, oppression, and economic control of Blacks constituted a source of power for many white people, including enabling those who would otherwise occupy a low status to see themselves as middle class.[25] However, Newton sees this position of "underclass" as a source of power. He held that because Black people in America compose a uniquely colonized community, comparable to colonized communities in other parts of the world while simultaneously located within the very center of the empire, the community is in a uniquely privileged position to destroy that empire. Specifically, Newton considered Black people in the U.S. to be in the ideal position to act as the vanguard for a global revolution against what he regarded as reactionary intercommunalism.[26]

In the early 1970s, a period when many groups were agitating for expanded political rights and the invasion of oppressed communities in Indochina by the United States, including its exploitative foray into emerging independent nations in Africa, the Panthers began to reimagine and reevaluate their ideological positions in light of the materiality of the activities of empire within oppressed communities. In addition, the shaping of Newton's ideas of revolutionary intercommunalism to embrace a collectivist epistemology was influenced by some of his experiences in his self-imposed exile to Cuba in the mid-seventies. As he articulates:

> [In Cuba] they are interested in their fields, and international politics. You get this singleness of purpose, from the university to the cane fields. You get the feeling you are a member of a collective, the whole country's collective, and you are working to make life better.[27]

The Panthers saw Cuba as a shining example of how revolutionary guerilla action could be led in a bid to achieve a more equitable society. They hoped that the Cuban government would allow them to establish an international base in Cuba and help train them to bring about a revolution in the United States.[28] These historical realities led the Panthers and other revolutionary nationalists to focus on resolving the tension regarding how to effectively locate Black nationalism in an international context and reconcile it with the larger goals of "Third World" anticolonialism and worldwide socialist revolution. Part of the BPP leader's response to this dilemma was to create what Eldridge Cleaver dubbed "embryonic sovereignty," using the Party's anticolonial vernacular, one that symbolically located Black people as part of a global anticolonial majority while acknowledging their unique position within the United States.[29] The concept of "embryonic sovereignty" was used to expose the axes of internal and external dynamics of colonialism, neocolonialism, and imperialism, such that an internal situation was generated to uphold antagonistic principles and practical politics to implode the oppressive structures of empire from within.

What Newton found interesting in the concept of collective epistemology at both the theoretical and practical levels includes the idea that social truths about the Black condition in the United States and about other subordinated groups across the world are shared as a common attitude, generated because of the colonial situation. It emphasizes the crafting of ideologies of an anticolonial coalition such that this becomes a cognitive disposition or attitude that is transferred from the individual agents within the oppressive social context to a broad spectrum of individuals that make up the social group. It is an emphasis on the social and political roles of knowledge acquisition, dissemination, and deployment in such a manner that it constitutes the very basis for negotiating terms of freedom or liberation from oppressive systems of the imperial state. In this context, group knowledge is understood as a source of socially located power—an aggregation of extrinsically attributable qualities of the mind shared as a uniting force for social mobilization and social understanding.[30] So, it is a reflection of the summative or binding philosophies that drives the cognitive states of groups and how this constitutes the basis of joint commitment or collective aspirations toward achieving social transformation.

In other words, collective epistemology, as embedded in Newton's idea of revolutionary intercommunalism, focuses on how group-based epistemological categories can be developed as alternatives to an oppressive sociopolitical order to transcend the experience of domination and subjugation within that order. This was a central concern within Newton's political epistemology. This collectivism also includes the sharing of the positive and negative consequences that are derived from the struggle against imperialist exploitation. In *Blood in My Eye*, George Jackson emphasizes similar sentiments about collective episte-mology when he avows that for one to develop revolutionary conscious-ness, one must learn how revolutionary consciousness can be raised to the highest point by stimuli from the vanguard elements. It must involve the recognition and appreciation of the decades of hard, sometimes dan-gerous work done in the name of revolution by the older socialist parties and oppressed groups within subjugated "colonies."[31] This is what he referred to as the "unitarian vision of the progressive movement." He believes that this "unitary vision" must encompass the "'search' for those elements in our present situation which can become the basis for joint action."[32]

From the analysis of the material conditions of Blacks in the United States and those of oppressed communities within the global polity, Newton divined that because the imperial state (empire) continues to transform itself into a power controlling the lands and political des-tinies of all peoples, especially those of oppressed communities, there is a need for Black revolutionaries to form political, epistemological, and revolutionary alliances with other militant revolutionaries across geospatial landscapes. Worthy of note here is the BPP's alliance with the Pan-Africanist movements in Africa.[33] In this instance, what was of particular interest to Newton was the political-military model of counterrevolutionary warfare designed and led by Kwame Nkrumah. In his *Handbook of Revolutionary Warfare*, Nkrumah situates the struggles of Black people against the forces of colonial and imperialist oppression in the context of the global Black struggle against oppres-sion. For instance, Nkrumah conceives of the Black Power movement, the militant revolutionary politics of the BPP in the United States, and the struggles of peoples of African descent in the Caribbean, South America, and elsewhere, as constituting an integral part of the African political-military revolutionary struggle.[34] As Nkrumah writes:

> The true dimension of our [the Pan-Africanist] struggle . . . is to pave the way for national reconstruction and to promote prosper-ity for the broad masses through an All-African struggle against colonialism and all the new manifestations of imperialism.[35]

Pan-Africanism, as conceived by Nkrumah, was based on the age-old aspiration for the unity of all peoples of African origin exploited as workers and as a race, which explains why any kind of victory attained in the process of this struggle must be viewed as a victory of all the revolutionary, oppressed, and exploited masses of the world who are challenging the capitalist, imperialist and neo-colonialist power structure.[36] Nkrumah was very clear that the ultimate revolution that would destroy Western imperialism has to be violent/militaristic in its approach, hence the need for a militarized Pan-African organization. In his view:

> In comparison, the Independent States of Africa are at present militarily weak. Unlike the imperialists and neo-colonialists, they have no mutual defense system and no unified command to plan and direct joint action. But this will be remedied with the formation of the All-African People's Revolutionary Army and the setting up of organizations to extend and plan effective revolutionary warfare on a continental scale. We possess the vital ingredient necessary to win—the full enthusiastic support of the broad masses of the African people [including Africans in diaspora] who are determined once and for all to end all forms of foreign exploitation, to manage their affairs, and to determine their future. Against such overwhelming strength organized on a Pan-African basis, no amount of enemy forces can hope to succeed.[37]

There is a form of epistemological independence that is generated in this image of revolutionary warfare. It is one which isolates the politically meaningful social reality from those that are extraverted. In other words, as a way of making peoples within the exploited colonies buy into the revolutionary philosophies of warfare, there must be an epistemological "acceptance" of the principles of engagement that would constitute the basis of group-based solidarity.

Newton thought highly of the revolutionary Pan-Africanist ideas of Nkrumah. In his essay "On Pan-Africanism or Communism," written in 1972, he had this to say about Nkrumah's Pan-Africanist ideas: "The brilliant Dr. Kwame Nkrumah, having identified and warned his people of the deviant dangers in neocolonialism, called for a united Africa. The unity that Dr. Nkrumah called for carried the demand of solidarity based upon certain principles: specifically, pooling resources from all separate countries of Africa into an all-African treasury."[38] This assertion by Newton was made at a time when he discovered that the global activities of the imperial state, through external and internal colonization efforts, have necessitated the formation of a global alliance to expose the real intentions of the agents of these oppressive Systems. He called for the elimination of all political, social, economic, and military bases that serve as a springboard for perpetuating the parasitic elements of the ideologies and praxis of empire within subjugated communities.

The Party looked to liberation struggles and revolutions around the world as inspiration and guidance for the Revolution that would one day emerge in the heart of the United States. All around the world, people were fighting for their freedom from foreign, usually colonial, domination. Africa, Asia, and Latin America were ablaze with the fiery light of rebellion.[39] This reality was exploited by Newton and the Panthers to make a call to the oppressed people of the world as a disparate collection of communities under siege. It entails the realization and affirmation of the fact that oppressed communities exist and nations are usurped, especially imperial nation-states. In this vein, communities, by way of definition, are a comprehensive collection of institutions that are supposed to serve the people. This is how the oppressed people of the world liberate their communities-through the redistribution of wealth and the pursuit of happiness.[40] It is no wonder, then, that "Power to the People" eventually became the slogan of the Black Panther Party.

As much as Newton praised Nkrumah's brilliance for coming up with this political epistemological revolutionary program that is extremely critical of the antics and politics of empire, he thought that it is limited in its application, especially when its tenets are considered in view of the conditions of Blacks in the United States. At the heart of Newton's critique of Pan-Africanism is the overemphasis placed by its progenitors and advocates on the historicization of the global Black experience as a monolith that is opposed to the philosophy of change that undergirds Newton's political epistemology, especially his emphasis on the principles of social contradictions that led to his formulation of revolutionary intercommunalism. Newton was more of the persuasion that historical realities and social trajectories may necessitate different instances of engagement and approaches to militaristic counterrevolution. Even though a global Black alliance can be formed, in principle, toward combating the forces of colonial/imperialist oppression, for Newton, the idea of Pan-Africanism is complicated by the limitations and complexities tied to the idea of creating a separate state for Black folks in the United States. As he inquires, "What does 'Pan-Africanism' mean to the Black Africans who did not live Nkrumah's dream but live in the real nightmare of U.S. economic/military might?"[41] What Newton is articulating here is the fact that the geospatial limitations of

Pan-Africanism do not make it specifically apropos in addressing the conditions of oppression of Black folks in the United States.

Newton would further advance his critique of Pan-Africanism to encompass his views on human culture, such that he imagined Pan-Africanism as upholding a monolithic view of African culture as a historically material immutable fact. Newton eventually submitted that Pan-Africanism was the highest expression of reactionary cultural nationalism.[42] In his view:

> Cultural nationalism deals with a return to the old culture of Africa and that we are somewhat freed by identifying and returning to this culture, to the African cultural stage of the 1100s or earlier. Somehow, they believe that they will be freed through identifying in this manner. As far as we are concerned, we believe that it's important for us to recognize our origins and identify with the revolutionary Black people of Africa and people of color throughout the world. But as far as returning, per se to the ancient customs, we don't see any necessity in this. And also, we say that the only culture that is worth holding is revolutionary—for change for the better.[43]

His critique of the nationalistic threshold that forms the basis of Pan-Africanism coincided with his appraisal of Black nationalism as a restricting framework for advocating revolutionary counter-resistance. For Newton, careful consideration of the condition of Blacks in the United States would reveal that they are only tied historically to Africa, which makes it impossible for them to lay any real claim to territory in the United States of Africa. Black Americans have only the cultural and social customs that have evolved from centuries of oppression. In other words, Blacks in the United States are not a subjugated colony in America alone, but an oppressed community inside the larger boundaries of the world. This is aptly captured in provocative questions raised by Newton, asking, "What, then, do the words 'Black nationalism' concretely mean to the U.S. Black? Not forming anything resembling a nation presently, shall U.S. Blacks somehow seize (or possibly be 'given') U.S. land and expect to claim sovereignty as a nation?"[44]

In the mid-seventies, when the Panthers were seeking to counter the multiple avenues of state violence against the leaders of the Party through imprisonment on trumped-up charges, clandestine "intelligence," or reactionary machinations of the FBI's COINTEL-PRO program, Newton began to broaden his vision of the political epistemological apparatus that would guide the Party's activities both locally and internally. He was more interested in building principles of alliances and social mobilization that looked beyond the analysis of historical material conditions toward a system of organizing that embraced the possibilities of present associations for building a liberating future. He was also interested in advancing a political epistemological framework that would bring oppressed people together within the global sphere as an ultimate source of strength. As he opined, "If however, we are speaking of eliminating exploitation and oppression, then the oppressed must begin with a united, worldwide thrust along the lines of oppressed versus oppressor."[45]

This is the thrust of his revolutionary intercommunalist ideas. Intercommunalism grew out of the Panthers' fundamental ideological position on internationalism: that the United States is not a nation but an empire that dominated and exploited the world and that its imperialism had transformed other nations into oppressed communities.[46] In the initial stages, the Panthers called themselves revolutionary nationalists. But then they realized that the politics of nation-states include genocidal violence and wars—there were many wars that had been fought for national liberation that were based mainly on capitalist-exploitative principles, and these wars of national liberation seemed to negate the very conditions of human flourishing. They reevaluated their position and found that it was necessary not to be nationalists, but internationalists. Nations ceased to exist when the ruling circle of the United States became imperialist, when America became an empire.[47]

It is crucial to note that revolutionary intercommunalism, as imagined by Newton, was not overly theoretical, nor was it understood as such by members of the BPP. It was designed as a political epistemology that required a direct application to the present realities in the material world, especially as it pertains to the experience of oppressed communities in the world. The party took some steps to implement the theory of revolutionary internationalism. Newton offered the National Liberation Front and Provisional Revolutionary Government of South Vietnam an undetermined number of troops to assist in their fight against American imperialism. Nguyen Thi Dinh, deputy commander of the South Vietnamese People's Liberation Armed Forces, accepted the offer in the following manner: "With profound gratitude, we take notice for your enthusiastic proposal; when necessary, we shall call for your volunteers to assist us."[48] In offering Panthers to fight in Vietnam, Newton invoked the spirit of international revolutionary solidarity.[49] In a very vociferous manner, Newton also declared the successes recorded by oppressed communities beyond the geographical borders of the United States that were putting into practice his ideas of revolutionary intercommunalism. He asserts thus:

> Some communities have begun doing this [practicalizing revolutionary intercommunalism]. They liberated their territories and have established provisional governments. We recognize them and say that these governments represent the people of China, North Korea, the people in the liberated zones of South Vietnam, and the people in North Vietnam. We believe their examples should be followed so that the order of the day would not be reactionary intercommunalism (empire) but revolutionary intercommunalism. The people of the world, that is, must seize the power from the small ruling circle and expropriate the expropriators, pull them down from their pinnacle and make them equals, and distribute the fruits of our labor, that have been denied us, in some equitable way.[50]

Newton made it clear that the actual power of revolutionary intercommunalism as a political epistemology rests on the fact that oppressed people can renegotiate their proximity to the hegemonic forces of colonial and imperial institutions, by any means necessary, to reclaim what originally belonged to them through the reordering of mindset and the reshaping of their worldview. This also demonstrates that revolutionary warfare, together with revolutionary epistemologies, are not merely designed to be a historical concept and a museum piece but principles and strategies that are real and achievable—especially when furnished and driven by a people whose imperialist subjugation had developed a strong basis for sympathetic alliances and revolutionary fraternities.[51] In this respect, the establishment of the international section of the BPP as an officially accredited revolutionary movement in Algiers was a major milestone, not only in the development of the Panthers but also in the history of African American international political alliance.[52]

What is truly unique and remarkable about viewing Newton's revolutionary intercommunalism as a kind of Black collectivist epistemology is that it fundamentally regards Blacks in the New World as well as in the diaspora as worthy epistemic agents who can transform their social conditions by the utilization of their cognitive, mental, and practical skills for revolutionary warfare. In this instance, Black subjects were accorded some form of epistemic responsibility that transcends just the interests of the individual. It focuses on the epistemic and political life of groups and how ideological frameworks can be designed to transform the lived experience or existential condition. Newton also demonstrated a very good understanding of the power that can be derived from the combination of political positioning and the development of radical political and social knowledge.[53]

Newton was not interested in pursuing political epistemology merely as a special case of social cognition but more as a set of values that should be directed toward material change, hence the emphasis he placed on Black revolutionaries understanding their place within social ontology as a central focus of the revolutionary struggle. Revolutionary intercommunalism as political epistemology is not construed solely as an embodiment of mentalist or abstract principles but as a system of thinking that is informed and contingent upon material social experiences, which is why it is directed toward the development of the Black community in the United States as well as of oppressed communities around the world. Thus, Newton's political epistemology essentially focuses on community development. This perspective assumes that the people in a community best understand their problems and the solutions that will work for them, and as such, they should be the ones to determine what battles should be fought against imperialist exploitation, and how.[54]

Through his political epistemology of revolutionary intercommunalism, Newton highlighted the connections between knowledge and social action. Knowledge, both in its abstract and practical forms, is directed toward achieving one goal—liberation from the oppressive antics, tactics, and policies of the state that seek to condemn Black people and Black communities to a life of hardship and recurrent dehumanizing schemes. This became the basis upon which Newton and the BPP engaged with the people. The people, in turn, formed an affinity and an affiliation with the BPP because they saw the Panthers as providing important models not only for political and social change but for profound personal transformations. The Black Panthers became masters at creating a radical visual and discursive language of affiliation and identification that expressed the need for personal involvement in liberatory social and political change.[55] It was something that the community needed to unleash its socially located power in order to organize as a united front to combat the forces of repression. Newton was able to discover that ignorance was partly responsible for how Black people were being oppressed indiscriminately within and outside the Black community. Many people do not know their rights and constitutional protections accorded to Blacks that could be used to engage with the state. For instance, when the Panthers began to patrol the police force within the Black communities in Oakland and surrounding neighborhoods in the late 1960s, members of the Black community were unsure about the legality of these patrols. But Newton made it a point of instruction to read out, in real time, the rules and laws that made such actions legally permissible, even to the shock of members of law enforcement who were not aware of the laws Newton was citing. Thus, he made education (education of members of the Black community) one of the cardinal programs of the BPP.

Newton was successful in communicating his political epistemological arguments to members of the Black community as well as to people of oppressed communities around the world because he often made structural comparisons of local discrimination with trans-geographical political oppression. He was remarkably skilled at analyzing larger structural situations and making them applicable to people's understanding of everyday cultural reality.[56] He also worked tirelessly to practically demonstrate how his ideas applied to conditions within the global polity, especially his envisioning of how technology would become a dominant tool that the empire would utilize to establish its global dominion throughout history. Looking at technological realities in contemporary society, one can only imagine the prophetic genius with which Newton predicted this in the late twentieth century. His emphasis on education was geared toward transformational learning, in a bid to get others within the movement to grasp how the political epistemologies and ideologies of the Party were changing with time, as well as the predictions of the future of the movement, based on present realities. This explains why he put so much effort into educating the youth about the painstaking process of revolutionary action against the empire. Newton clearly articulated this in a conversation he had with J. Herman Black, Erik H. Erikson, and Kai T. Erikson in Oakland, California, on March 31, 1971, later published under the title, *In Search of Common Ground*, where he asserted thus:

> Young people generally feel that the role of the revolutionary is to define a set of actions and sets of principles that are easy to identify and are absolute. But what I was trying to explain to them was the process: revolution is a contradiction between the old and the new in the process of development. Anything can be revolutionary at a particular point in time, but most of the students don't understand that. And most other people don't understand it either.[57]

It is in pursuit of this understanding that he vigorously accentuated education as one of the central programs within the Panthers' Ten-Point Program. Newton believed that education is a vehicle for achieving both individual and social transformation. He was quite successful in developing educational theories and in his distinctive approach to communicating his ideas to others such as other notable revolutionary leaders. He also grounded his abstraction in material examples and was constantly reformulating his ideology to address Black self-determination and self-education.[58]

In sum, the exposition in this chapter is an attempt to study Newton seriously as a philosopher—more specifically as a Black political epistemologist—while exploring the epistemological arguments that span his writings, speeches, and ideas. A political epistemologist is someone who believes that there is a connection that exists between the phenomenon of human knowledge and its application to social reality in ways that are politically relevant to aspects of human life. In every sense of that definition, Newton can be categorized as an important Black political epistemologist for insisting that political and revolutionary ideas must be the very basis from which Black people, in alliance with other oppressed groups in the world, should negotiate the conditions of their lives to ensure that they live freely and authentically. It is the condition for fighting back against the empire "by any means necessary." As a political epistemologist, Newton understood and appreciated the social value of knowledge, evident in the ways he organized members of the BPP and other allied revolutionary groups beyond the borders of the United States around his political-philosophical systems. His philosophy is geared toward challenging the powers of empire, and providing an avenue for the understanding of how hegemonic societies transform themselves into global exploitative elements as well as forces of mass oppression. Newton is an important Black political epistemologist who created revolutionary intercommunalism as an anti-imperialist and anti-colonial epistemology out of a rigorous examination of the existential conditions of Black folks in the United States and the exploitation of oppressed communities in the global sphere by the imperial state and forces of colonial capitalist interests. Although Newton is not often acknowledged as a philosopher in contemporary scholarship, this work makes a case for re-imagining this genius Black intellectual as a Black political epistemologist.

10

Kathleen Neal Cleaver on Black Feminism, Black Knowledge, and Black Resistance

It is impossible to give an accurate historical account of the struggles of Black folks against forced labor, systemic oppression, colonial exploitation, orchestrated dehumanization, and the tribulations evinced by the tripartite categories of class, race, and gender without emphasizing the role that Black women have played in heralding this history. As tumultuous and challenging as the twentieth century was with respect to the struggle for civil rights and the movement to affirm the humanity of Black people, Black women threw themselves into the struggle and resisted the systems of dehumanization with the goal of achieving absolute and unconditional freedom for members of the race. Kathleen Neal Cleaver[1] is one such Black woman, an important figure in this period given her unique membership in a Black radical organization at a time when Black women were not fully regarded as social forces to be reckoned with in terms of activism and radical resistance. In this chapter, I aim to highlight the thoughts and activism of K. Cleaver, who was the first woman to become a highly visible leader in the Black Panther Party and one of the few Black women to emerge as a nationwide symbol of the Black Power movement.[2] Her membership in one of the most radical Black organizations during the modern civil rights movement provided her with an uncompromising anticolonial view of the world as well as the ability to effectively analyze the interconnection and tensions between Black feminism, Black epistemology, and Black resistance.

Through her radical activism and involvement in the organizational systems that challenged the repressive power structure of the United

States, K. Cleaver's contributions to Black progress place her among the most courageous Black women of the modern civil rights era. Even at a very young age, she had developed an uncanny understanding of the systems of difference and segregation that encapsulated social structures in the United States and the ways in which these structures were maintained along racial, gender, and class lines in order to restrict Black families to a life of poverty and underachievement. As she reflects in *Lighting the Fires of Freedom,* "I was trained from the time I was three years old, in a community in which the challenge to segregation was very alive. My father was very much a part of it, and my mother was very much a part of it, all before I was born."[3]

So, by her condition of birth into a deeply segregated community in Alabama, the Deep South, she was acutely aware of the demarcations, hierarchies, and lines of existence that were drawn and the repressive nature of the conditions of life for Black people. Her circumstance of birth and family lineage brought her into the awareness of radical resistance to a system of segregation that, as she puts it, "was very alive." Such awareness also reveals her genius and intellectual gifts, especially the ability to decipher the structural inequalities and the systems of dehumanization that were immixed with social realities for Black families in her early years. This familial exposure to Black resistance would continue beyond her formative years and crystalize into an intense and relentless passion for the liberation of Black people from both psychological and material systems of oppression that were instituted to prevent members of this group from pursuing a meaningful existence.

In many of her writings and speeches, she advocated a positive movement toward the liberation of Black people from the chains of coloniality, oppression, and mental and material slavery, but she emphasized that this upward trajectory must begin with the radical reshaping of Black knowledge and the unraveling of the Black self, which had been bastardized and colonized by the experience of slavery and the rush to accept the façade of assimilation into white middle-class values as the harbinger of Black prosperity, especially in this period. The aspirational aspects of the civil rights era, in terms of the promise of assimilation, weakened the resolve of the Black community to unite around a central message of destroying the yoke of racial capitalism and its erosion of Black self-determination.

K. Cleaver understood that Black knowledge, specifically Black knowledge of the self, ought to be seen as fundamental and a foundation upon which any liberatory praxis or philosophy of radical resistance could be constructed. Therefore, she vehemently attacked one of the most potent propaganda machines of the United States government—miseducation—as the first apparatus that needed to be destroyed if Black people would ever be able to galvanize, organize, and resist the throes of the colonizing experience in the New World. She insisted that in order for Black knowledge to be directed at achieving Black liberation, there had to be what she regarded as "a confrontation" with distorted scholarship or twisted intellectual conclusions that demeaned Black people and provided information that undermined the intellectual accomplishments and gifts of members of the race.[4]

In her reflections on what should be the task of Black intellectual inquiry in the context of imperialist exploitation and colonial manipulations of the repressive state, she emphasized the importance of Black self-determination. This advocacy of Black self-determination has both historical and contemporary dimensions, signified by her insistence that a movement for Black liberation with the Black Power movement must challenge all the preconceived notions of Blacks as beings that are incapable of determining their own destiny. It is an emphasis on the need to eschew the false historical, colonial, and ethnological categories of animality and ignorance, which have been projected and ascribed to Blacks throughout the Western articulation of human history as a necessary condition for reconceptualizing Blackness in a new light, especially within the Black community. This is echoed in K. Cleaver's expression in an interview with Henry Louis Gates Jr. in 1997, where she articulated that what appealed to her about the Black Panther Party "was that it took the position of self-determination and articulated it in a local community structure."[5]

In other words, she took the interiorization of the project of liberation seriously because she saw its potential to change the Black community by transforming the minds of Black people, and its relevance in helping them create a spirit of independence from the conceptual schemes and existential apparatus that are tainted by phenomenological and ontological assumptions of inferiority. This radical stance impacted how the Panthers and the advocates of Black liberation engaged with the questions of freedom and struggle for justice and equality during this period. By using such historical analyses to make a case for Black self-determination, K. Cleaver was able to advocate a liberatory praxis aimed at intellectual freedom and self-assertion, which proved useful for the Panthers' goal of recruiting young Black revolutionaries who were unafraid of challenging the oppressive power schemes of the repressive state.

The emphasis on the connections between Black resistance, Black epistemology, and the community in the reflections of K. Cleaver is instructive. She is unequivocal in her stance that Black liberation and revolution must begin with the achievement of self-determination, which is not to be realized in isolation but rather in community with other Black people and minority populations suffering from structural inequalities on the basis of class, race, and gender. As she writes in "Women, Power and Revolution":

> Those of us who were drawn to the early Black Panther Party were just one more insurgent band of young men and women who refuse to tolerate the systematic violence and abuse being meted out to poor Blacks, to middle-class Blacks, and to any old ordinary Blacks. When we looked at our situation, when we saw violence, bad housing, unemployment, rotten education, unfair treatment in the courts, as well as direct attacks from the police, our response was to defend ourselves.[6]

The emphasis here is on the ubiquity of the structural and systemic inequalities that affect Black people as a group and the necessity of resisting this as a group or as a community. This is another important aspect of K. Cleaver's contributions to the development of Black knowledge, especially her analyses of how the goals of anticolonial activism and the development of an anticolonial epistemology transcend the politics of gender that are quite common in current feminist scholarship.

One of the most troubling theses in the development of Black feminist epistemology in the last four decades is the thesis of standpoint theory. As an epistemological project, standpoint theory focuses on the personalization of knowledge as a form of exclusive individuality, which is commonly advocated in Black feminist thought. For instance, in "Learning from the Outsider Within: The Sociological Significance of Black Feminist Thought," and in "The Social Construction of Black Feminist Thought," Patricia Hill Collins advanced the view of the unique standpoint that Black women possess.[7] Other feminist scholars such as Kelly Oduro, Monica Allen, and Brenda J. Allen have expressed similar views, arguing that Black women hold a unique perspective into understanding the world; this view of the world is grounded in their lived experience and provides them with a vantage point from which to analyze and challenge systems of power.[8] Feminist standpoint theory and Black feminist thought are used as lenses to centralize Black women's experiences in the analyses of social problems in a myriad of social contexts. This view is concerning because it takes women's material experience and the supposed epistemic advantage that ensues from it as an essentialist universalizable claim to knowledge, according to which women are afforded automatic epistemic privilege simply for the fact of being women.[9] It has also created a situation in which the epistemic views and experiences of members of other oppressed social groups, such as Black men, have been discountenanced as lacking credibility, on the basis that they are not grounded in the reality of the lives of women.

While it is true that K. Cleaver extolled the feminist's role in the civil rights struggle in the latter parts of the twentieth century, her emphasis was not focused on the destructive projection and demonization of Black men, who were revolutionaries and utterly committed their lives and died for the liberation of Black people. It is a radically different account from what is propagated in contemporary Black feminist scholarship about the Black Panthers and the Black Power movement. In feminist accounts, the role of Black women in the Black radical tradition has been framed around the narrative that the orientation of Black male revolutionaries during the civil rights era and within the Black radical tradition was patriarchal, sexist, or discriminatory against women.[10]

For instance, in *Remaking Black Power* Ashley Farmer argues that the Black Panther Party was sexist and patriarchal until the Black women who were later recruited transformed the Party from within. Farmer argues that from 1967 to 1975, the Panther women expanded the party's gendered imaginary and organizing ethos through their debate over Black womanhood and theorized new ideas about the Black Revolutionary Woman as a way to challenge the Panthers' patriarchal political imaginary.[11] Similarly, Mary Phillips, in "The Feminist Leadership of Ericka Huggins in the Black Panther Party," argues that "the sexism in the Black Power movement, isolated Black women."[12] Although such narrative accounts have been made popular in recent Black feminist scholarship, they are directly contradicted by the first-hand account of the reality of the situation offered by K. Cleaver, who was one of the earliest women recruited into the Black Panther Party. K. Cleaver was interested in focusing not on a feminist analysis of gender dynamics and its acrimonious analytical lens but on the larger contributions of women to the project of liberating Black people, both in the United States and in places where subjugated peoples were struggling to gain freedom from the chains of colonial domination. She expressed this sentiment in her reflections on "The Feminist Role in a Race-Based Civil Rights Struggle," stating that "despite finding strength in the passion of the Black struggle and benefiting from legislation passed in response to the civil rights movement, feminists offer no substantial attack against racism."[13]

In "Women, Power and Revolution," K. Cleaver offered insightful commentary on the question of gender within the Black Panther Party, highlighting how this was not considered in isolation from all the other issues of structural injustice that the Party was combating in society at large. She described the "young women and men who flocked to the front lines of the war against segregation [and structural injustice as focused on] contesting the remaining legacy of racial slavery."[14] In other words, the focus of young Black men and women, during this early phase of the BPP, was on the social structure as a whole and how the conditions that impose restrictions on Black lives could be eliminated. According to K. Cleaver, "What they sought to eliminate were the legal, social, psychological, economic, and political limitations still being imposed on [the human rights of Blacks, and on their rights as citizens. That was the context in which [they] fought to remove limitations imposed by gender, clearly aware that it could not be fought as a stand-alone issue."[15] She made it clear that the women in the BPP were intentional about rupturing the projection of socially designed gender roles for women, and they took a revolutionary stance on this as a problem of the larger society and not particularly a problem within the Party.

This is why she asserted that she never liked it when she was asked the question "What is the woman's role in the Black Panther Party?" She further described how she would typically respond to such an irritating question:

> I'd give a short answer: "It's the same as men." We are revolutionaries, I'd explain. Back then, I didn't understand why they wanted to think of what men were doing and what women were doing as separate. It's taken me years, literally about twenty-five years, to understand that what I really didn't like was the underlying assumption motivating the question. The assumption held that being part of a revolutionary movement was in conflict with what the questioner had been socialized to believe was appropriate conduct for a woman.[16]

It is clear that she found the projection of social norms of gender and its undermining of the role of women misplaced as the Party was not merely trying to replicate the discriminatory structures and gender oppression found in society. She asserted that the gender relations and orientation within the Party were different from those of society, which is why she maintained that those who critiqued the gender dynamics in the Party as oppressive toward women did not take external and internal factors on social relations into consideration. Tracye A. Matthews's view on this issue is worthy of note:

> The Party's theory and praxis with regard to issues of gender and sexuality should be viewed as an ongoing, non-linear process that was affected by factors both internal and external to the organization. This analysis of gender ideology offers insights into the internal politics of Black communities, especially relations of power between and among men and women, and the myriad ways in which these dynamics influence political movements and popular perceptions of them.[17]

Matthews insists that there was something distinctive about gender relations within the Black Panther Party; it was the stance of the Party leadership not to duplicate the gender relations that existed in the larger society. She further noted that the reality of the world and social context in which the Party existed were extremely misogynist and authoritarian, and this was part of what inspired members of the Party to fight against it.

K. Cleaver clarified that when women suffered hostility, abuse, neglect, and assault, this was not something arising from the policies or structure of the Black Panther Party; it arose out of what was going on in the world. So, being a member of the Black Panther Party made a significant difference in the sense that women's membership in the Party placed them in a position to contest such treatment whenever it occurred.[18] It also created a space whereby women were not only empowered but encouraged to put their intellect and skills to good use and to bring about the liberation of African-descended people.[19] To this end, Tracye A. Matthews is right to point out that the politics of the Black Panther Party cannot be reduced to a monolithic party line on "the woman question," or a linear progression from an overtly and overwhelmingly sexist organization to a pro-Black feminist/womanist one. But a more accurate account of the gender dynamics within the Party must pay attention to internal conflict as well as agreement, overt as well as covert manifestations of this dialogue, the changes that occurred over time, the diversity of individual experiences, and internal as well as external influences.[20]

Kathleen Cleaver's Anticolonial Reflections as an Epistemology of Social Change

For K. Cleaver, thinking radically about the world is not merely an abstract reality but a practical reality that involves the immersion of one's self, the totality of one's self, into the process of negotiating social realities, resisting social structures, and imagining new pathways. This is a mode of existing and resisting that was influenced by Frantz Fanon. She, as well as other members of the Black Panther Party, drew their articulation of Black agency and self-determination from Fanon, in particular his sociogenic principle. This articulation emphasizes a radical recasting and redefinition of Black subjectivity, grounding it in the Black experience and the Black self, devoid of any accretions or allusions of alterity and the grandeur of being as delineated within the colonial or Eurocentric imaginary. She made this very clear in her reflections in "And the Beat Goes On," asserting that the Panthers "identified with Fanon's analysis of how violence and racism intertwined in the colonial scheme and with his psychological insight into the way revolutionary violence aided the colonized in reclaiming the dignity that white racism denied."[21] In other words, the philosophical insights of Fanon were seen as a pathway to self-determination and liberation.

What emerged from this quest to achieve psychological renewal and social transformation for Black subjects was a genuine anticolonial worldview, which maintained that authentic liberation and freedom cannot be achieved if there is no attempt made to first purge the distorted ideas and negative perceptions about Blackness and the intellectual heritage of Black folks. By taking this approach and maintaining such a disposition about social reality, K. Cleaver and other members of the Black Panther Party were able to embark on one of the most important goals toward Black freedom, which was the revamping of the existing ideals, concepts, and structures of society, especially those that were not consistent with the Black lived experience and not aligned with the goals of liberation. One of these restructured ideas was the concept of leadership. Black women played an integral part in the day-to-day activities of the Black Panther Party, helped shape its agenda, had significant input into its programs, and occupied important leadership roles within the party structure. Despite this, society still viewed them through a hegemonic structural lens as subservient.[22] But K. Cleaver describes this as a misunderstanding of the political epistemology of the Panthers, which was focused on transforming dominant social ideas or concepts that were problematic and counterproductive to the social programs that the Panthers were aiming to actualize.

A good example of this is how the Panthers redefined, reframed, and reimagined the concept of leadership, which was radically different from how it was understood and deployed by society. As K. Cleaver acknowledges, although society has a conceptual structure that is called leadership, members of the Black Panther Party created a different structure of organizing that was not leadership. This new structure was revolutionary. They were not interested in a mere hierarchization of power or social status but on a radical revamping of the social structure. In other words, they were trying to make themselves revolutionaries, and in fact, this was how they functioned.[23] This was an attractive proposition by the Panthers because they collectively believed that "revolutionaries are not interested in the normal operating of society. A revolutionary is the one that transforms that. The way in which they do it is by creating revolutionary movements, revolutionary concepts, revolutionary ideas."[24] In "Back to Africa," K. Cleaver clarifies why the radical view of social concepts such as leadership is contradictory to the goals of Black liberation and within social movements. She asserts that:

There [are] different ways in which movements function as opposed to a military, a corporation, a government. The kind of leadership notions that most people have come from corporate structures. Military, states, corporations. Social justice activism does not use that structure, and social justice activism does [not] use the kind of people who are leaders in those contexts. Leadership is not a viable concept in the context of a revolution. Which means that when you say "leadership" that [is] all nice, well, and good, but civil rights are the rights of citizens, so if you [are] a citizen you have these rights. So that was that whole dynamic. We are second-class citizens, but we [are] not really citizens like the other people[;] . . . therefore we want to get our civil rights.[25]

It is apparent from her articulations that the notion of "leadership" was eschewed because of its assumption of hierarchy. So, the Panthers adopted a more inclusive and equitable orientation of a revolutionary.

Another important aspect of K. Cleaver's anticolonial reflection that points toward social change is her critique of racial capitalism. In his seminal text *Black Marxism: The Making of the Black Radical Tradition*, Cedric Robinson used the term "racial capitalism" to describe "the development, organization and expansion of capitalist society [in

Europe and in other states that practiced the feudal system of political power, such as the United States, that] pursued essentially racial dimensions," using the force of violence.[26] In other words, racial capitalism highlights the production of difference in accordance with the production of capital, usually through violence.[27] It is "a powerful heuristic, one that not only sheds light on the persistence of supremacist phantasmagoria in white identity, but also calls into question the introjection of racialist hierarchization in bourgeoisies of color."[28]

The discursive framework for the development of the theory of racial capitalism theoretically grounds and connects the histories of Black social exclusion and colonialism to the contemporary economic-material predicament of Black populations.[29] Using this model as a framework for understanding the expansion of empire within the American context, the Panthers developed a dialectic of the structural relation between the Black community and the dominant white community as an exploitative relation that continues to alienate Black people from the means of production. Accordingly, racial capitalism is a fundamental cause of racial and socioeconomic inequities that are especially detrimental to members of marginalized communities.[30] It is a system of capital whereby the proceeds from social production and the system of wealth creation are unequally distributed across racial lines. Even though schemes and political ideals are put in place to mask the lines of inequalities and nondistribution of social goods, the material conditions and their affective states (material force) are too devastating to ignore.

Within this framework, "as a material force then, it could be expected that racialism would inevitably permeate the social structures emergent from capitalism."[31] These kinds of schemes to disguise or conceal the devastating effects of structuralized racism and the racialized distribution of wealth or capital are very prevalent within a capitalist form of democracy. For K. Cleaver, a critique of the social systems and power structure within a capitalist democracy, as practiced in the United States, must take into cognizance the fact that such a society must construct an underclass (subservient class) in order to properly function. She regards America's capitalist form of democracy, or "commercial democracy," as she likes to call it, as a system that needs the underclass, like poor Black people and members of marginalized communities, or a middle class to function properly.[32]

This explains why she considers the presence of a significant underclass, masses of solid working people, and an affluent middle class among Black people as emblematic of the fact that they are neither liberated nor integrated and have become a fragmented population, scattered throughout all levels of society, from the Pentagon to the prison yard. In this scenario, equality, even though it is espoused in legal structures, remains but an ideal that is never to be realized. In other words, inequality becomes an important factor that is designed as part of the system in order for it to work. In such a system, people are generally stratified into classes, such that some will be at the top and others will be at the middle and bottom of the social hierarchy. Those who are at the bottom are left scrambling and struggling to reach the upper level following a zealous (but unrealistic) commitment to make money.[33] It is a cycle of exploitation that will continue to replicate itself until a new path is forged from either within or outside the socially determined framework.

The goal of K. Cleaver's critique of the capitalist and commercialized democratic social framework in the United States is to make a connection between the evolution of new epistemic dispositions (mental attitudes) and social change. She makes a case for why individuals with a revolutionary mindset are the ones that can bring about social change. She considers the aim of the revolution as social change, which entails the fundamental and permanent elimination of certain types of discrimination and separation based on race, class, and gender. It is, both as an ideal and as a material condition, fundamentally seeking to achieve social justice through methods that will change the social, political, and economic reality of the people who choose to participate in the revolutionary transformation of society.[34] She argues that people who have a revolutionary mindset are not trapped in the illusion of maintaining the social status quo and the unrealistic commitment to making money; they rather, demand change.[35] This demand for change is only going to be realized if those (the underclass) who have been trapped in the idea of a structure based on financial rewards and financial incentives come to terms with the fact that they are being exploited, revolt against the way the system works, and embrace a different idea. This is why the Panthers held a mantra that says: "Power to the people."[36]

The idea of "Power to the People" entails a holistic consideration of methods of resistance to the structures of oppression that include group solidarity as a social force and violence as a strategy, if that is going to result in the rupturing of material structures and systems of oppression and bring about the respect for the dignity and human rights of members of marginalized groups. It is through group solidarity that K. Cleaver advocates a way of Black radical resistance, made of up of what she regarded as "the rainbow coalition" (allies pulled together from Black and Brown peoples within and outside the United States) working together in solidarity with the aim of transforming society and achieving freedom.[37] Her view of Black resistance emphasizes the community over the individual because fighting back against powerful oppressive governments and their insidious schemes would be more effective through the force of a coalition.

In the discourse on Black knowledge and the struggles for social change through an anticolonial praxis, K. Cleaver is an important voice, exemplifying the important role Black women played in the Black Power era. One cannot divorce her activism and revolutionary philosophies from the fact that she deeply cares about the liberation of Black people and other oppressed peoples. This is very apparent in many of her writings. She fundamentally believes that "respecting the liberty and dignity of the disempowered and dispossessed is critical to ensuring social justice for everyone."[38] In contemporary society, the struggle to ensure justice for everyone continues, and this chapter's exploration of the reflections of K. Cleaver serves as a model for mapping the strategies, pitfalls, and possibilities of resistance, even in a world consumed by endemic violence.

Conclusion

The Task and Future
of Black Epistemology

This work, through its advocacy of Black epistemology as a new subdisciplinary focus in Africana thought, makes a case for a different approach to doing Africana philosophy in the twenty-first century. It is a work that is much needed in this historic moment, when books and ideas focusing on the subject of race are being banned and outlawed by those in power in the United States. What has been demonstrated in this book is that Black intellectual gifts will continue to thrive even in the most repressive and dehumanizing situations. Black knowledge will always survive the antics and politics of those who stand to oppose it. This book uncovers a rich treasure of Black knowledge within intellectual history and makes a case for a specialized engagement of the ideas produced by Black thinkers under a disciplinary concentration: Black epistemology.

Black epistemology is considered mainly from the standpoint of embodied subjectivity to encompass the Black lived experience, Black agency, and the connections between an epistemic agent and social properties in the world. It is characterized as "the study or theory of the knowledge generated out of the African American existential condition, that is, of the knowledge and cultural artifacts produced by African Americans based on African American cultural, social, economic, historical, and political experience."[1] In other words, Black epistemology in an anti-Black world is not focused on an investigation of the nature of phenomenal experience or the nature of knowledge for the sake of it because Black subjects do not have the luxury of wallowing in empty existential abstractions in a world that persistently seeks to trivialize what it means to exist as a Black person and ultimately negate Black existence. This implies that the ever-present threat to Black existence in an anti-Black society inadvertently conditions this form of epistemological production to seek ways of improving the Black condition.

Black epistemology employs methodologies, ideas, and theories developed by Black thinkers to address issues related to the Black condition both in African and African diasporic contexts. It rejects the extraverted epistemological posture advocated in earlier Africana philosophical scholarship which breeds a "victim" orientation. The orientation that is put forward in this book favors approaches focusing on efforts by African Americans and Blacks in the diaspora to shape their destiny (Africana/Black agency). It surveys the interpretation of agency and epistemic authority in contemporary scholarship through a framework of analysis that explores the effects of historical forces in shaping current conditions (continuing historical influences). In looking at representative Black thinkers from the eighteenth through the twentieth centuries, this work utilizes multiple analytical methods and modes of presentation to articulate the complexities and importance of Black epistemological contributions to the lives of people of African descent.

Through the emphasis on knowledge formation and the global alliance of Black political epistemologies, this book explores aspects of historical and continuing cultural and political linkages between Africans in Africa and Africans in the Diaspora.[2] What is crucial in how the discourse of Black epistemology is approached in this work is that it encompasses the gamut of epistemes and knowledge that speak specifically to the Black existential condition. These include the spectrum of philosophical ideas developed by Black intellectuals, touching on the robustness of the Black experience, culture, genius, and ideas, including forms of Black intellectual creations that explore the architecture of Black struggles against the powerful forces of oppression, slavery, colonialism, racism, and imperialism in an anti-Black society. Thus, Black epistemology is focused on understanding and grappling with the truth of the Black condition and the Black lived experience. It is a practical epistemology that uncovers practical solutions to the numerous problems that confront Black people.

In this work, I have argued against the pretentiousness of race-neutral scholarship under the regime of multidisciplinarity and philosophical pluralism.[3] For instance, in "A Future for Africana (Post-) Analytic Philosophy," Paul C. Taylor characterizes the epistemological thrust of Africana scholarship as that which should focus on pushing

"the boundaries of [Western] analytic philosophy," because "we cannot simply write off the entire approach as bankrupt."[4] He maintains
that Africana/Black philosophers need to push these boundaries toward
what he refers to as a "post-analytic" philosophy.[5] I consider this a misguided preoccupation because it characterizes the thrust of Africana/
Black scholarship as a field of inquiry that exists primarily to do the
bidding of "Western analytic philosophy."

What Taylor conceives as the epistemological thrust of Africana philosophy is essentially a rehabilitative project that aims to identify the
limitations of a disciplinary formation that does not take Black intellectual thought seriously. It is difficult to conceive of the plausibility of
such a project as advocated by Taylor (and other scholars sympathetic to
this worldview), especially "in an academic environment in which Black
philosophers are regularly characterized as not doing 'real' philosophy
in virtue of their choosing to grapple with the topic of racial injustice
and related themes."[6] This proposal that Taylor puts forward assumes
that the "relentless" pushing of the Western canon by Black philosophers
would have some effect on pulling the discipline of Africana/Black philosophy from its current position of liminality within the philosophical
edifice to a position of equanimity. As a critique to Taylor's claims,
Tommy J. Curry notes that "since the 1970s Black philosophers have
criticized, attacked, and attempted to reform the discipline with little
effect."[7]

Thus, my work offers arguments against such proposals for an
epistemological project in Africana philosophy, insisting that the epistemological goals of Black philosophy and its success are not going
to be found in their ability to change the disciplinary programs of
knowledge, since it is difficult to imagine that the white majority in
mainstream philosophy is going to miraculously change after almost
fifty years of being confronted with its anthropological limitations
and illusory concepts.[8] In "Black Critics and the Pitfalls of Canon
Formation," Cornel West offers a set of arguments similar to that of
Taylor, maintaining that for any serious discussion or canon formation of the Africana/Black philosophical edifice to take place, Black
philosophers must first focus on a wholesale reconsideration of the
philosophical canon already in place (the Western philosophical
canon).[9] He considers this an important task that Africana/Black philosophers should embark upon because of its epistemological promise
of breaking new grounds of knowledge through a constant "struggle" against and critique of the "established" Western philosophical canon.[10] West insists that Black thinkers or philosophers should

mainly focus on the "demanding efforts of pursuing dedisciplinizing modes of knowing that call into question the very boundaries of the disciplines themselves."[11]

What West suggests here, as the task of Africana philosophy, is a reconstructionist project that operates on an extraverted epistemology under the guise of interdisciplinarity or trans-disciplinary scholarship. Lucius Outlaw echoes West's arguments, asserting that Black philosophers should focus their efforts on the reconstruction of the history of Western philosophy and its relation to peoples on the African continent and Blacks generally. This is imagined as a pathway for generating intersecting or intercultural philosophical praxis that, in the end, does not prioritize the ideas of important figures within Black intellectual history. Although Outlaw believes that such an endeavor ought to recover and rehabilitate the thoughts of African-descended thinkers from earlier periods, and to significantly move to deconstruct and revise narratives of the histories of philosophical enterprises in the Western context. This suggestion runs into problems when we consider that most of the African-descended thinkers that Outlaw references were not interested in having such trans-disciplinary narratives of the history of philosophy, especially within the Western or Euro-American canon.[12] Furthermore, "the majority of cross-cultural/multicultural research seems to emphasize problems or pathology, cultural deprivation, adjustments, pluralism, interpersonal relationships, and tensions [often] associated with Black people."[13] Its major weakness consists of the fact that it does not offer a humanizing vision of Blackness, which is of primary concern in this work.

The discourse of Black epistemology that I imagine for the future of Africana philosophy does not make knowledge within this intellectual enterprise subservient to Western philosophy. It opposes philosophical systems that seek to undermine Black genius and Black intellectual creativity through disguised schemes of "trans-disciplinary" or "intersecting" scholarship. It also does not favorably consider intellectual proposals that offer a reductionist account of Black genius or Black intellectual creativity. I have argued against epistemological reductionism in Africana/Black philosophy, which undermines the serious philosophical considerations that Black philosophers have given to discussions about the acquisition and utilization of knowledge as a programmatic element for racial transformation and uplift, especially the reduction of the gamut of knowledge produced by Black intellectuals throughout human history to mere "critiques" of racism and group oppression or to philosophies of survival. Such descriptions of the task of Black philosophy, especially by those who write from a standpoint that is outside of the Black experience, do not capture the deeper substance of Black philosophical reflection through the history of white racialized oppression against nonwhite peoples in the global sphere. They are an attempt to make Black philosophers appear shallow and single-minded. Black philosophers are more than this.

The thrust of this work is to expand the frontiers of knowledge within Africana philosophy by examining questions concerning what it means to conceive of Black subjects as knowledgeable beings within systems that did not historically categorize them as human. It also examines how the uniqueness of the Black experience, both in African and African diasporic contexts, shaped social knowledge production as well as the formation of political epistemologies to mold the destinies and improve social outcomes for Black folks.[14] Thus, by the very ways in which the phenomenon of human knowledge is examined concerning the Black subject, in this work it is disrobed from the usual garb of abstractions in which it is clothed in the present order of knowledge. It is more focused on the social and practical value of human knowledge, especially in the manner that Black leaders of social movements and philosophers have understood the phenomenon. Contrary to recent trends in Africana philosophical scholarship in which knowledge production by Black intellectuals is projected as something that should be "in the service" of dominant systems of knowledge, this work argues for a renewed sense of intellectual positioning within the discourse of Africana/Black philosophy that takes on a new orientation primarily focused on the Black subject as occupying a place of salience in philosophical musings. In other words, the Black subject must be considered and seen as the grounding from which we should understand and determine which social problems or issues deserve to be centered and how we should engage in philosophical theorizing.

In the manner that Black epistemology is considered in this work, the Black subject has been made alive to its social context of knowledge-formation (the situatedness of knowledge). This work also offers a perspective on what the expression of subjectivity looks like when expressed in liberated terms as an existential embodiment. It does not prioritize the divination of systems of oppression and social practices conscripted within the dominant frames of knowledge as the "norm" of understanding the world as it is rather than as it appears. Rather, it seriously engages with the thoughts of Black thinkers as important philosophical roadmaps for fashioning the future of Africana/Black scholarship, drawing from a rich legacy of epistemological production within Black intellectual history.

Notes

CHAPTER 1

1. See William R. Jones, "Crisis in Philosophy," *The Proceedings and Addresses of the American Philosophical Association* 47 (1973): 118–125; William R. Jones, "The Legitimacy and Necessity of Black Philosophy: Some Preliminary Considerations," *The Philosophical Forum* 9, no. 2 (1977): 149–160; and Cornel West, "Philosophy and the Afro-American Experience," *The Philosophical Forum* 9, nos. 2–3 (Winter–Spring 1977–1978): 117–148. It needs to be mentioned here as well that Leonard Harris's edited anthology, *Philosophy Born of Struggle: Anthology of Afro-American Philosophy from 1917* (Dubuque, IA: Kendall Hunt Publishing, 1983), is one of the pioneering works that sought to establish an Afro-American perspective or worldview in philosophy. In this compilation, Harris provided a select bibliography of Afro-American works in philosophy. Though not an exhaustive list, it was a definitive attempt at forging a Black philosophical tradition and a documentation of the published philosophical reflections of Black people from the earliest parts of the twentieth century. Other important (although representative) publications in this regard include August Meier's *Negro Thought in America 1880–1915: Racial Ideologies in the Age of Booker T. Washington* (Ann Arbor: University of Michigan Press, 1963); Howard Brotz's edited volume *African-American Social and Political Thought 1850–1920* (London: Routledge, 2017); Dorothy Sterling's edited volume *We Are Your Sisters: Black Women in the Nineteenth Century* (New York: W. W. Norton, 1984).

2. For Jones, what is at stake in delineating the praxis for Black philosophical scholarship has to do with epistemic authority: the authority of Blacks to describe reality as they perceive it. With this understanding at play, "Blacks announce their own inferiority if they do not force the established philosophies to revalidate themselves and reconstruct their normative apparatus in light of the black perspective." See William R. Jones, "The Legitimacy and Necessity of Black Philosophy," 157.

3. Although West claims that his intention was to interrogate the Afro-American past and critically evaluate Afro-American responses to crucial challenges in the present—while attempting to understand the Afro-American experience in order to enhance and enrich the lives of Afro-Americans—he fails to see how his subscription to the Eurocentric or Western philosophical paradigm as the normative or axiomatic principle for achieving his goal is deeply problematic and counterintuitive. See Cornel West, "Philosophy and the Afro-American Experience," 148.

4. William R. Jones, "The Legitimacy and Necessity of Black Philosophy," 157.

5. I use the term "Blackness" in this work in a broad sense of identity-category and the lived experience of African-descended peoples across the globe—in the African *diasporas*. There is a form of power that comes with conceiving of "Blackness" in this fluid sense, which accrues from the richness of the Black experience, not as a monolith but as an ever-evolving axiomatic reference to the experiential world at different stages of earthly metamorphosis. This characterization of Blackness is similar to what Eric Dyson refers to in "Tour(é)ing Blackness" as "the plasticity of Blackness": the way that this notion conforms to such a bewildering array of identities and struggles—and defeats the attempt to bind its meanings to any one camp or creature—makes a lot of Black folks nervous and defensive. In "Forty Million Ways to Be Black," Touré Neblett argues that the concept of Blackness should not to be looked at from a monolithic perspective because such a perspective would not capture the richness of Black identity. In his view, there is no univocal view of authentic Blackness because the possibilities for Black identity are infinite. To say that something or someone is not Black—or is inauthentically Black—is to sell Blackness short. This explains why Michelle M. Wright, upon her critical reading of Paul Gilroy's *The Black Atlantic*, argues that "any truly accurate definition of an African diasporic identity, then, must somehow simultaneously incorporate the diversity of Black identities in the diaspora yet also link all those identities to show that they indeed constitute a diaspora rather than an unconnected aggregate of different peoples linked only by name." See Eric Dyson, "Tour(é)ing Blackness," in *Who's Afraid of Post-Blackness? What It Means to Be Black Now*, ed. Touré Neblett (New York: Free Press, 2011), xi–xviii; Touré Neblett, "Forty Million Ways to Be Black," in *Who's Afraid of Post-Blackness?*, 5; Michelle Wright, *Becoming Black: Creating Identity in the African Diaspora* (Durham: Duke University Press, 2004), 2; Paul Gilroy, *The Black Atlantic: Modernity and Double-Consciousness* (Cambridge, MA: Harvard University Press, 1993); Manning Marable and Vanessa Agard-Jones, eds., *Transnational Blackness: Navigating the Global Color Line* (New York: Macmillan Palgrave, 2008).

6. In current convention, the term "Black" is capitalized when used as a reference for Black people as a racial and ethnic group. However, I have retained references to lowercase "black" in direct quotations in order to retain the voice of the original authors. I have applied this approach where this occurs throughout the text.

7. Vincent Harding, "The Vocation of the Black Scholar and the Struggles of the Black Community," *Harvard Educational Review*. Monograph Series. No. 2 (1974): 14.

8. Barbara Ransby, "Remembering Vincent G. Harding (1931–2014)," *Souls: A Critical Journal of Black Politics, Culture, and Society* 16, nos. 1–2 (2014): 140–142.

9. Some of the original citations in this chapter make use of the term "negro"

as a colloquial reference for Black people. I have retained the original term as used by the authors but provided the more updated reference [Black] in brackets. I have applied this approach where this occurs throughout the book.

10. Harold Cruse, *The Crisis of the Negro Intellectual* (New York: Quill, 1984), 451.

11. Harold Cruse, *The Crisis of the Negro Intellectual*, 451.

12. The essay under this title, "Africana Philosophy," published in *The Journal of Ethics* 1, no. 3 (1997): 265–290, is a substantial revision of "African, African American, Africana Philosophy," published in *Philosophical Forum* 24, nos. 1–3 (Fall–Spring 1992–1993): 63–93. This same essay is also published in revised form in Lucius Outlaw, *On Race and Philosophy* (New York: Routledge, 1996).

13. Lucius Outlaw, "Africana Philosophy," 265.

14. Lucius Outlaw, "Africana Philosophy," 267.

15. Lucius Outlaw, *On Race and Philosophy*.

16. Carter G. Woodson, *The Mis-Education of the Negro* (Washington, DC: Associated Press, 1933), xiii.

17. Ama Mazama, "Introduction: Special Issue of JBS: Celebrating the 30th Anniversary of the First Doctoral Program in Black Studies," *Journal of Black Studies* 49, no. 6 (September 2018): 529.

18. Lewis R. Gordon, "Disciplinary Decadence and the Decolonisation of Knowledge," *Africa Development* 39, no. 1 (2014): 86.

19. Lewis R. Gordon, "Disciplinary Decadence," 86.

20. Lewis R. Gordon, *Bad Faith and Antiblack Racism* (New Jersey: Humanities Press, 1995), 131.

21. Lewis R. Gordon, *Bad Faith and Antiblack Racism*, 135.

22. Lewis R. Gordon, *Bad Faith and Antiblack Racism*, 136.

23. Lewis R. Gordon, *Existentia Africana: Understanding Africana Existential Thought* (New York: Routledge, 2000), 7.

24. Lewis R. Gordon, *Existentia Africana*, 9.

25. Frantz Fanon, *Black Skin, White Masks*, trans. Richard Philcox (New York: Grove Press, 2008), 114.

26. Derek Kelly, "The Logic of Black Philosophy," *Southern Journal of Philosophy* 10 (Spring 1972): 87.

27. Derek Kelly, "The Logic of Black Philosophy," 87.

28. Tommy J. Curry, "The Derelictical Crisis of African American Philosophy: How African American Philosophy Fails to Contribute to the Study of African-Descended People," *Journal of Black Studies* 42, no. 3 (2011): 317.

29. Tommy J. Curry, "The Derelictical Crisis of African American Philosophy," 320.

30. Molefi Kete Asante, "The Relentless Pursuit of Discipline: An Africological March Toward Knowledge Liberation," *Journal of Black Studies* 49, no. 6 (2018): 537.

31. The term "Blackness" is used here to signify its commonsense usage, which denotes people who have been racially positioned as Black and the lifeworlds or lived experiences these people have constructed. For instance, in *The Challenge of Blackness*, Lerone Bennett raises the question: what is the true meaning of Blackness? He goes on to define Blackness as "the universe of values, attitudes, and orientations that rises, like dew, from the depths of Black ancestral experience and pulls us toward distant shores of our Black destiny." In "The Case of Blackness,"

Fred Moten argues for an understanding of Blackness that moves beyond the accentuation of pathology. He considers this a crucial task because, as he sees it, the cultural and political discourse on Black pathology has been so pervasive that it could be said to constitute the background against which all representations of Blacks, Blackness, or the color black take place. Moten further stresses that in grappling with the notion of Blackness, one must recognize that its manifestations have changed over the years, though it has always been poised between the realms of the pseudo-social scientific, the birth of new sciences, and the revolting impulse that is at the heart of the Black radicalism that strains against it. See Fred Moten, "The Case of Blackness," *Criticism* 50, no. 2 (Spring 2008): 177–218. See also Lerone Bennett Jr., *The Challenge of Blackness* (Chicago: Johnson Publishing Company, 1972), 34.

32. Sylvia Wynter, "A Black Studies Manifesto," *Forum N.H.I.: Knowledge for the 21st Century* 1, no. 1 (Fall 1994): 6.

33. Jason R. Ambroise and Sabine Broeck, "Black Knowledges/Black Struggles: An Introduction," in *Black Knowledges/Black Struggles: Essays in Critical Epistemology*, eds. Jason R. Ambroise and Sabine Broeck (Liverpool: Liverpool University Press, 2015), 7.

34. Boaventura de Sousa Santos, *The End of the Cognitive Empire: The Coming of Age of Epistemologies of the South* (Durham: Duke University Press, 2018), 7

35. Miranda Fricker, *Epistemic Injustice: Power and the Ethics of Knowing* (Oxford: Oxford University Press, 2007), vii.

36. Miranda Fricker, *Epistemic Injustice*, 5

37. Miranda Fricker, *Epistemic Injustice*, 25.

38. Under Jim Crow laws and customs, Negros [Blacks] were painfully and constantly made aware that they lived in a society dedicated to the doctrine of white supremacy and to the idea that Negros [Blacks] were less than human. "Jim Crow" became synonymous with a complex system of racial laws and customs that ensured white social, legal, and political domination. Blacks were segregated, deprived of their right to vote, and subjected to abuse, discrimination, and violence without redress in the courts. This period was epitomized by a plethora of "Whites Only" signs on virtually every form of public convenience. This period of legalized Jim Crow in the South, and Jim Crow by custom in the North, lasted from 1877 to 1964, and ended with the passage of the Civil Rights Act of 1964 and the Voting Rights Act of 1965. These two revolutionary congressional bills were the direct result of what has come to be known as the civil rights movement, which began in the 1940s. However, many states made efforts to circumvent or avoid enforcement of these laws. See Cecil J. Hunt II, "The Jim Crow Effect: Denial, Dignity, Human Rights, and Racialized Mass Incarceration," *Journal of Civil Rights and Economic Development* 29, no. 1 (2016): 22.

39. Tommy J. Curry, "This Nigger's Broken: Hyper-Masculinity, the Buck, and the Role of Physical Disability in White Anxiety Toward the Black Male Body," *Journal of Social Philosophy* 48, no. 3 (Fall 2017): 338.

40. What Fricker failed to recognize in her analysis is that the racism and anti-Black misandry at play in this scenario greatly overshadow and undermine any intimations of the agency she wishes to attribute to the Black male figure within a racist society. Anti-Black misandry consists of the projection of negative stereotypes onto Black males that make it difficult or impossible to ascribe the

characteristics or traits of humanity to them. In "Killing Boogeymen," Tommy J. Curry describes anti-Black misandry as "the cumulative assertions of Black male inferiority due to errant psychologies of lack, dispositions of deviance, or hyper-personality traits (e.g., hyper-sexuality, hyper-masculinity) which rationalize the criminalization, phobics and sanctioning of Black male life. These ideas are part of the group-based racial consciousness of white America and part of the social fabric and mythology of racism." In other words, the caricaturized portrayal of Black men that is borne out of hatred for members of this social group is what is referred to as anti-Black or racist misandry. Within the field of Black Male Studies, the concept of anti-Black misandry has generated a considerable amount of discussion. For instance, in his work geared toward the understanding of the Black male experience, Derrick Blooms describes anti-Black racism as encompassing "the ways that Black men are racialized, simultaneously as invisible and hypervisible, and problematized in U.S. society." This perspective is consistent with that of William A. Smith, Jalil Bishop Mustaffa, Chantal M. Jones, Tommy J. Curry, and Walter R. Allen in "'You Make Me Wanna Holler And Throw Up Both My Hands!'" where they describe anti-Black misandry as "an exaggerated pathological aversion toward Black boys and men created and strengthened in societal, institutional, and individual ideologies, practices," and behaviors that are mostly driven by different manifestations of hatred of Black men. This form of hatred functions on the dual axes of race and sex/gender. In "Racial Battle Fatigue and the MisEducation of Black Men: Racial Microaggressions, Societal Problems, and Environmental Stress," William A. Smith, Man Hung, and Jeremy D. Franklin argue that what is identified as anti-Black misandry includes the gendered and racialized forms of discrimination that Black men experience, such that they are deemed hypersexual beasts requiring the most brutal forms of societal control while being simultaneously seen as an inferior member of a "non-human" race. This is why William A. Smith, Tara J. Yosso, and Daniel G. Solórzano, in "Racial Primes and Black Misandry on Historically White Campuses," assert that the intersecting identities of Black men are a double burden due to race (i.e., anti-Black racism) and gender (i.e., Black misandry or anti-Black male attitudes and oppression). In this instance, the anti-Black misandric treatment of members of this group requires that Black men carry the burden of two negative social identities as they move through society, one as a member of the African American race (i.e., anti-Black racism and stereotypes) and the other as a Black male (i.e., Black misandry or anti-Black male ideologies, stereotypes, and oppression), with hyper-masculine and oversexed features that make it impossible for society to see them as something nonviolent, nonthreatening, and above all, *human*. See Derrick R. Brooms, *Being Black, Being Male on Campus: Understanding and Confronting Black Male Collegiate Experiences* (New York: SUNY Press, 2017), 19; William A. Smith, Man Hung, and Jeremy D. Franklin, "Racial Battle Fatigue and the MisEducation of Black Men: Racial Microaggressions, Societal Problems, and Environmental Stress," *The Journal of Negro Education* 80, no. 1 (Winter 2011): 66; William A. Smith, Tara J. Yosso, and Daniel G. Solórzano, "Racial Primes and Black Misandry on Historically White Campuses: Toward Critical Race Accountability in Educational Administration," *Educational Administration Quarterly* 43, no. 5 (December 2007): 559; William A. Smith, Jalil Bishop Mustaffa, Chantal M. Jones, Tommy J. Curry, and Walter R. Allen, "'You Make Me Wanna Holler and Throw Up Both My Hands!': Campus Culture, Black

Misandric Microaggressions, and Racial Battle Fatigue," *International Journal of Qualitative Studies in Education* 29, no. 9 (2016): 1189–1209; Tommy J. Curry, "Killing Boogeymen: Phallicism and the Misandric Mischaracterizations of Black Males in Theory," *Res Philosophica* 95, no. 2 (April 2018): 235–272; William A. Smith, "Toward an Understanding of Black Misandric Microaggressions and Racial Battle Fatigue in Historically White Institutions," in *The State of the African American Male in Michigan: A Courageous Conversation*, eds. Eboni M. Zamani-Gallaher and Vernon C. Polite (East Lansing: Michigan State University Press, 2012), 265–277.

41. José Medina, "Toward a Foucaultian Epistemology of Resistance: Counter-Memory, Epistemic Friction, and Guerrilla Pluralism," *Foucault Studies*, no. 12 (October 2011): 32.

42. See Stephen C. Ferguson II, Chapter 5: "What's Epistemology Got to Do with It?: The 'Death of Epistemology' in African American Studies," in *Philosophy of African American Studies: Nothing Left of Blackness* (New York: Palgrave Macmillan, 2015), 159–192.

43. Stephen C. Ferguson II, *Philosophy of African American Studies*, 192.

44. Stephen C. Ferguson II, *Philosophy of African American Studies*, 166.

45. Joe R. Feagin, *Racist America: Roots, Current Realities, and Future Reparations,* 3rd ed. (New York: Routledge, 2014), xiii.

46. See, for instance, Keisha N. Blain, Christopher Cameron, and Ashley D. Farmer, "The Contours of Black Intellectual History," in *New Perspectives on the Black Intellectual Tradition,* eds. Keisha N. Blain, Christopher Cameron, and Ashley D. Farmer (Illinois: Northwestern University Press, 2018), 3–16.

47. José Medina, *The Epistemology of Resistance: Gender and Racial Oppression, Epistemic Injustice, and Resistant Imaginations* (Oxford: Oxford University Press, 2017), 16–17.

CHAPTER 2

1. This hegemonic posture of Western philosophical praxis that seeks to universalize subjective knowledge claims has been described by Michael A. Peters and Carl Mika as "the blindness of Western philosophy." This blindness consists of the uncritical knowledge attribution that conveys the idea that philosophical thinking, within the Western tradition, is a neutral entity, which is actually not the case. In "Through the Crucible of Pain and Suffering," George Yancy describes this blindness as evidence of the narcissism of Western philosophy, which is heralded by the specter of racism as well as the unacknowledged limits of white forms of knowing. In this regard, Yancy argues that the characterization of whiteness as the transcendental norm is productive of a form of ignorance endemic to Western philosophical practices that are myopic and hegemonic. This is why he believes that an alternate philosophical paradigm such as African American philosophy should be seen as a gift, as a critical counter-narrative that can be deployed to fissure Western philosophy's narcissism. In a similar vein, Francis A. Akena, in "Critical Analysis of the Production of Western Knowledge," argues that Western philosophy's attempt to universalize its epistemic principles, and its perspective on issues and relation of ideas, is a vehicle for achieving the colonization of knowledge within non-Eurocentric societies. He especially notes that "European colonizers have defined legitimate

knowledge as Western knowledge, fundamentally European colonizers' ways of knowing. [It is] often taken as objective and universal knowledge. Arriving with the colonizers and influenced by Western ethnocentrism, Western knowledge imposed a monolithic worldview that [put] power and control in the hands of Europeans. It delegitimized other ways of knowing as savage, superstitious, and primitive." Meanwhile, in *The Invention of Women*, Oyèrónké Oyewùmí exposes how knowledge schemes developed within the Western cultural praxis are limited in their assumption of universalism formed from a particularist epistemological prism; the significance of this observation is that one cannot assume the social and epistemological organization of one culture (the dominant West included) to be universal, or the interpretations of the experiences of one culture to explain another one. See Cecil Foster, *Blackness and Modernity: The Colour of Humanity and the Quest for Freedom* (London: McGill-Queen's University Press, 2007), 123; see also Michael A. Peters and Carl Mika, eds., *The Dilemma of Western Philosophy* (New York: Routledge, 2018), 2; George Yancy, "Through the Crucible of Pain and Suffering: African-American Philosophy as a Gift and the Countering of the Western Philosophical Metanarrative," in *The Dilemma of Western Philosophy*, eds. Michael A. Peters and Carl Mika (New York: Routledge, 2018), 19; Oyèrónké Oyewùmí, *The Invention of Women: Making an African Sense of Western Gender Discourses* (Minneapolis: University of Minnesota Press, 1997), 10; Francis A. Akena, "Critical Analysis of the Production of Western Knowledge and Its Implications for Indigenous Knowledge and Decolonization," *Journal of Black Studies* 43, no. 6 (2012): 600.

2. Tendayi Sithole, "The Concept of the Black Subject in Fanon," *Journal of Black Studies* 47, no. 1 (2016): 35.

3. Cecil Foster, *Blackness and Modernity*, 125.

4. Emmanuel Eze, *On Reason: Rationality in a World of Cultural Conflict and Racism* (Durham: Duke University Press, 2008), 171.

5. Calvin Warren, "Black Nihilism and the Politics of Hope," *The New Centennial Review* 15, no. 1 (Spring 2015): 241.

6. George Yancy, *Black Bodies, White Gazes: The Continuing Significance of Race in America* (New York: Rowman & Littlefield, 2017), xxx (emphasis mine).

7. W.E.B. Du Bois, *The World and Africa and Color and Democracy (The Oxford W. E. B. Du Bois)*, ed. Henry Louis Gates Jr. (New York: Oxford University Press, 2007), 1.

8. W.E.B. Du Bois, *The World and Africa* , xxxi.

9. Robert Dunn, "Some Observations on the Psychological Differences which Exist among the Typical Races of Man," *Transactions of the Ethnological Society of London* 3 (1865): 21.

10. Melissa Stein, *Measuring Manhood: Race and the Science of Masculinity, 1830–1934* (Minneapolis: University of Minnesota Press, 2015), 45.

11. Melissa Stein, *Measuring Manhood*, 48.

12. The classification of human groups (Caucasians and the colored races) into varieties, or races, was attempted by eighteenth- and early nineteenth-century naturalists, but they were unable to formulate a common index to distinguish one race from another. "To visually identify differences was one thing, but to determine a method for measurement and an index for tracing affinities among the various races was a far more vexatious undertaking." For the nineteenth-century anthropologist, anthropometry, or anatomical measurement, became a

focal point (hence the birth of craniology and craniometrics during this period). See John S. Haller Jr., *Outcasts from Evolution: Scientific Attitudes of Racial Inferiority, 1859–1900* (Carbondale: Southern Illinois University Press, 1971), 3, 96.

13. Buckner H. Payne (Ariel), *The Negro: What is His Ethnological Status?* (Cincinnati: Published for the Proprietor, 1867), 4.

14. Although Ariel sets out to disprove the prevalent myths among the white racial intelligentsia concerning the descendance of Black folks from Ham. As he argues in *The Negro: What is His Ethnological Status*, "We have shown (1.) that Ham was not made a negro, neither by his name, nor the curse (or the supposed curse) of his father Noah. (2.) We have shown that the people of India, China, Turkey, Egypt (Copts), now have long, straight hair, high foreheads, high noses and every lineament of the white race; [biological markers of a superior race] and that these are the descendants of Ham. (3.) That, therefore, it is impossible that Ham could be the father of the present race of Negroes." This overemphasis on biological/physiological markers of the human will be used to construct the image of the savage in sociological studies of indigenous or ethnic populations during this period. A case in point is the work by James Greenwood, *Curiosities of Savage Life*, which argues that as a rule, the skull of the Negro [Blacks] is remarkably long; it rarely approaches the broad type, and never exhibits the roundness of other races—the distinguishing features of a savage race which makes it incapable of achieving any form of civilization. Greenwood goes further to argue that "in no stage of his existence does the savage appear so as entirely to please us, his civilized brethren. I don't know that this was ever observed to have a depressing effect on the savage mind, nor, in my humble opinion, should it do so. Whatever our notions may be to the contrary, the savage never yet had reason to regard civilization as a particularly lovely thing." See Buckner H. Payne (Ariel), *The Negro*, 6, 45; James Greenwood, *Curiosities of Savage Life* (London: S. O. Beeton, 1863), 6.

15. Buckner H. Payne (Ariel), *The Negro*, 25.

16. Samuel George Morton, *Types of Mankind: or, Ethnological Researches, Based Upon the Ancient Monuments, Paintings, Sculptures, and Crania of Races, and Upon their Natural, Geographical, Philological, and Biblical History*, 7th ed. (Philadelphia: Lippincott, Grambo & Co., 1855), xxx.

17. Samuel George Morton, *Types of Mankind*, xxxiii.

18. In his discussion of the relation between biological classification of humans and race, Chamberlain draws from August Forel, a well-known psychiatrist at that time, whom he quotes thus: "Even for their own good the blacks must be treated for what they are, an absolutely subordinate, inferior, lower type of men, incapable themselves of culture." See Houston Stewart Chamberlain, *The Foundations of the Nineteenth Century*, vol. 1 (London: John Lane Company, 1911), 289–290.

19. Stephen Jay Gould, *The Mismeasure of Man* (New York: W. W. Norton & Company, 1996), 142.

20. Peter K. J. Park, *Africa, Asia, and the History of Philosophy: Racism in the Formation of the Philosophical Canon, 1780–1830* (Albany: State University of New York Press, 2013), xii.

21. John S. Haller Jr., *Outcasts from Evolution*, 26.

22. David Hume, *Essays and Treatises on Several Subjects* (London, 1758); quoted in Aaron Garrett, "Hume's Revised Racism Revisited," *Hume Studies* 26, no. 1 (April 2000): 171–172.

23. John S. Haller Jr., *Outcasts from Evolution*, 27.

24. John S. Haller Jr., *Outcasts from Evolution*, 27.

25. According to John Graham, "when Johann Caspar Lavater died in 1801, a leading British periodical, *The Scots* Magazine (LXIII, 79) quite rightly acknowledged that he had been for many years, one of the most famous men in Europe. Part of his fame rested on his capable and conscientious performance of duties as a pastor and a religious writer, roles which made him loved and respected by his fellow citizens of Zurich, who literally flocked about him in the streets. But his fame was based more firmly, albeit more questionably, on his *Essays on Physiognomy*." See John Graham, "Lavater's Physiognomy: A Checklist," *The Papers of the Bibliographical Society of America* 55, no. 4 (Fourth Quarter, 1961): 297.

26. J. C. Lavater, *Physiognomy, or the Corresponding Analogy Between the Conformation of the Features and the Ruling Passions of the Mind: Being a Complete Epitome of the Original Work of J.C. Lavater* (London: William Tegg, 1866), 96.

27. Some scholars like Tayyab Mahmud believe that the Enlightenment period was essentially bad for people of color because "the Enlightenment and liberalism on the one hand, and slavery and colonialism on the other, hegemonic forces in Europe fashioned strategies of exclusion, grounded in a racial dichotomy between human and sub-human, or civilized and savage." See Tayyab Mahmud, "Colonialism and Modern Constructions of Race: A Preliminary Inquiry," *University of Miami Law Review* 53, no. 1219 (1999): 1221.

28. See Immanuel Kant and Friedrich Christian Starke, *Menschenkunde: oder Philosophische Anthropologie (1831)* (Whitefish, MT: Kessinger Publishing, 2010) (emphasis added).

29. Joe L. Kincheloe, "The Struggle to Define and Reinvent Whiteness: A Pedagogical Analysis," *College Literature* 26, no. 3 (1999): 164.

30. Joe L. Kincheloe, "The Struggle to Define and Reinvent Whiteness," 164.

31. Joseph Agnew, "Know-Where: Geographies of Knowledge of World Politics," *International Political Sociology* 1, no. 2 (2007): 141.

32. Lindon Barrett, *Racial Blackness and the Discontinuity of Western Modernity* (Chicago: University of Illinois Press, 2014), 4. See also Sylvia Wynter, "Unsettling the Coloniality of Being/Power/Truth/Freedom: Towards the Human, After Man, Its Overrepresentation—An Argument," *CR: The New Centennial Review* 3, no. 3 (Fall 2003): 257–337; and Nelson Maldonado-Torres, "On the Coloniality of Being: Contributions to the Development of a Concept," *Cultural Studies* 21, nos. 2–3 (2007): 240–270.

33. René Descartes, *Key Philosophical Writings,* trans. Elizabeth S. Haldane (Hertfordshire: Wordsworth Editions Limited, 1997), 280.

34. Mack C. Jones also stressed the important point that those who construct knowledge for control often fail to appreciate the fact that knowledge that serves the interest of one cannot serve the interest of another. See Mack C. Jones, *Knowledge, Power and Black Politics: Collected Essays* (New York: SUNY Press, 2014), 45.

35. Tommy J. Curry elaborated more on this: in his view, "when Black thinkers are not seen as the primary theoreticians of their own thought, they become the

unnamed casualties of disciplinary warfare—martyrs in the battles to maintain (white) philosophical legitimacy." See Tommy J. Curry, "On Derelict and Method: The Methodological Crisis of African-American Philosophy's Study of African-Descended Peoples under an Integrationist Milieu," *Radical Philosophy Review* 14, no. 2 (2011): 150.

CHAPTER 3

1. See Thomas Carlyle, *Occasional Discourse on the Nigger Question* (London: Thomas Bosworth, 1853), 44; Archibald Alison, *History of Europe from the Commencement of the French Revolution in 1789 to the Restoration of the Bourbons in 1815* (Paris: Baudry's European Library, 1842), 275.

2. William D. P. Bliss, ed., *The Encyclopedia of Social Reform* (New York: Funk and Wagnalls, 1897), 928.

3. Although, the critiques of feminist epistemology were not yet developed during the period of Wheatley's life, I believe that her experience and treatment by the white power structure, in terms of her status as a knower, fits into what has been described in contemporary Black feminist scholarship as the subjugation of the knowledge of the Black female within a context where knowledge acquisition and understanding are deeply impacted by social structures such as race, class and gender. Subjugated knowledge includes understandings of knowledge or creative ideas that are produced by the Black female subject and obscured by hegemonic theories, perspectives, and practices. Black female intellectuals such Angela Davis and Patricia Hill Collins have used terms like "controlling images" to describe the stereotypes used to subordinate African American women not only in the discourse of knowledge but also in society. In "The Colonial Roots of the Racial Fetishization of Black Women," Caren Holmes discusses how colonizers in America perceived Black men and women as subhuman byproducts of manifest destiny. This perception informed how slaves were stripped of their agency and desire; they were dehumanized, morally, physically, intellectually, and sexually. In this context, Black slaves were sexualized as animals through the institutionalized system of chattel slavery. Black slave women considered most capable of producing children were commonly referred to as "breeders" and were bought and sold based on their reproductive efficiency. There were no remote considerations for them as intellectually gifted humans. See Caren Holmes, "The Colonial Roots of the Racial Fetishization of Black Women," *Black & Gold* 2, no. 2 (2016): 3. See also Carolyn Martin Shaw, "Disciplining the Black Female Body: Learning Feminism in Africa and the United States," in *Black Feminist Anthropology: Theory, Politics, Praxis, and Poetics*, ed. Irma McClaurin (New Brunswick, NJ: Rutgers University Press, 2001); Diann H. Painter, "The Black Woman in American Society," *Current History* 70, no. 416 (May 1976): 224; Patricia Hill Collins, *Black Feminist Thought: Knowledge, Consciousness, and the Politics of Empowerment* (New York: Routledge, 1991); Patricia Hill Collins, *Fighting Words: Black Women and the Search for Justice* (Minneapolis: University of Minnesota Press, 1998); Angela Davis, *Women, Race, and Class* (New York: Vintage Books, 1981); Rupe Simms, "Controlling Images and the Gender Construction of Enslaved African Women," *Gender and Society* 15, no. 6 (December 2001): 879–897.

4. William H. Robinson, *Phillis Wheatley and Her Writings* (New York: Garland Publishing, 1984), 10.

5. Jemima Pierre, "Slavery, Anthropological Knowledge, and the Racialization of Africans," *Current Anthropology* 61, no. 22 (2020): 220. doi:10.1086/709844.

6. G. Herbert Renfro, *Life and Works of Phillis Wheatley: Containing her Complete Poetical Works, Numerous letters, and a Complete Biography of this Famous Poet of a Century and a Half Ago* (Washington, DC: Robert L. Pendleton, 1916), 11.

7. In "Our Phillis, Ourselves," Joanna Brooks argues that the examination of Phillis Wheatley by the Boston intelligentsia was a landmark event not only for her but also for all Black people because it fundamentally challenged the myth of the inferiority of the Black race that was prevalent during this period. She describes the examination scene as compelling—the scenario of the Black poet and her white judges—a powerful image that encapsulates the Enlightenment-era controversies over the intellectual capacity of Black people. See Joanna Brooks, "Our Phillis, Ourselves," *American Literature* 82, no. 1 (2010): 1–28.

8. Henry Louis Gates Jr., *The Trials of Phillis Wheatley: America's First Black Poet and her Encounters with the Founding Fathers* (New York: Basic Civitas Books, 2003), 5.

9. Henry Louis Gates Jr., *The Trials of Phillis Wheatley*, 26–27.

10. Henry Louis Gates Jr., *The Trials of Phillis Wheatley*, 44.

11. Thomas Jefferson, *Notes on the State of Virginia, Written in the Year 1781* (Paris: Publisher not identified, 1782), 255.

12. Thomas Jefferson, *Notes on the State of Virginia*, 257.

13. This is quoted in Chas. Fred Heartman, ed., *Phillis Wheatley: Poems and Letters* (Miami: Mnemosyne Publishing, 1969), 269.

14. Phillis Wheatley, *Poems on Various Subjects, Religious and Moral* (Denver: W. H. Lawrence & Co., 1887), 9.

15. John C. Shields, *The Collected Works of Phillis Wheatley* (New York: Oxford University Press, 1988), ix–x.

16. John C. Shields, *The Collected Works of Phillis Wheatley*, 238.

17. Babacar M'Baye, "The Pan-African and Puritan Dimensions of Phillis Wheatley's Poems and Letters," in *New Essays on Phillis Wheatley*, eds. John C. Shields and Eric D. Lamore (Knoxville: University of Tennessee Press, 2011), 272–274.

18. Phillis Wheatley, *Poems on Various Subjects*, 13.

19. As quoted in Phillis Wheatley, *Phillis Wheatley: Complete Writings*, ed. Vincent Carretta (New York: Penguin Books, 2001), 7.

20. William H. Robinson, *Phillis Wheatley and Her Writings* (New York: Garland Publishing, 1984), 48.

21. Julian D. Mason Jr., ed., *The Poems of Phillis Wheatley* (Chapel Hill: University of North Carolina Press, 1966), xxxvii.

22. Julian D. Mason Jr., *The Poems of Phillis Wheatley*, xxxvi

23. Phillis Wheatley, *Phillis Wheatley: Complete Writings*, 159.

24. Phillis Wheatley, "Letter to Reverend Samson Occum," *The Connecticut Gazette*, March 11, 1774. Published in Bob Blaisdell, ed., *Female Abolitionists* (New York: Dover Publications, 2021), 1.

25. Phillis Wheatley, "Letter to Occum," 1.

26. Phillis Wheatley, "Letter to Occum," 1.

27. Phillis Wheatley, "Letter to Occum," 1.

28. Phillis Wheatley, *Phillis Wheatley: Complete Writings*, 93.

29. Phillis Wheatley, *Poems on Various Subjects,* 104.

30. Some scholars have provided additional commentary on the identity of S. M. the Young African Painter as referred to in Wheatley's Poems on Various Subjects. He has been described as Scipio Moorhead, the artist who drew the engraving of Wheatley that was printed on her volume of poetry in 1773. He was believed to be an enslaved young man of African descent who lived near the author in Boston during that period. See Elliot C. Mason, "Phillis Wheatley Peters' Fugitive Poetics of Freedom," *Textual Practice* (2022): 9; Eleanor Smith, "Phillis Wheatley: A Black Perspective," *Journal of Negro Education* 43, no. 3 (1974): 401–407. doi:10.1080/0950236X.2022.2150289.

31. Phillis Wheatley, *Poems on Various Subjects,* 104.

32. Charmaine A. Nelson, *The Color of Stone: Sculpting the Black Female Subject in Nineteenth-Century America* (Minneapolis: University of Minnesota Press, 2007), 116.

33. Phillis Wheatley, *Poems on Various Subjects,* 14.

34. David Waldstreicher, *The Odyssey of Phillis Wheatley: A Poet's Journeys through American Slavery and Independence* (New York: Farrar, Straus and Giroux, 2023), 38.

35. David Waldstreicher, *The Odyssey of Phillis Wheatley,* 38–39.

36. Phillis Wheatley, *Poems on Various Subjects,* 14.

37. Chas. Fred Heartman, ed., *Phillis Wheatley,* 33.

CHAPTER 4

1. Frederick Douglass, *Life and Times of Frederick Douglass Written by Himself: His Early Life as a Slave, His Escape from Bondage and his Complete History to the Present Time* (Boston: Park Publishing Co., 1881).

2. It should be noted that Broadus N. Butler's essay, "Frederick Douglass: The Black Philosopher in the United States: A Commentary," published in 1983, constitutes a landmark in the consideration of Douglass's thoughts in the philosophical arena as they address conceptual and analytical questions from a humancentric perspective. In his essay, Butler describes Douglass's philosophy as a humanistic philosophy to be distinguished from any form of systematic thought, given that "whether Douglass [was] consciously engaged in formal philosophy or making philosophical expression through poetry, speech, or literature, his Black American cosmological, metaphysical, epistemological, [and] ethical conceptions and modalities tend, in the final analysis, to be humanicentric [sic] as distinguished from system-centric thought." The thrust of this chapter goes a step further than what Butler endeavored to achieve in his essay. Here, an attempt is made to consider the significance of Black self-knowledge as a social epistemological category in the thoughts of Frederick Douglass, especially considering the legacy of Douglass's struggle to free himself from the debilitating conditions of slavery through the display of tactfulness, sage wisdom, guile, intelligence, and self-knowledge, which speaks to the importance of subjective principles of self-transformation in a social epistemic context. See Broadus N. Butler, "Frederick Douglass: The Black Philosopher in the United States: A Commentary," in *Philosophy Born of Struggle: Anthology of Afro-American Philosophy from 1917,* ed. Leonard Harris (Dubuque: Kendall/Hunt Publishing, 183), 6.

3. The term "career" was used by Frederick Douglass to refer to the period when he was held in the bondage of American slavery. It does not precisely equate to the contemporary understanding of a profession in which one receives a formalized training.

4. Ivy G. Wilson, "On Native Ground: Transnationalism, Frederick Douglass, and 'The Heroic Slave,'" *PMLA* 121, no. 2 (March 2006): 454.

5. Frederick Douglass would later criticize the American School of Ethnology on this point for attempting to deny the Black body of any ontological and transcendental meaning. However, In Douglass's reading of the American School of Ethnology, the black body c. 1855 has not been emptied of transcendental meanings; rather, it is supercharged with them. In other words, the monogenist account of human origins that had served the abolitionist cause so well, Douglass recognizes, is propped up only by the weakening fiat of a literalist biblical history, and science, in his estimation, has not yet delved systematically enough either to affirm or deny the monogenist account—which makes Douglass's critique of the American School of Ethnology simultaneously more confident and more anxious. Douglass thus seems to understand the context that his text addresses as something of a vacuum of epistemic authority in which objective truth cannot find a place to hang its hat, which creates a certain rhetorical situation, indeed, a situation in which the rhetoricity of all knowledge-claims is somewhat uncomfortably exposed. In "The Claims of the Negro Ethnologically Considered," Douglass ridicules the logic of American ethnologists ("the scholars of America") as lacking in common sense. He arrives at this conclusion through the following line of reasoning: "Man is distinguished from all other animals, by the possession of certain definite faculties and powers, as well as by physical organization and proportions. He is the only two-handed animal on the earth—the only one that laughs, and nearly the only one that weeps. Men instinctively distinguish between men and brutes. Common sense itself is scarcely needed to detect the absence of manhood in a monkey, or to recognize its presence in a Negro." This implies that the colonial system of oppression and dehumanization, in this this period, thrived on a mischaracterization of the Black subject, and Douglass was adamant in his attempt to challenge such ethnological assumptions. He goes further to argue in this essay that having been "tried by all the usual, and all the unusual tests, whether mental, moral, physical, or psychological, the Negro is a Man—considering him as possessing knowledge, or needing knowledge, his elevation or his degradation, his virtues, or his vices—whichever road you take, you reach the same conclusion, the Negro is a Man." See Frederick Douglass, "The Claims of the Negro Ethnologically Considered," in *Frederick Douglass: Selected Speeches and Writings*, ed. Philip S. Foner (Chicago: Lawrence Hill Books, 1999), 284. See also Jared Hickman, "Douglass Unbound," *Nineteenth-Century Literature* 68, no. 3 (December 2013): 327–333.

6. Frederick Douglass, *Narrative of the Life of Frederick Douglass, an American Slave* (New York: Penguin Books, 2014), 48. First published by The Anti-Slavery Office, Boston, 1845.

7. Frederick Douglass, "An Address to the Colored People of the United States," in *Frederick Douglass: Selected Speeches and Writings*, 119.

8. Frederick Douglass would go on to claim that America has no choice but to accept and welcome the genius of Black folks as well as their scholarship projected into the world through their newfound or re-acquired self-reflectivity. As

he logically affirms, "If the American people could endure the negro's presence while a slave, they certainly can and ought to endure his presence as a free-man. If they could tolerate him when he was a heathen, they might bear with him when he is Christian, a gentleman and a scholar." See Frederick Douglass, "Lessons of the Hour: An Address Delivered in Washington D.C., on 9 January, 1894," in *The Frederick Douglass Papers: Series One; Speeches, Debates, and Interviews, Volume 5, 1881–95*, eds. John W. Blassingame and John R. McKivigan (New Haven: Yale University Press, 1992), 599.

9. Frederick Douglass, "The Claims of the Negro Ethnologically Considered," in *Frederick Douglass: Selected Speeches and Writings*, 284.

10. Douglass locates his earlier intimations of freedom in his acquisition of reading skills and in the act of reading itself, in particular his reading of a volume titled *The Columbian Orator*. Compiled by Caleb Bingham and published in 1797, *The Columbian Orator* contained a variety of pieces designed to instruct in the ornamental and useful art of eloquence. See Shelley F. Fisher and Carla L. Peterson, "'We Hold these Truths to be Self-Evident': The Rhetoric of Frederick Douglass's Journalism," in *Frederick Douglass: New Literary and Historical Essays*, ed. Eric Sundquist (Cambridge: Cambridge University Press, 1990), 190.

11. Frederick Douglass, *My Bondage and My Freedom*, 1st ed. (Miller, Orton & Mulligan, 1885; New York: Barnes & Noble Books, 2005), 125.

12. David W. Blight, *Frederick Douglass: Prophet of Freedom* (New York: Simon & Schuster, 2018), 45.

13. Frederick Douglass, "Letter to Thomas Auld," *The Liberator*, September 22, 1848, in *Frederick Douglass: Selected Speeches and Writings*, 115.

14. Frederick Douglass, *My Bondage and My Freedom*, 42. See also Frederick Douglass, "The Claims of the Negro Ethnologically Considered."

15. This notion of "epistemology of ignorance" is substantively different from how Charles W. Mills uses the term in his essay on "White Ignorance." In his essay, Mills utilized this concept to refer to the articulation of cognitive norms from an individualistic-epistemological standpoint, such that the dynamic of what is considered as a particularly pervasive form of ignorance, what could be called white ignorance, could be linked to white supremacy. As he puts it, "the phrase 'white ignorance' implies the possibility of a contrasting 'knowledge,' a contrast that would be lost if all claims to truth were equally spurious, or just a matter of competing discourses." Thus, in the way Mill conceives of this concept, the distinction between the domain of knowledge and ignorance consists of the bifurcation between what is known as such and what is not. However, my usage of the term does not merely refer to what is known or unknown; rather, it refers to the false categories of knowledge and being/unbeing that are forcefully systematized as a form of social epistemology and power to undermine the condition and lives of Black folks, especially in antebellum America. Whereas Mills argues that "mapping an epistemology of ignorance is for [him] a preliminary to reformulating an epistemology that will give us genuine knowledge," I argue that the mapping of such an epistemology of ignorance clearly depicts the weaponization of ignorance—a violently imposed system of unknowing on Black slaves (within the context of nineteenth-century America) in order to make them subservient in all existential considerations. Thus, the "success" of the American slave system was largely dependent on keeping Black slaves ignorant through extremely forceful and legal means (especially antiliteracy laws

codified in the slave codes). In *Self-Taught: African American Education in Slavery and Freedom*, Heather A. Williams, points out that "placing antiliteracy laws in dialogue with the words of enslaved people enables an examination of the tensions that slave literacy provoked between owned and owner. Masters made every attempt to control their captives' thoughts and imaginations, indeed their hearts and minds." Williams asserts further that "maintaining a system of bondage in the Age of Enlightenment depended upon the master's being able to speak for the slave, to deny his or her humanity, and to draw a line between slave consciousness and human will. The presence of literate slaves threatened to give lie to the entire system. Reading indicated to the world that this so-called property had a mind, and writing foretold the ability to construct an alternative narrative about bondage itself. Literacy among slaves would expose slavery, and masters knew it." This was why the white slave owners implemented severe forms of punishment including death to any Black slave who dared to transgress the boundaries of unknowledge or the domain of ignorance which are regarded as part of the natural state for the slave. Yet, Mills argues in "White Ignorance" that "white ignorance need not always be based on bad faith" because "you can have white racism, in particular white cognizers, in the sense of the existence of prejudicial beliefs about people of color without (at the same time and place) white domination of those people of color having been established; and you can also have white domination of people of color at a particular time and place without all white cognizers at that time and place being racist." Mills believes that what he refers to as "racialized causality" can give rise to two dimensions of white ignorance: first, for a straightforward racist cognizer, and second "for a nonracist cognizer who may indirectly form mistaken beliefs (e.g., that after the abolition of slavery in the United States, blacks generally had opportunities equal to whites) because of the social suppression of pertinent knowledge, though without prejudice himself." This view does not correspond with the ethnological assumptions and hypothesis customarily held by white America in the nineteenth century about Blacks, specifically Black slaves, as biologically inferior and undeserving of equal opportunities with whites. The ethnological assumptions about Blacks during this period do not allow for this individualistic-communalistic bifurcation that Mills points to in his discussion of racialized causality in relation to the prevalence of white racism and epistemology of ignorance (especially when detailing the racist-on-nonracist epistemic ascriptions of what he regards as "white ignorance"). Mills also seems to equate white disillusionment with white ignorance, although he considers this a case of epistemic failure or a flaw, rather than as evidence of white power/privilege at work. However, with respect to my usage of the term "epistemology of ignorance," this idea of "mistaken belief," which Mills wants to classify as an example of epistemic failure or cognitive deficiency, means something entirely different. It would reinforce white power to remake reality (calling things that are not, as though they were), including relegating (through the sheer power of white imagination) Black beings to an unnatural state of slavery (and its enforced domain of ignorance) while falsely (or "mistakenly") describing it as the natural state, the natural condition of all Blacks. It is also important to note that the view of race/racism as a fungible trait of whiteness that Mills promotes in "White Ignorance" is quite different from the view he holds in an earlier essay, "Revisionist Ontologies: Theorizing White Supremacy." In that essay, Mills considers race/racism as a product of an enclosed political system that should be treated "as a particular mode of domination, with its special norms for allocating benefits and burdens, rights and duties, its own ideology, and an internal logic at least semi-autonomous, influencing law, culture, and consciousness." On this account, whiteness or the violence of white racism cannot be excused as a form of mistakenly held systems of beliefs or practices that brutally dehumanize an entire otherized race—the Black race, especially when it is noted that the enforcement of the American slave codes and other legal codes upholding and defending the institution of slavery was contingent on the belief that the "state of ignorance" was natural state or condition of the Black slave. However, despite laws and customs in American slave states prohibiting enslaved Black people from learning to read and write, a small percentage managed, through ingenuity and will, to acquire a degree of literacy in the antebellum period. In "'We Slipped and Learned to Read:' Slave Accounts of the Literacy Process, 1830–1865," Janet Cornelius argues that the fact that Black slaves were able to achieve literacy even in a context where "ignorance" was weaponized against them represents the hallmark of Black genius and evidence of the capacity to reclaim their Black agency and personhood that are totally denied under the American institution of slavery. See Charles W. Mills, "White Ignorance," in *Race and Epistemologies of Ignorance*, eds. Shannon Sullivan and Nancy Tuana (New York: SUNY Press, 2007): 13–38; Charles W. Mills, "Revisionist Ontologies: Theorizing White Supremacy," *Social and Economic Studies* 43, no. 3 (September 1994): 108; Heather A. Williams, *Self-Taught: African American Education in Slavery and Freedom* (Chapel Hill: The University of North Carolina Press, 2005): 17; Janet Cornelius, "'We Slipped and Learned to Read': Slave Accounts of the Literacy Process, 1830–1865," *Phylon* 44, no. 3 (1983): 171–186.

16. William Goodell, *The American Slave Code* (New York: Arno Press, 1969), 251.

17. William Goodell, *The American Slave Code*, 252.

18. William Goodell, *The American Slave Code*, 251.

19. William H. McClendon, "The Black Perspective of Frederick Douglass," *The Black Scholar* 3, nos. 7–8 (1972): 8.

20. Frederick Douglass, *Narrative*, 92.

21. Frederick Douglass, *Narrative*, 80.

22. Frederick Douglass, *My Bondage and My Freedom*, 305.

23. Frederick Douglass, *My Bondage and My Freedom*, 73.

24. Frederick Douglass, *My Bondage and My Freedom*, 117.

25. Frederick Douglass, *My Bondage and My Freedom*, 117.

26. Frederick Douglass, *Narrative*, 42 (italics were in the original but the emphasis here is mine).

27. Frederick Douglass, *Narrative*, 42.

28. Angela Davis, *Lectures on Liberation* (Los Angeles, CA: National United Committee to Free Angela Davis, 1971), 1.

29. Frederick Douglass, *My Bondage and My Freedom*, 118.

30. Frederick Douglass, *My Bondage and My Freedom*, 118.

31. David W. Blight, *Frederick Douglass: Prophet of Freedom*, 40.

32. Frederick Douglass, *Narrative*, 73.

33. It is important to note that Douglass's usage of the term "man" in talking about the "self-made man" is not intended to be sexist. He was using the term in

a generic sense to conform with nineteenth century-etiquette in writing, whereby the term "man" was often used for the designation of the human species. See Harrison Allen, *A System of Human Anatomy, Including Its Medical and Surgical Relations* (Philadelphia: Henry C. Lea's Son & Co., 1884); Arthur De Gobineau, *The Inequality of Human Races* (New York: G. P. Putnam's Sons, 1915); W. H. Fowler, "Lectures on Anthropology," *Nature* 50, no. 1294 (August 16, 1894): 387–396.

34. Frederick Douglass, "'Self-Made Men,' An Address Delivered in Carlisle, Pennsylvania, March 1893," in George Barr, et al., *The Speeches of Frederick Douglass: A Critical Edition* (New Haven: Yale University Press, 2018), 420.

35. Waldo E. Martin, "Images of Frederick Douglass in the Afro-American Mind: The Recent Black Freedom Struggle," in *Frederick Douglass: New Literary and Historical Essays*, ed. Eric Sundquist (Cambridge: Cambridge University Press, 1990), 275.

36. Waldo E. Martin, "Images of Frederick Douglass," 275.

37. Frederick Douglass, *Narrative*, 42.

38. Frederick Douglass, "Self-Made Men," 420–421.

39. Frederick Douglass, *Narrative*, 34.

40. Frederick Douglass, *Narrative*, 34.

41. Frederick Douglass, "The Heroic Slave," in *Narrative*, 151.

42. Frederick Douglass, "The Heroic Slave," 151.

43. Ivy G. Wilson, "On Native Ground," 458.

44. See, for example, Annalisa Coliva, *The Varieties of Self-Knowledge* (London: Palgrave Macmillan, 2016); Brie Gertler, ed., *Privileged Access: Philosophical Accounts of Self-Knowledge* (New York: Routledge, 2016); Peter Carruthers, *The Opacity of the Mind: An Integrative Theory of Self-Knowledge* (Oxford: Oxford University Press, 2011); Annalisa Coliva, *The Self & Self Knowledge* (Oxford: Oxford University Press, 2012).

45. Frederick Douglass, "Letter to Thomas Auld," 113.

46. Frederick Douglass, "Letter to Thomas Auld," 113.

CHAPTER 5

1. Lindsey N. Kingston, *Fully Human: Personhood, Citizenship, and Rights* (Oxford: Oxford University Press, 2019), 1.

2. Ida B. Wells, *Crusade for Justice: The Autobiography of Ida B. Wells*, ed. Alfreda Duster (Chicago: University of Chicago Press, 2020), 42.

3. Ida B. Wells, *Crusade for Justice*, 51.

4. Eve L. Ewing, "Foreword," to *Crusade for Justice: The Autobiography of Ida B. Wells*, by Ida B. Wells and ed. Alfreda M. Duster (Chicago: The University of Chicago Press, 2020), vii–viii.

5. Ida B. Wells, *Crusade for Justice*, 61.

6. Ida B. Wells, *The Light of Truth: Writings of An Anti-Lynching Crusader*, ed. Mia Bay (New York: Penguin, 2014), 221–222.

7. Ida B. Wells, *The Light of Truth*, 229.

8. The fifteenth amendment to the U.S. Constitution (1870) prohibited the denial of voting rights based on race, color, or previous status of servitude. According to the Historical Society of the New York Courts, "the 15th Amendment, however, was limited. It did not provide protections against discrimination based on sex

or economics, leaving the door open for states to exclude women and the impoverished from the polls and from being full citizens and participants in American democracy." See National Archives, "15th Amendment to the U.S. Constitution: Voting Rights (1870)," https://www.archives.gov/milestone-documents/15th -amendment; Historical Society of the New York Courts, "15th Amendment," https://history.nycourts.gov/democracy-teacher-toolkit/civil-rights-and-reconst ruction/15th-amendment-2/.

9. Ida B. Wells, *The Light of Truth*, 228.

10. Melba Joyce Boyd, "Canon Configuration for Ida B. Wells-Barnett," *The Black Scholar* 2, no. 1 (1994): 8.

11. Ida B. Wells, *The Light of Truth*, 222.

12. Tommy J. Curry, "The Fortune of Wells: Ida B. Wells-Barnett's Use of T. Thomas Fortune's Philosophy of Social Agitation as a Prolegomenon to Militant Civil Rights Activism," *Transactions of the Charles S. Peirce Society: A Quarterly Journal in American Philosophy* 48, no. 4 (2012): 472.

13. It deserves to be mentioned that it is impossible to chronicle the history of antilynching activity in the United States without ascribing significant credit to Ida B. Wells-Barnett. She was a central figure in the civil rights movement from the 1890s until her death in 1931. She was a leader of the antilynching movement in the nineteenth century, a cause to which she came after a brief but memorable career of militant journalism in defense of the Black community. See William F. Pinar, "Black Protest and the Emergence of Ida B. Wells," *Counterpoints* 163 (2001): 461; Ida B. Wells-Barnett, *Southern Horrors: Lynch Law in All Its Phases* (New York: New York Age Print, 1892). Sourced from: Schomburg Center for Research in Black Culture, Manuscripts, Archives and Rare Books Division, The New York Public Library. "Southern horrors," New York Public Library Digital Collections, accessed July 28, 2003, https://digitalcollections.nypl.org/items /634281e0-4abc-0134-346c-00505686a51c.

14. Ida B. Wells, *The Light of Truth*, 218.

15. Charles F. Robinson II, "Anti-miscegenation Laws," *Encyclopedia of Arkansas*, February 13, 2020, accessed July 6, 2023, https://encyclopediaofarkan sas.net/entries/anti-miscegenation-laws-3508/.

16. Ida B. Wells, *The Light of Truth*, 222.

17. Ida B. Wells, *The Light of Truth*, 228.

18. Ida B. Wells-Barnett, "Lynch Law in America," *Arena*, January 1900, 15–24. Cited in *The Light of Truth*, 394.

19. Akiko Ochiai, "Ida B. Wells and Her Crusade for Justice: An African American Woman's Testimonial Autobiography," *Soundings: An Interdisciplinary Journal* 75, nos. 2/3 (1992): 370.

20. Ida B. Wells, *Crusade for Justice*, 61.

21. Martha Hodes, "The Sexualization of Reconstruction Politics: White Women and Black Men in the South after the Civil War," *Journal of the History of Sexuality* 3, no. 3 (1993): 402.

22. Ida B. Wells, *Crusade for Justice*, 56.

23. Anne M. Brubaker, "Who Counts? Urgent Lessons from Ida B. Wells's Radical Statistics," *American Quarterly* 74, no. 2 (2022): 271.

24. Ida B. Wells, *Crusade for Justice*, 173.

25. Ida B. Wells, *Crusade for Justice*, 173.

26. Anne M. Brubaker, "Who Counts?" 266.

27. In many sections of her written essays, articles, and her autobiography, Wells-Barnett was very critical of the American legal system, especially of its failure to protect Black men and women accused of committing crimes, according to the principle of equal protection before the law, which assumes every accused person to be innocent until proven guilty in a competent court of law. The inadequacy of the law to provide this protection propelled her movement to make lynching a national issue. She worked very hard and drew both national and international awareness to the issue, such that several states in both the North and South eventually passed antilynching laws. The issue also became one that the federal government of the United States had to deal with as Congress attempted but failed to pass federal antilynching legislation in 1900. Her efforts contributed to a decrease in the number of lynchings compared to the years prior to her antilynching activism. The failure of American law was well demonstrated by the fact that most white men who held political office tacitly supported these murderous acts, as they were used to police the color line. In some cases investigated by Ida B. Wells-Barnett, she discovered that even members of law enforcement such as the police, sheriffs, judges, and other officers of the court also participated in the lynching of Black people. This implies that Black people were generally seen as being outside of the law and that the law can only be what murderous white people want it to be. In "Outlawry: Ida B. Wells and Lynch Law," David Squires argues that this is the same logic underpinning Revolutionary-era claims to popular sovereignty, which declares that since white people substantiate law, they can repudiate it. This logic explains why many white people, including law enforcement officers, continue to contravene criminal and constitutional law when it engages with Black people. There is a very important subtext in Wells-Barnett's critique of American law, which has to do with how the projection of criminalization on Black men as "rapists" has made it possible for their destruction and death through legal and extrajudicial means. This is a theme that is now being explored in the emergent area of research known as Black Male Studies. Some representative works in this area include Tommy J. Curry, *The Man-Not: Race, Class, Genre, and the Dilemmas of Black Manhood* (Philadelphia: Temple University Press, 2017); Adebayo Oluwayomi, "The Man-Not and the Inapplicability of Intersectionality to the Dilemmas of Black Manhood," *The Journal of Men's Studies* 28, no. 2 (2020): 183–205; Tamari Kitossa, *Appealing Because He Is Appalling: Black Masculinities, Colonialism, and Erotic Racism* (Alberta, Canada: University of Alberta Press, 2021); Tommy J. Curry, "Killing Boogeymen: Phallicism and the Misandric Mischaracterization of Black Males in Theory," *Res Philosophica* 95, no. 2 (2018): 235–272; Tracey Owens Patton and Julie Snyder-Yuly, "Any Four Black Men Will Do: Rape, Race, and the Ultimate Scapegoat," *Journal of Black Studies* 37, no. 6 (2007): 859–895; Tommy J. Curry, "He's a Rapist, Even When He's Not: Richard Wright's Account of Black Male Vulnerability in the Raping of Willie McGee," in *The Politics of Richard Wright: Perspectives on Resistance*, eds. Jane Gordon and Cyrus Ernesto Zirakzadeh (Lexington: University of Kentucky Press, 2018), 132–154; D. Marvin Jones, *Race, Sex, and Suspicion: The Myth of the Black Male* (New York: Praeger, 2005); Dalitso Ruwe, "Eugenic Caricatures of Black Male Death from the Nineteenth- to Twenty-First Centuries," *Theory & Event* 25, no. 3 (2022): 665–688. In "The Sexualization of Reconstruction Politics," Martha Hodes argues that the extralegal killings of Black men by white mobs

and militias through lynchings were utilized as a tool to ensure that they would never possess any civil rights. This was an important theme in the work of Ida B. Wells-Barnett. She contended that lynching could be "explained" by drawing a connection between the law and white Southern resentment at giving Black males their freedom, the right to vote, and fair representation under civil rights law in the United States. Wells-Barnett buttressed the fact that the denial of these rights to Black males was ultimately aimed at the intentional destruction of Black manhood. She "maintained that accusations of the rape of white women had been unknown to Black men prior to emancipation." This only became a popularized social theory only after emancipation and post-Reconstruction. A critical study of the works of Ida B. Wells-Barnett also reveals the contradiction of the notion in popular Black feminist discourse that Black men do not support Black women to succeed. Wells-Barnett's life exemplifies how Black men support Black women—this contradicts the current discussion in feminist scholarship claiming that Black men historically have not been supportive of Black women, as exemplified in works such as Michael Awkward, "Black Feminism and the Challenge of Black Heterosexual Male Desire," *Souls* 2, no. 4 (2000): 32–37; Patricia Hill Collins, "The Social Construction of Black Feminist Thought," *Signs* 14, no. 4 (1989): 745–773; Allison Wiltz, "Why Are Black Men So Quiet about the Things That Matter to Black Women?" *Zora*, March 3, 2022, accessed July 11, 2023, https://zora.medium.com/why-are-black-men-so-quiet-about-the-things-that-matter-to-black-women-a8a5a865ec35; Thomas Kochman, *Black and White: Styles in Conflict* (Chicago: University of Chicago Press, 1981); Carol B. Stack, "The Culture of Gender: Women and Men of Color," *Signs* 11, no. 2 (1986): 321–324. In a very instructive section of her autobiography, Ida B. Wells-Barnett writes about her indebtedness to the Black men who provided her with boundless support when her newspaper office was destroyed and she was exiled from the South. As she puts it, "They had destroyed my paper, in which every dollar I had in the world was invested. They had made me an exile and threatened my life for hinting at the truth. I felt that I owed it to myself and my race to tell the whole truth. So with the splendid help of T. Thomas Fortune and Jerome B. Peterson [two prominent and successful Black men], owners and editors of the *New York Age*, I was given an opportunity to tell the world for the first time the true story of Negro lynchings, which were becoming more numerous and horrible. Had it not been for the courage and vision of these two men, I could never had made such headway in emblazoning the story to the world." The case speaks for itself. See Ida B. Wells, *Crusade for Justice*, 54; Martha Hodes, "The Sexualization of Reconstruction Politics: White Women and Black Men in the South after the Civil War," *Journal of the History of Sexuality* 3, no. 3 (1993): 416; Paula J. Giddings, *Ida: A Sword among Lions: Ida B. Wells and the Campaign against Lynching* (New York: Amistad, 2008), 6; David Squires, "Outlawry: Ida B. Wells and Lynch Law," *American Quarterly* 67, no. 1 (2015): 141–163.

28. Wells-Barnett's desire for the law to protect the interest of all was highlighted in the public transportation system and her failed attempt to seek legal redress. In May 1884, her civil rights activism began when she sought legal redress against the Chesapeake, Ohio and Southwestern Railroad after its employees, a conductor and baggage man, physically assaulted her by dragging her from a seat in the "Ladies' Car" and eventually put her off the train

in Shelby County, Tennessee, for refusing to sit in a "first class" segregated smoking car. In the initial prosecution of her case in December 1884, a judge, who was a Union army veteran, awarded her a settlement of five hundred dollars, but the railway company appealed the court's decision to the state supreme court. The Tennessee Supreme Court reversed the decision. This case gave the signal that Black rights were not going to be protected or defended under the law. After Wells-Barnett lost the case against Southwestern Railroad for discriminating against her and physically assaulting her for refusing to ride in a segregated car, she would go on to call for militant Black self-defense. She urged Black people to fight back and protect themselves, militantly with guns if the American legal system would not provide them with much-needed protection against racist white violence. As Miriam Decosta-Willis documents in *The Memphis Diary of Ida B. Wells*, "as early as this 1800 diary, Wells stakes out a staunchly militant position on the side of the Black victims of White mob rule. Her tone is the same militant and uncompromising one that will later get her run out of Memphis with a price on her head." Wells would urge Blacks to resist violence, with force if necessary, arguing with characteristic intensity that a Winchester rifle should have a place of honor in every Black home. See Miriam Decosta-Willis, ed., *The Memphis Diary of Ida B. Wells* (Boston: Beacon Press, 1995), xiii; Ida B. Wells, "The Requirements of Southern Journalism," *A.M.E. Zion Church Quarterly* (January 1893): 96; Stephanie Athley, "Race in Feminism: Critiques of Bodily Self-Determination in Ida B. Wells and Anna Julia Cooper," *Trotter Review* 17, no. 1 (2007): 119; Paula J. Giddings, *Ida: A Sword Among Lions.*

29. The theme of white Christianity's complicity in racism in the nineteenth century was thinly veiled in the work of Ida B. Wells-Barnett. She critiqued the Christian churches in the United State for being hypocritical when it came to caring for and loving one's neighbor, which are central to the Christian faith. In "Crusade for Justice," she avows that "white people forget Christianity and good breeding when dealing with those who belong to the darker races" and that "the Christian churches of the South refuse to admit Negro [Black] communicants into their houses of worship save in the galleries or in the back seats." Her critique of white Christians was developed from years of her advocacy and campaigning to stop lynchings at Christian gatherings and community events, and through other speaking and writing mediums. In the initial stages of her campaign, she was under the impression that ignorance was the principal problem for why white Christians were not antagonistic to the brutal lynchings of other human beings. As she writes, "I had been indulging in the belief that Christian bodies on this side of the water needed only to know that over a thousand black men, women and children had been hanged, shot and burned to death by white mobs in America, to be willing to do what they could to put a stop to such infamy." But she quickly realized that this was a mistaken belief because the so-called Christians were actual participants and spectators in the lynching rituals. See Ida B. Wells, *Crusade for Justice*, 65, 131, and 161.

30. Deborah L. Rhode, "Leadership Lessons from a Heroic, if 'Difficult' Woman: A Tribute to Ida B. Wells," *Tennessee Journal of Law and Policy* 14, no. 2 (2020): 479.

31. Ida B. Wells, *Southern Horrors and Other Writings: The Anti-Lynching Campaign of Ida B. Wells, 1892–1900*, ed. Jacqueline Jones Royster (Boston: Bedford/St. Martin, 1997), 23.

32. Anne M. Brubaker, "Who Counts?" 266.

33. Christopher Waldrep, "War of Words: The Controversy over the Definition of Lynching, 1899–1940," *The Journal of Southern History* 66, no. 1 (2000): 76.

34. Paul H. Stuart, "From the Archives: Ida B. Wells-Barnett Confronts 'Excuses for Lynching' in 1901," *Journal of Community Practice* 28, no. 3 (2020): 216

35. Ida B. Wells, *The Light of Truth*, 220.

36. Dorothy Sterling, "Afterword," in *The Memphis Diary of Ida B. Wells*, ed. Miriam Decosta-Willis (Boston: Beacon Press, 1995), 192.

37. Ida B. Wells, *Crusade for Justice*, 345.

38. Ida B. Wells, *Crusade for Justice*, 345.

39. Ida B. Wells, *Crusade for Justice*, 328.

40. Ida B. Wells, *Crusade for Justice*, 328.

41. Ida B. Wells, *Crusade for Justice*, 313.

42. Ida B. Wells-Barnett's work in defense of women aligned with that of the women's movement of the nineteenth century, supporting the activism of some of the leaders of the women's rights movement such as Lucy Stone, Julia Ward Howe, and Susan B. Anthony in their bid to secure the rights of full citizenship and civil rights in the United State for women (mostly white women). But not all of these white women supported her as a Black woman. In the early stages of the women's movement, white women leaders were strongly opposed to the inclusion of Black women in the quest to seek the full rights of citizenship in the United States. Wells-Barnett wrote about how she was personally criticized by Susan B. Anthony for wanting to marry Ferdinand Lee Barnett because she believed that marriage would prevent Wells-Barnett from becoming an effective suffragist and activist. Another important piece of evidence supporting the fact that some powerful white women were very antagonistic of Wells-Barnett is the well-documented controversy between her and Frances E. Willard—the Wells-Barnett/Willard controversy, which centered on the horrors of white lynchings in the 1890s in America. Willard, just like many white people during this period, seemed to be open to the idea that Black men deserved to be lynched based on the myth of the Black male rapist; but Wells-Barnett's empirical and data-based investigation showed that this was not the case. The cry of "rape" was a pretext for lynching that was repeated so often that even Black people had begun to believe it. But the more Wells-Barnett studied the statistics, the more she became convinced that these mob murders were still another way to "destroy the Black race" and restore white supremacy in the South. So, the Wells-Barnett/Willard debate was essentially about white women's support for the practice of lynching and competing claims concerning white women's sexual desire for Black men, which complicates their gendered identity as either a morally superior, passive victim of abuse or a willing participant in interracial sexual desire and activity. As Maegan Parker argues in "Desiring Citizenship: A Rhetorical Analysis of the Wells/Willard Controversy," "the Wells/Willard controversy underscores the way in which race, sexual desire, and gender identity mutually constituted one another in turn-of-the-century reform campaigns for women's suffrage and black men's full enfranchisement." This was a spirited debate that received broad coverage both at home and abroad and lasted for several years. As Parker observes,

Wells-Barnett began challenging Willard's characterization of Black men in 1891 and continued to publicly refute her racist remarks until Willard's death in 1898. Various speeches, letters, newspaper articles, and pamphlets, in addition to several interviews given by the women in both the United States and the United Kingdom, comprise the dispute. See Maegan Parker, "Desiring Citizenship: A Rhetorical Analysis of the Wells/Willard Controversy," *Women's Studies in Communication* 31, no. 1 (2008): 56–57; Dorothy Sterling, "Afterword," in *The Memphis Diary of Ida B. Wells*, 191.

43. Ida B. Wells, *The Light of Truth*, 14. Sourced from: Ida B. Wells, "Woman's Mission," *New York Freeman*, December 26, 1885.

44. Paula J. Giddings, *Ida: A Sword Among Lions*, 3.

45. It is possible that contemporary readers and writers of the works of Ida B. Wells-Barnett may consider these notions under the framework of feminism or Black feminism given the development of critiques regarding the different axes of oppression such as race, class, gender, sexuality, identity, and group membership or affiliation. But such considerations would be ahistorical since this movement, at least around the time of Wells-Barnett's life, was centered primarily on white women and its advocates actively argued for the exclusion of Black women. As Tommy J. Curry notes in "The Fortune of Wells," "Recent scholarship depicts Wells-Barnett as a pragmatist feminist whose interests aligned with the social awareness of white figures like Jane Addams or John Dewey. Such claims are not only revisionist but largely inventions of white American scholars seeking to establish continuity between Black and white figures in an era defined by Jim Crow segregation, lynching and the mass murder of Black citizens. Believing that their 'theory' is sempiternal, these scholars have no problem retroactively attributing and/or describing the lives of said thinkers under the conceptual milieu of our present day." In addition, some of the white women who were credited with the early waves of the feminist movement deeply disliked Wells-Barnett for her militant activism. Her method of activism was very off-putting to contemporaries because of her gender and race. Many white women leaders of social reform organizations in the nineteenth century and at the turn of the twentieth century did not expect to be criticized or challenged by a Black woman. But this did not deter Wells-Barnett from achieving the great things she did in spite of the criticisms, mischaracterization, and character assassination she experienced. See Tommy J. Curry, "The Fortune of Wells: Ida B. Wells-Barnett's Use of T. Thomas Fortune's Philosophy of Social Agitation as a Prolegomenon to Militant Civil Rights Activism," 460; Deborah L. Rhode, "Leadership Lessons from a Heroic, if 'Difficult' Woman," 491.

46. Ellesia Blaque, "Black Ink: Writing Black Power with the Words of David Walker, Ida B. Wells, and Malcolm X," *Counterpoints* 406 (2012): 13.

47. Patricia A. Schechter, *Ida B. Wells-Barnett and American Reform* (Chapel Hill: The University of North Carolina Press, 2001), 34.

48. Hollie Pich, "Various, Beautiful and Terrible: The Life and Legacy of Ida B. Wells-Barnett," *Australasian Journal of American Studies* 34, no. 2 (2015): 61.

CHAPTER 6

1. W.E.B. Du Bois, *The Souls of Black Folk* (New York: Penguin Books, 2018), 14.

2. W.E.B. Du Bois, *The Souls of Black Folk*, 3.

3. Carol M. Taylor, "W.E.B. Du Bois's Challenge to Scientific Racism," *Journal of Black Studies* 11, no. 4 (1981): 451.

4. Many notable American scientists and anthropologists contributed to the development of this theory of scientific racism and wrote treatises that defended eugenics as a scientific mechanism that would ultimately save the white race from persecution. For instance, David S. Jordan, in "The Blood of the Nation" (1902), argued in favor of eugenics because "in selective breeding with any domesticated animal or plant, it is possible, with a little attention, to produce wonderful changes for the better." So, eugenics should be applied to make "wonderful changes" to the racial groupings in the United States claiming that "almost anything may be accomplished with time and patience [and American scientists need] to select for posterity those individuals which best meet our needs [needs of the white race] or please our fancy, and to destroy those with unfavorable qualities." Wesley C. George, in "The Biology of the Race Problem," even makes it clear that the scientific (or pseudo-scientific) racism of the eugenics movement was borne out of "the need to protect the white race and our [white] civilization." When the assumptions that motivated this racist theory are considered critically, they reveal some racial anxieties that may have stimulated its development. After Reconstruction, amendments (the Thirteenth, Fourteenth, and Fifteenth Amendments) were ratified by the United States Congress, which granted former slaves some social, political, and economic freedoms. This created a social crisis, with the struggle for labor at its epicenter, since former slaves now worked as paid laborers and not free laborers as they had in the previous social order and political economy of slavery. White people, especially powerful ones, devised a new means at the turn of the century to create a barrier to halt Black progress and upward economic mobility by developing a new science known as eugenics, heavily drawn from the prejudiced naturalist theory of social Darwinism. See Lester Frank Ward, *Pure Sociology: A Treatise on the Origin and Spontaneous Development of Society* (New York: Macmillan, 1914); David S. Jordan, *The Blood of the Nation: A Study of the Decay of Races through the Survival of the Unfit* (Boston: American Unitarian Association, 1902), 13; Wesley Critz George, "The Biology of the Race Problem," cited in *Documents of American Prejudice: An Anthology of Writings on Race from Thomas Jefferson to David Duke*, ed. S. T. Joshi (New York: Basic Books, 1999), 180.

5. See Carol M. Taylor, "W.E.B. Du Bois's Challenge to Scientific Racism," 452. In *Darkwater*, Du Bois describes this succinctly, writing that when you "say to a people: 'the one virtue is to be white,' . . . and the people rush to the inevitable conclusion, 'Kill the [Black person].'" See W.E.B. Du Bois, *Darkwater: Voices from Within the Veil* (New York: Schocken Books, 1969), 34.

6. David Graeber and David Wengrow, *The Dawn of Everything: A New History of Humanity* (New York: Farrar, Straus and Giroux, 2021), 21.

7. Albert Edward Wiggam, "The New Decalogue of Science," cited in *Documents of American Prejudice: An Anthology of Writings on Race from Thomas Jefferson to David Duke*, ed. S. T. Joshi (New York: Basic Books, 1999), 176.

8. W.E.B. Du Bois, "The Conservation of Races," in *The Oxford W.E.B. Du Bois Reader*, ed. Eric J. Sundquist (New York: Oxford University Press, 1996), 38.

9. W.E.B. Du Bois, "Race Intelligence," in *The Oxford W.E.B. Du Bois Reader*, 197.

10. Saidiya Hartman, *Scenes of Subjection: Terror, Slavery, and Self-Making in Nineteenth-Century America* (Oxford: Oxford University Press, 1997); 119.

11. W.E.B. Du Bois, *The Negro* (London: Oxford University Press, 1970-first edition, 1915), 139–140.

12. W.E.B. Du Bois, "Phylon: Science or Propaganda," *Phylon* 5, no. 1 (1944): 7.

13. W.E.B. Du Bois, "Phylon," 9.

14. See Eric J. Sundquist, ed., *The Oxford W.E.B. Du Bois Reader*, 354–362.

15. W.E.B. Du Bois, *Black Folk, Then and Now: An Essay in the History and Sociology of the Negro Race* (New York: Octagon Books, 1973), ix.

16. W.E.B. Du Bois, *Black Folk, Then and Now*, 20

17. See Eric J. Sundquist, ed., *The Oxford W.E.B. Du Bois Reader*, 355.

18. W.E.B. Du Bois, "The Study of the Negro Problems," *Annals of the American Academy of Political and Social Science* 11, no. 1 (1898): 10.

19. W.E.B. Du Bois, "The Study of the Negro Problems," 603.

20. W.E.B. Du Bois, "The Study of the Negro Problems," 361.

21. W.E.B. Du Bois, "The Study of the Negro Problems," 361.

22. The idea of Black epistemic authority would inform Du Bois's Pan-Africanism as an ideological formation that seeks to bring together Black communities across the globe to demand political and economic rights from oppressive imperialist economies or colonial political entities such as the United States and Great Britain. In a string of essays published in *The Crisis* magazine in 1921, Du Bois called for the first Pan-African Congress, designed for the interests of the darker peoples in the world. It was at the Peace Conference in Paris, February 1919, that this call was first made. Du Bois conceived of this congress as a forum that would serve "the purpose of raising peoples to intelligence, self-knowledge and self-control, their intelligentsia of right ought to be recognized as the natural leaders of their groups." Du Bois's call for the Pan-African congress was inspired by his unflinching belief that genuine Black progress in an anti-Black world could only be achieved through an emphasis of Black self-determination and knowledge schemes that emphasize Black intellectual and spiritual gifts. This is why he decried any attempt, intellectual or otherwise, that demonizes Blackness in any fashion. According to Du Bois, "the insidious and dishonorable propaganda which, for selfish ends, so distorts and denies facts as to represent the advancement and development of certain races of men as impossible and undesirable should be met with widespread dissemination of the truth." This is the truth of knowledge of history that would show the enormous contributions of Black folks to human civilization. In *The Negritude Movement*, Reiland Rabaka argues that "invoking the Africana intellectual tradition, at least in its modern guise, takes us back to Du Bois, who is almost universally regarded as the preeminent intellectual of the modern African world. Arguably more than any other continental or diasporan African intellectual from the period spanning 1895 to the emergence of the Negritude movement in the mid- to late 1930s, Du Bois's discourse—whether via his Pan-Africanism, sociology, historiography, radical politics, poetry, short stories, or novels—was dominant and extremely influential." Du Bois was renowned for placing people of African descent at the center of history, and this contributed to his influence in the Africana intellectual tradition in the modern moment. See W.E.B. Du Bois's *The Crisis* 23, no. 1 (November 1921): 510 and *The Crisis* 21, no. 5 (March 1921): 198–199; Reiland Rabaka, *The Negritude Movement: W.E.B. Du Bois, Leon*

Damas, Aimee Césaire, Leopold Senghor, Frantz Fanon, and the Evolution of an Insurgent Idea (New York: Lexington Books, 2015), 4; *W.E.B. Du Bois on Africa*, ed. Eugene F. Provenzo and Edmund Abaka (California: Left Coast Press, 2012); Patricia W. Romero, "W.E.B. DuBois, Pan-Africanists, and Africa 1963–1973," *Journal of Black Studies* 6, no. 4 (June 1976): 321–336.

23. W.E.B. Du Bois, *The Gift of Black Folk: The Negroes in the Making of America* (Oxford: Oxford University Press, 2007), 117.

24. Anthony Monteiro, "W. E. B. Du Bois and the Study of Black Humanity: A Rediscovery," *Journal of Black Studies* 38, no. 4 (March 2008): 600.

25. W.E.B. Du Bois, "My Evolving Program for Negro Freedom," *Clinical Sociology Review* 8, no. 1 (1990): 33.

26. W.E.B. Du Bois, "My Evolving Program," 32.

27. For this claim, I rely on the research work carried out by Aldon Morris in *The Scholar Denied: W. E. B. Du Bois and the Birth of Modern Sociology*, which argued that Du Bois was the first social scientist to establish a sociological laboratory where systematic empirical research was conducted to determine the scientific causes of racial inequality. Morris considered this as "an intriguing, well-kept secret regarding the founding of scientific sociology in America. The first school of scientific sociology in the United States was founded by a black professor located in a historically black university in the South. This reality flatly contradicts the accepted wisdom." He goes on to affirm that "the black sociologist, scholar, and activist W.E.B. Du Bois developed the first scientific school of sociology at Atlanta University, a historically black institution of higher learning located in the heart of Atlanta's black community." See Aldon D. Morris, *The Scholar Denied: W.E.B. Du Bois and the Birth of Sociology* (Oakland, CA: University of California, 2015), 1–2.

28. Du Bois explicates further: "This program at Atlanta, I sought to swing as on a pivot to one of scientific investigation into social conditions, primarily for scientific ends: I put no emphasis on specific reform effort, but increasing and widening emphasis on the collection of a basic body of fact concerning the social condition of the American Negro." W.E.B. Du Bois, "My Evolving Program," 33.

29. Aldon D. Morris, *The Scholar Denied*, 3.

30. Aldon D. Morris, *The Scholar Denied*, 3–4.

31. Aldon D. Morris, *The Scholar Denied*, 4.

32. Aldon D. Morris, *The Scholar Denied*, 4.

33. Today, the University of Pennsylvania takes great pride in associating itself with the name and person of Du Bois by naming a student dorm after him, "W.E.B. Du Bois College House," in the hope of documenting the "history of the Black presence at Penn." This was not their disposition in 1896 toward Du Bois, one of the most brilliant and gifted Black scholars that ever lived. They were so embarrassed that they had to hire a Black male scholar during this period that they made sure his name was not publicly displayed on any official documentation as a hired faculty member of the University. Du Bois himself wrote about the horrible treatment by this University in his autobiography: "I was nominated to the unusual status of 'assistant' instructor. Even at that there must have been some opposition, for the invitation was not particularly cordial. . . . I was given no real academic standing, no office at the University, no official recognition of any kind.

My name was eventually omitted from catalogue; I had no contact with students, and very little with members of the faculty, even in my own department." As difficult as this experience and the condition of engagement were for him, he accepted this offer for the principal reason that it would allow him to study Black people, whom he deeply cared about. See W.E.B. Du Bois, *The Autobiography of W.E.B. Du Bois: A Soliloquy on Viewing My Life from the Last Decade of Its First Century*, ed. Herbert Aptheker (New York: International Publishers, 1968), 194.

34. Sharon D. Jones-Eversley and T. Lorraine T. Dean, "After 121 Years, It's Time to Recognize W.E.B. Du Bois as a Founding Father of Social Epidemiology," *The Journal of Negro Education* 87, no. 3 (2018): 232.

35. See W.E.B. Du Bois, *The Autobiography of W.E.B. Du Bois*, 194; W.E.B. Du Bois, *Darkwater*, 20.

36. Aldon Morris, "The Sociology of W.E.B. Du Bois as a Weapon of Racial Equality: Pioneering Scientific Social Research at Historically Black Colleges and Universities," *Quaderni di Sociologia* 83, no. 64 (2020): 3.

37. Aldon Morris, "The Sociology of W.E.B. Du Bois as a Weapon of Racial Equality," 4.

38. Du Bois is widely regarded as one of the most successful Black intellectuals of the twentieth century and his extraordinary scholarship and engagement with the problems of the Black condition occupies a central place in Black intellectual history. However, some scholars have presented the idea that Du Bois is the pioneer of the scientific study of the condition of Black folks during this period, especially the emphasis on the deployment of empiricism to challenge false social categories of dehumanization that were being projected on Black people. See works such as: Dan S. Green and Edwin D. Driver, "W.E.B. DuBois: A Case in the Sociology of Sociological Negation," *Phylon* 37, no. 4 (1976): 308–333; Joseph Jakubek and Spencer D. Wood, "Emancipatory Empiricism: The Rural Sociology of W.E.B. Du Bois," *Sociology of Race and Ethnicity* 4, no. 1 (2017): 14–34; Lee W. Formwalt, "W.E.B. Du Bois in Turn-of-the-Century Atlanta, 1897–1910," *Soc* 50 (2013): 180–169. A more accurate chronology of this historical legacy should show that Ida B. Wells-Barnett was the first Black intellectual to pioneer the method of empirical investigation of the conditions of Black folks.

39. W.E.B. Du Bois, *Efforts for Social Betterment Among Negro Americans*, a Social Study made by Atlanta University Publications, no. 14 (Atlanta: The Atlanta University Press, 1909), 5.

40. W.E.B. Du Bois, "My Evolving Program for the Negro," in *W.E.B. Du Bois: A Reader*, ed. David Levering Lewis (New York: Henry Holt, 1995), 618.

41. Werner J. Lange, "W.E.B. Du Bois and the First Scientific Study of Afro-America," *Phylon* 44, no. 2 (1983): 138.

42. W.E.B. Du Bois, "The Laboratory in Sociology at Atlanta University," W.E.B. Du Bois, in *W.E.B. Du Bois: A Reader*, 167.

43. Earl Wright II, *The First American School of Sociology: W.E.B. Du Bois and The Atlanta Sociological Laboratory* (New York: Routledge, 2016), 18.

44. Earl Wright II, *The First American School of Sociology*, 19.

45. Whitney Battle-Baptiste and Britt Rusert, eds., *W.E.B. Du Bois's Data Portraits: Visualizing Black America* (New York: Princeton Architectural Press, 2018), 9.

46. Whitney Battle-Baptiste and Britt Rusert, eds., *W.E.B. Du Bois's Data Portraits*, 35.

47. Dan S. Green and Edwin D. Driver, eds., *W.E.B. Du Bois on Sociology and the Black Community* (Chicago: The University of Chicago Press, 1980), 12.

48. W.E.B. Du Bois and Augustus Granville Dill, eds., *The College-Bred Negro American*, Atlanta University Publications, no. 15 (Atlanta: The Atlanta University Press, 1910). As cited in Earl Wright II, *The First American School of Sociology*, 55.

49. Earl Wright II, *The First American School of Sociology*, 55.

50. W.E.B. Du Bois, "Sociology Hesitant," *boundary 2* 27, no. 3 (2000): 40.

51. W.E.B. Du Bois, *Black Folk, Then and Now: An Essay in the History and Sociology of the Negro Race* (New York: Octagon Books, 1973), 210.

CHAPTER 7

1. Frantz Fanon, *Black Skin, White Masks,* trans. Richard Philcox (New York: Grove Press, 1952), 203.

2. Frantz Fanon, *Black Skin, White Masks,* xii.

3. Fanon used the term *comparaison* in French Creole to highlight ways in which the color-line creates an alienating existential condition for the Black subject.

4. Frantz Fanon, *Black Skin, White Masks,* 185–186

5. W.E.B. Du Bois, *The Souls of Black Folk* (Oxford World's Classics) (Oxford: Oxford University Press, 2007), 8.

6. Some scholars have claimed that Fanon's anticolonial project or epistemology was focused on "rehabilitating" or "reclaiming" the concept of humanism in its universal form. Although these views have become popularized in the available scholarship on Fanon, they are not consistent with his writings. For instance, Gili Kliger, in "Humanism and the Ends of Empire, 1945–1960," opines that one of Fanon's objectives was to reclaim humanism in its universal form since his anticolonial critique captures humanism as problematic both in content and in form but as something that can be revamped. However, this does not mirror Fanon's true feelings or position on the question of whether we need to engage with the notion of humanism and other ideological constructs developed within the problematic Eurocentric context. An example of this is Fanon's expression in *Wretched of the Earth*, where he admonishes thus: "Let us leave this Europe [and its ideological creations] which never stops talking of man yet massacres him at every one of its street corners." It is difficult to see how Fanon is being read as calling for a "revamping" of this ideological construct when he appears more concerned about departing from it. I think Nelson Maldonado-Torres was correct, in "On the Coloniality of Human Rights," to point out that "damnation" is the starting point from which Fanon considers the possibility of a new concept of the human. Instead of inclusion in the existing dominant humanism, Fanon argues for "a new start," "a new way of thinking," and for the creation of a "new man." Given this understanding of Fanon, if there is to be a humanism, it is one that has to emerge from this "new humanity" and one "written into the objectives and methods of the struggle." This leans more toward Fanon reinitiating the process through which we arrive at a shared notion of the human, rather than relying on already existing ideas about it. See Gili Kliger, "Humanism and

the Ends of Empire, 1945–1960," *Modern Intellectual History* 15, no. 3 (2018): 781; Frantz Fanon, *The Wretched of the Earth* (New York: Grove Press, 2004), 235; Nelson Maldonado-Torres, "On the Coloniality of Human Rights," *Revista Crítica de Ciências Sociais* 114 (2017): 123–124.

7. Frantz Fanon, *Black Skin, White Masks,* 185–186.

8. Gili Kliger, "Humanism and the Ends of Empire, 1945–1960," 781.

9. Lewis Gordon, *What Fanon Said: A Philosophical Introduction to His Life and Thought* (New York: Fordham University Press, 2015), 103–104.

10. See Karen Ng, "Humanism: A Defense," *Philosophical Topics* 49, no. 1 (Spring 2021): 145–164; Stefan Kipfer, "Comparison and Political Strategy: Internationalism, Colonial Rule and Urban Research After Fanon," *Urban Studies* 59, no. 8 (2021): 161.

11. Frantz Fanon, *Black Skin, White Masks,* 204.

12. Frantz Fanon, *Black Skin, White Masks,* 14.

13. I regard this as an anticolonial move rather than a decolonial move because in the myriad of views that are categorized as part of the framework of critical decolonial scholarship currently, there is a tendency to place an overemphasis on the project of "rehabilitating" problematic hegemonic ideas in the hope of keeping open the lines of communication with erstwhile oppressive systems of thought such as the mental verse of coloniality and its dehumanizing modal logic. For instance, in their work *On Decoloniality: Concepts, Analytics, Praxis,* Walter D. Mignolo and Catherine E. Walsh describe what they conceive as the "decolonial praxis" as having to do with "relationality," "in the ways that different local histories and embodied conceptions and practices of decoloniality . . . can enter into conversations and build understandings that both cross geopolitical locations and colonial differences." In this framing of decoloniality, the oppressed or subjugated being will always be beholden to the antics and schemes of the oppressor and its dehumanizing philosophies of accentuations of reality. There is also the unnecessary task of the decolonial method, or movement for decolonization, that is not consistent with the spirit of Fanon's work. Fanon's ultimate objective was to destroy and utterly decimate the intellectual categories that sustain the structure of empire and coloniality in the world because those ideas and concepts are considered as pernicious or harmful to the mental and holistic wellbeing of subjugated peoples. In his later work, *The Politics of Decolonial Investigations,* Walter Mignolo devoted a significant part of this book to engaging with Eurocentric ideas, trying to understand the transcendental conscious experience as described by Edmund Husserl and how that contrasts with a decolonial understanding. For instance, he writes thus: "I am underlining two distinct lifeworlds, in one of which phenomenology emerges in the heart of Europe, and in the other coloniality emerges in the Southern American Andes, where the majority of the population are Pueblos Originarios of ancient Andean civilizational descent." Here is a question that needs to be raised about the praxis of "relationality" as highlighted in the decolonial praxis—why is the *comparaison* (to use the words of Fanon) needed? Why do we always have to engage epistemologically, phenomenologically, or even ontologically from this place of "two-ness" in the Du Boisean sense? Fanon sees this as part of the trap of the oppressive systems of coloniality, such that dangerously violent ideas are presented as "redeemable," and in the process aspects of such ideas are retained,

thereby allowing harmful systems to continue to reinforce themselves. He was clear about this in *The Wretched of the Earth*, where he asserts that "although fundamentally racist, the Western bourgeoisie generally manages to mask this racism by multiplying the nuances, thereby enabling it to maintain intact its discourse on human dignity in all its magnanimity." A more accurate reading of Fanon reveals that he is more interested in rupturing these cycles of alterity and sublimation—to introduce invention into life. This is the crux of the anticolonial move in the thoughts of Fanon. See Walter D. Mignolo and Catherine E. Walsh, *On Decoloniality: Concepts, Analytics, Praxis* (Durham: Duke University Press, 2018), 1; Walter D. Mignolo, *The Politics of Decolonial Investigations* (Durham: Duke University Press, 2021), 469; Frantz Fanon, *The Wretched of the Earth*, trans. Ricard Philcox (New York: Grove Press, 1963), 109; Adebayo Ogungbure, "Dialectics of Oppression: Fanon's Anticolonial Critique of Hegelian Dialectics," *Africology: The Journal of Pan African Studies* 12, no. 7 (2018): 216–230.

14. Oladipo Fashina, "Frantz Fanon and the Ethical Justification of Anti-Colonial Violence," *Social Theory and Practice* 15, no. 2 (1989): 182.

15. Oladipo Fashina, "Frantz Fanon and the Ethical Justification," 185.

16. Oladipo Fashina, "Frantz Fanon and the Ethical Justification," 185–186.

17. David Marriot, "Inventions of Existence: Sylvia Wynter, Frantz Fanon, Sociogeny, and 'the Damned,'" *The New Centennial Review* 11, no. 3 (Winter 2011): 46.

18. Frantz Fanon, *The Wretched of the Earth*, 110.

19. Frantz Fanon, *The Wretched of the Earth*, 90.

20. Frantz Fanon, *The Wretched of the Earth*, 6.

21. Carolyn Ureña, "Decolonial Embodiment: Fanon, the Clinical Encounter, and the Colonial Wound," *Disability and the Global South* 6, no. 1 (2019): 1641.

22. Frantz Fanon, *A Dying Colonialism* (New York: Grove Press, 1965), 43.

23. Bashir Abu-Manneh, "Who Owns Frantz Fanon's Legacy?" *Catalyst: Journal of Theory and Strategy* 5, no. 1 (2021): 4.

24. Frantz Fanon, *The Wretched of the Earth*, 108.

25. Frantz Fanon, *Black Skin, White Masks*, 73.

26. Henry Louis Gates Jr., "Critical Fanonism," *Critical Inquiry* 17, no. 3 (1991): 458.

27. Frantz Fanon, *Alienation and Freedom*, eds. Jean Khalfa and Robert J. C. Young (New York: Bloomsbury Academic, 2021), 169.

28. Frantz Fanon, *Alienation and Freedom*, 174.

29. Frantz Fanon, *Alienation and Freedom*, 174.

30. Frantz Fanon, *Black Skin, White Masks*, 186.

31. Frantz Fanon, *Black Skin, White Masks*, 93.

32. Frantz Fanon, *Black Skin, White Masks*, 45.

33. Glen Sean Coulthard, *Red Skin, White Masks: Rejecting the Colonial Politics of Recognition* (Minneapolis: University of Minnesota Press, 2014), 140.

34. Frantz Fanon, *The Wretched of the Earth*, 158–159.

35. Messay Kebede, "The Rehabilitation of Violence and the Violence of Rehabilitation: Fanon and Colonialism," *Journal of Black Studies* 31, no. 5 (May 2001): 541.

36. Zenon Ndayisenga, "Fanon on the Arbitrariness of Using Violence: An Inevitable for Both Colonialism and Decolonization," *Journal of Black Studies* 53, no. 5 (2022): 465–466.

37. Lou Turner, "Black Thought and Black Reality," *Ufahamu* 10, no. 3 (1980): 103.

38. Frantz Fanon, *Black Skin, White Masks*, 206.

39. Frantz Fanon, *Black Skin, White Masks*, xii.

40. Frantz Fanon, *Black Skin, White Masks*, xviii.

41. Frantz Fanon, *Black Skin, White Masks*, xviii.

42. Sylvia Wynter, "Towards the Sociogenic Principle: Fanon, Identity, the Puzzle of Conscious Experience, and What It is Like to Be 'Black,'" in *National Identities and Sociopolitical Changes in Latin America*, eds. Mercedes F. Durán-Cogan and Antonio Gómez-Moriana (New York: Routledge, 2001), 31.

43. Frantz Fanon, *Black Skin, White Masks*, xv.

44. Albert Memmi, Thomas Cassirer, and G. Michael Twomey, "The Impossible Life of Frantz Fanon," *The Massachusetts Review* 14, no. 1 (Winter 1973): 11.

45. Frantz Fanon, *The Wretched of the Earth*, 239.

46. Joshua Gregory, "Whiteness and/as War," *Psychoanalysis, Culture & Society* 27 (2022): 302.

47. Sylvia Wynter, "Towards the Sociogenic Principle: Fanon, Identity, the Puzzle of Conscious Experience, and What It Is Like to Be 'Black,'" in *National Identity and Social Change: Latin America Between Marginalization and Integration*, eds. Mercedes Durán-Cogan and Antonio Gómez-Moriana (Minneapolis: University of Minnesota Press, 1999), 60.

48. Frantz Fanon, *Toward the African Revolution*, trans. Haakon Chevalier (New York: Grove Press, 1964), 31.

49. Sylvia Wynter, "Towards the Sociogenic Principle," 31.

50. Frantz Fanon, *The Wretched of the Earth*, 15.

51. Frantz Fanon, *Toward the African Revolution*, 40–41.

52. Frantz Fanon, *Black Skin, White Masks*, 96.

53. Frantz Fanon, *Black Skin, White Masks*, 102.

54. Frantz Fanon, *Black Skin, White Masks*, 102.

CHAPTER 8

1. Steve Biko, "We Blacks," in *I Write What I Like* (Johannesburg: Heinemann Publishers, 1978), 28.

2. Steve Biko, "We Blacks," 28.

3. Steve Biko, "We Blacks," 28.

4. Steve Biko, "We Blacks," 29.

5. Steve Biko, "We Blacks," 30.

6. Steve Biko, *I Write What I Like* (London: The Bowerdean Press, 1978), 27.

7. Kogila Moodley, "The Continued Impact of Black Consciousness in South Africa," *The Journal of Modern Studies* 29, no. 2 (1991): 237.

8. This remark by Biko is part of a broader point he makes about the central thesis of Black Consciousness philosophy. The complete thought is as follows: "At the heart of this kind of thinking is the realization by the blacks that the most potent weapon in the hands of the oppressor is the mind of the oppressed." See Steve Biko, *I Write What I Like*, 68.

9. Steve Biko, "We Blacks," 46.

10. Steve Biko, "We Blacks," 32.

220 / Notes to Chapter 8

11. Steve Biko, "The Definition of Black Consciousness," in *The African Philosophy Reader*, eds. P. H. Coetzee and A. P. Roux (London: Routledge, 1998), 360.

12. Steve Biko, "The Definition of Black Consciousness," 360.

13. The radical ideas of Fanon and other revolutionary Black thinkers became available at the most critical juncture in the liberation struggle of Azania. This was a time when the political attitudes and activities of the Blacks were dominated by general apathy and fear after the banning of the ANC and the PAC by the South African government. At the time, the predominant currents of thought, prior to the emergence of the Black Consciousness philosophy, were represented by the underground liberation organizations, the ANC and the PAC. The ANC's political philosophy was a combination of liberal nationalism and Christian reformist ideas that became the inspiration and basis of an ANC document called the Freedom Charter. The political ideology of the PAC was an orthodox type of African nationalism that projected the basic concepts of Anton Lembede, the founding member and first president of the ANC Youth League. The ideological orientation of the PAC also reflected the pan-Africanist principles of George Padmore and Kwame Nkrumah. See Thomas K. Ranuga, "Frantz Fanon and Black Consciousness in Azania (South Africa)," *Phylon* 47, no. 3 (1986): 182, 186.

14. For instance, one can draw poignant similarities between the philosophical ideas of Steve Biko and revolutionary thinkers in African diaspora like Kwame Nkrumah, who developed the anticolonial political thought system known as "consciencism," or conscientization. Basically, conscientization refers to a system whereby people become critically aware of the possibilities of their life situation, systematically and sustainably examine the alternatives, and confidently adopt the most effective method and means of social and radical development. Specifically, and quite relevantly for the South African case, systems of conscientization were definitely in place for the oppressed communities under the weight of colonial exploitation. See Ali A. Abdi, "Identity Formations and Deformations in South Africa: A Historical and Contemporary Overview," *Journal of Black Studies* 30, no. 2 (November 1999): 150.

15. Gail M. Gerhart, *Black Power in South Africa: The Evolution of an Ideology* (Berkeley, CA: University of California Press, 1978), 291.

16. Tendayi Sithole, *Steve Biko: Decolonial Meditations of Black Consciousness* (New York: Lexington Books, 2016), 3.

17. Steve Biko, *I Write What I Like*, 29.

18. Shannen L. Hill, *Biko's Ghost: The Iconography of Black Consciousness* (Minneapolis: University of Minnesota Press, 2015), 6.

19. Tendayi Sithole makes reference to the power in Biko's writing styles in his investigation of the thrust of Biko's political epistemology as an exercise in self-definition. He affirms that, while looking at Biko's thought, another form of politics emerges through the politics of writing, that is, the politics of self-definition. It is through writing that Biko defines the political course of Black Consciousness and advocates the forms of life that should be pursued. In this form of writing, the definition of the self is not in the narcissistic sense, but the self as that which is living for the other. See Tendayi Sithole, *Steve Biko: Decolonial Meditations of Black Consciousness*, 7.

20. Derek Hook, *The Mind of Apartheid: A Critical Psychology of the Postcolonial* (New York: Routledge, 2012), 22.

21. Hashi K. Tafira, *Black Nationalist Thought in South Africa: The Persistence of an Idea of Liberation* (New York: Palgrave Macmillan, 2016), 2.

22. Derek Hook, *The Mind of Apartheid*, 23.

23. Derek Hook, *The Mind of Apartheid*, 25.

24. Steve Biko, *I Write What I Like*, 48.

25. Robert Fatton Jr., *Black Consciousness in South Africa: The Dialectics of Ideological Resistance to White Supremacy* (New York: State University of New York Press, 1986), 78.

26. Vuyisile Msila, "Stephen Biko's Philosophy and Its Pedagogical Implications in South Africa," *Creative Education* 4, no. 8 (2013): 492.

27. Daniel Magaziner, "'Black Man, You Are on Your Own!' Making Race Consciousness in South African Thought, 1968–1972," *The International Journal of African Historical Studies* 42, no. 2 (2009): 226.

28. Ian M. Macqueen, *Black Consciousness and Progressive Movements under Apartheid* (South Africa: University of KwaZulu-Natal Press, 2018), 6.

29. Ian M. Macqueen, *Black Consciousness*, 225.

30. Ian M. Macqueen, *Black Consciousness*, 4.

31. Ian M. Macqueen, *Black Consciousness*, 5.

32. Xolela Mangcu, *Biko: A Life* (London: I. B. Tauris & Co., 2012), 272.

33. It is undeniable that ideas play a role in politics. If we broadly define "ideas" as synonymous with something like beliefs or people's reasons for acting, then I think it is clear that the only real way we have of explaining action is by an appeal to the reasons, beliefs, or ideas of the actor. See Scott Althaus, Mark Bevir, Jeffrey Friedman, Helene Landemore, Rogers Smith, and Susan Stokes, "Roundtable on Political Epistemology," *Critical Review: A Journal of Politics and Society* 26, nos. 1–2 (2014): 6, 11.

34. Steve Biko, *I Write What I Like*, 49.

35. Steve Biko, "Black Consciousness and the Quest for a True Humanity," *Ufahamu: A Journal of African Studies* 8, no. 3 (1978): 18.

36. Michael Cloete, "Steve Biko: Black Consciousness and the African Other— The Struggle for the Political," *Angelaki: Journal of the Theoretical Humanities* 24, no. 2 (2019): 106.

37. Derek Hook, *The Mind of Apartheid*, 26.

38. Steve Biko, "Black Consciousness and the Quest for a True Humanity," 19.

39. Lindy Wilson, "Bantu Stephen Biko: A Life," in *Bounds of Possibility: The Legacy of Steve Biko & Black Consciousness*, eds. N. Barney Pityana, Mamphela Ramphele, Malusi Mpumlwana, and Lindy Wilson (Cape Town: David Philip Publishers, 1991), 27.

40. Xolela Mangcu, *Biko: A Life*, 33.

41. Biko picked his way through numerous books, including Carmichael's; surely, then, he had noted the role that consciousness played there. "A new consciousness among black people," Hamilton and Carmichael wrote, "will make it possible for us [Black people] to proceed." This consciousness would provide a "sense of people hood" from which progress would come. See Daniel R. Magaziner, *The Law and the Prophets: Black Consciousness in South Africa, 1968–1977* (Athens: Ohio University Press, 2010), 50; Stokely Carmichael and Charles Hamilton, *Black Power: The Politics of Liberation in America* (New York: Vintage Books, 1967), viii.

42. Ramathate T. Dolamo, "The Legacy of Black Consciousness: Its Continued Relevance for Democratic South Africa and Its Significance for Theological Education," *HTS Teologiese Studies/Theological Studies* 73, no. 3 (2017): 3.

43. Robert Fatton Jr., *Black Consciousness in South Africa*, 75.

44. Steve Biko, *I Write What I Like*, 68.

45. Steve Biko, *I Write What I Like*, 144.

46. Cited in Mpiyakhe Dhlamini, "Black Consciousness in Modern SA: The Inferiority Complex (Part 1)," *Rational Standard*, March 21, 2018, https://ratio nalstandard.com/black-consciousness-in-modern-sa-the-inferiority-complex -part-1/.

47. Huey P. Newton, *Revolutionary Suicide* (New York: Harcourt Brace Jovanovich, 1973), 4.

48. Huey P. Newton, *Revolutionary Suicide*, 4.

49. Brian Richardson, "The Making of a Revolutionary," *International Socialism: Quarterly Journal of the Socialist Workers*, Issue 70, 1996, http:// pubs.socialistreviewindex.org.uk/isj70/huey.htm

50. Derek Hook, *The Mind of Apartheid*, 23.

51. Steve Biko, *I Write What I Like*, 145.

52. Huey P. Newton, *Revolutionary Suicide*, 164.

53. Hashi K. Tafira, *Black Nationalist Thought in South Africa*, 5.

54. In 1945, Chief Obafemi Awolowo, a Nigerian nationalist, political leader, and a principal participant in the struggle for Nigerian independence, penned one of his most influential books, *The Path to Nigerian Freedom* (Faber & Faber, 1966), in which he was highly critical of British policies of indirect colonial administration and called for rapid moves toward self-government and the Africanization of administrative posts in Nigeria. He later expanded his critique of the colonial structures of power, indicting this system for the conditions of economic, political, and social oppression within African states/nations between the late fifties and early sixties. In *The Problems of Africa: The Need for Ideological Reappraisal* (Macmillan Education, 1977), he argued for the need for African states to do everything in their power to end political oppression, economic exploitation, and human degradation, which are the essential characteristics of alien or colonial rule. In a similar vein, Leopold Sedar Senghor, president of the Republic of Senegal from 1960 to 1981, focused his intellectual concerns toward a critique of the so-called superior European civilization, which was used as a justification by colonial empires to exploit and pillage the states and nations of Africa. In *Freedom: Negritude and Humanism* (Editions du Seuil, 1964), Senghor engaged in a critique of European civilization and offered a moral challenge to its pretension of superiority over the peoples it continues to brutally colonize within Africa and the African diaspora. His obsession with the mapping of the geography of the black race took him, as we know, beyond the more readily acknowledged Diaspora of the Americas and the Caribbean to the subcontinent of India, Papua New Guinea, and the South Sea Islands. Kwame Nkrumah, for his part, was deeply concerned about the unspeakable inhuman nature of European imperialism and colonialism, and he made it his life's mission to battle against its insidious political mechanisms and the self-abrogation of authority that drives this system of oppression and exploitation. In *Revolutionary Path*, Nkrumah describes the colonial existence under imperialist conditions as that which "necessitates a fierce and constant struggle for emancipation from the yoke of colonialism and exploitation. The aim of all colonial governments in Africa and elsewhere should be the struggle for raw materials; and not only this, but the colonies have become a dumping ground, and colonial peoples the false recipients, of manufactured goods of the

industrialists and capitalists of Great Britain, France, Belgium and other colonial powers who turn to the dependent territories which feed their industrial plants. This is colonialism in a nutshell." In a bid to overcome colonial rule in Africa, Nkrumah argues for a national solidarity of colonial peoples driven by their determination to end the political and economic power of colonial governments. This also involves the critical analysis of colonial policies, the colonial mode of production and distribution, and of imports and exports. This is to serve as a rough blueprint of the processes by which colonial peoples can establish the realization of their complete and unconditional independence. Julius Nyerere, president of Tanzania from 1963 to 1964, is another important scholar who expressed deep anticolonial sentiments during this period. By the late 1960s Tanzania was one of the world's poorest countries. Like many others it was suffering from a severe foreign debt burden, a decrease in foreign aid, and a fall in the price of commodities. Nyerere called for an alternative vision in resolving this problem that does not rely on the West. His solution was based on the collectivization of agriculture, which was largely inspired by his philosophy of the family as a unit—Ujamaa—a strategy he described in his *Crusade for Liberation*, Oxford University Press (1978). This helped to build a large-scale movement for nationalization built on indigenous African values. Under this system, people were encouraged to live and work on a co-operative basis in organized villages or *ujamaa* (meaning 'familyhood' in Kiswahili). It fundamentally informed his belief that African traditional values should be cultivated to reinforce the idea of African solidarity and unity. This trajectory of thinking is radically different from the kind of thought systems previously imposed by the structures of European modernity. Consequently, Nyerere argued in *Ujamaa: Essays on Socialism* (Oxford: Oxford University Press, 1968), thus: "We have to keep the concept of Africa, as one unit, before our people all the time. In our schools, we must teach our children that they are Africans as well as Liberians or Tanzanians. Through our newspapers and radios, we must extend knowledge of other parts of our continent, and ensure that all our people know how much they have in common with each other." See Julius Nyerere, *Ujamaa: Essays on Socialism* (Dar es Salaam: Oxford University Press, 1973), 19; Wole Soyinka, "Senghor: Lessons in Power," *Research in African Literatures* 33, no. 4, (Winter 2002): 1; Kwame Nkrumah, *Revolutionary Path* (London: Panaf Books, 1973), 15; Julius Nyerere, *Crusade for Liberation* (Oxford: Oxford University Press, 1978); Kandioura Dramé, "Introductory Notes," *Callaloo* 13, no. 1 (Winter 1990): 12–13; Kwame Nkrumah, *Neo-colonialism: The Last Stage of Imperialism* (Bedford: Panaf Books, 1974); Charles Martin, "Nkrumah's Strategy of Decolonization: Originality and Classicism," *Présence Africaine* 85, no. 1 (1975): xv; Julius Nyerere, *Freedom and Socialism: A Selection from Writings & Speeches, 1965–1967* (Dar es Salaam: Oxford University Press, 1968).

55. Hashi K. Tafira, *Black Nationalist Thought in South Africa*, 8.

56. Hashi K. Tafira, *Black Nationalist Thought in South Africa*, 2.

57. Huey P. Newton, *Huey Talks to the Movement* (Boston: New England Free Press, 1968), 7.

58. Huey P. Newton, *Huey Talks to the Movement*, 8

59. Huey P. Newton, *The Huey P. Newton Reader*, eds. David Hilliard and Donald Weise (New York: Seven Stories Press, 2002), 317.

60. Huey P. Newton, *Revolutionary Suicide*, 4.

61. Huey P. Newton, *Revolutionary Suicide*, 4.

62. It is important to clarify that the concept of revolutionary suicide does not mean that black revolutionaries like Huey P. Newton are suicidal. What this means, as described by Newton, is that before black revolutionaries die, they must ask this crucial question: how shall we live? He proceeded to describe how this question should be answered: "I say with hope and dignity; and if premature death is the result, that death has a meaning reactionary suicide can never have. It is the price of self-respect." Newton, in his own words, clarified this further: "Revolutionary suicide does not mean that I and my comrades have a death wish; it means just the opposite. We have such a strong desire to live with hope and human dignity that existence without them is impossible. When reactionary forces crush us, we must move against these forces, even at the risk of death; even though my struggle might have harmed my health, even killed me, I looked upon it as a way of raising consciousness." See Huey P. Newton, *Revolutionary Suicide*, 5–7; Meserette Kentake, "Ten Revolutionary Quotes by Huey P. Newton," *Kentake Page: A Love Affair With Black History* (August 22, 2016), accessed on January 31, 2025, https://kentakepage.com/ten-revolutionary-quotes-by-huey-p-newton/.

63. Writing about "Raising Consciousness" of Black peoples, especially the recognition of the importance of words in consciousness-raising, Newton recognized the power in using spoken words to advance Black Consciousness. He believed that words could be used not only to make Blacks prouder but to make whites question and even reject concepts they had always unthinkingly accepted. According to Newton, "one of our prime needs was a new definition for 'policeman.' A good descriptive word, one the community would accept and use, would not only advance Black consciousness, but in effect control the police by making them see themselves in a new light." The fundamental thinking here has to do with waging psychological warfare against the oppressor by capturing the Black mind and rescuing power from the grip of the oppressor. This takes Biko's remark that "the most potent weapon in the hands of the oppressor is the mind of the oppressed" and flips it around thus: the most potent weapon in the hands of the oppressed is the mind of the oppressor. See Huey P. Newton, *Revolutionary Suicide*, 163–165, 175; Steve Biko, *I Write What I Like: Selected Writings* (Chicago: The University of Chicago Press, 2002), 68.

64. Huey P. Newton, *Revolutionary Suicide*, 5.

65. Quoted in Donald Wood, *Biko* (New York: Henry Holt and Company, 1978), xii.

66. Steve Biko, *I Write What I Like*, 6.

67. Tendayi Sithole, *Steve Biko: Decolonial Meditations of Black Consciousness*, 10.

68. Tendayi Sithole, *Steve Biko: Decolonial Meditations of Black Consciousness*, 12.

69. Huey P. Newton, "War Against the Panthers: A Study of Repression in America" (PhD diss., University of California, Santa Cruz, June 1, 1980), 24.

70. Huey P. Newton, "War Against the Panthers," 17.

71. Huey P. Newton, "War Against the Panthers," 18.

72. David Hilliard, *The Black Panther Party: Service to the People Programs* (Albuquerque: University of New Mexico Press, 2008), 3.

73. Hashi K. Tafira, *Black Nationalist Thought in South Africa*, 15.

74. Stokely Carmichael, *Stokely Speaks: Black Power Back to Pan-Africanism* (New York: Vintage Books, 1965), 42.

75. Stokely Carmichael, *Stokely Speaks*, xiv.

76. Stokely Carmichael, *Stokely Speaks*, 97.

77. Steve Biko, *I Write What I Like*, 68.

78. Hashi K. Tafira, *Black Nationalist Thought in South Africa*, 25.

CHAPTER 9

1. Elaine Brown, "Introduction to the 2019 Edition," in *The New Huey P. Newton Reader*, eds. David Hilliard and Donald Weise (New York: Seven Stories Press, 2019), 22.

2. Huey P. Newton and Erik H. Erikson, *In Search of Common Ground* (New York: W. W. Norton & Co., 1973), 133.

3. Bobby Seale, *Seize the Time: The Story of the Black Panther Party and Huey P. Newton* (Baltimore, MD: Black Classic Press, 1970), 393.

4. Huey P. Newton, "Dialectics of Nature," in *The New Huey P. Newton Reader*, eds. David Hilliard and Donald Weise, 311.

5. Huey P. Newton, *Revolutionary Intercommunalism and the Right of Nations to Self-Determination*, ed. Amy Gdala (Wales, UK: Superscript, 2004), 31.

6. According to Amy Gdala, Huey P. Newton's exposition of the concept of Revolutionary intercommunalism (RI) is the most progressive, most logical, and most hopeful political idea since Ghandi developed the principle of nonviolent direct action. In this vein, she considers Newton's dialogues on intercommunalism as the quintessence of permanent revolution on the noumenal plane, beckoning to mankind to struggle without end, a struggle without which their lives would be wasted in history. See Huey P. Newton, *Revolutionary Intercommunalism*, 20, 33.

7. Huey P. Newton, "War Against the Panthers," 4.

8. Albert Wirz and Andreas Eckert, "The Scramble for Africa: Icon and Idiom of Modernity," in *From Slave to Empire: Europe and the Colonisation of Black Africa 1780–1880s*, ed. Olivier Pétré-Grenouilleau (New York: Routledge, 2004), 133–153.

9. Huey P. Newton, *Revolutionary Intercommunalism*, 29.

10. Huey P. Newton, *Revolutionary Intercommunalism*, 29.

11. Huey P. Newton, *Revolutionary Intercommunalism*, 32.

12. Elaine Brown, "Introduction to the 2019 Edition," 23.

13. Huey P. Newton, *Revolutionary Intercommunalism*, 25.

14. Judson L. Jeffries, *Huey P. Newton: The Radical Theorist* (Jackson: University Press of Mississippi, 2002), 62.

15. Although the Panthers kept their revolutionary nationalist views intact during Huey Newton's imprisonment, that changed upon his release in August 1970. Reflecting the impact of an increasingly global consciousness on his thinking, Newton once again transformed the Black Panther ideology but retained the basic elements of revolutionary nationalism as far as coalition politics was concerned. The new Panther ideology represented a transition to revolutionary internationalism. See Charles E. Jones, ed., *The Black Panther Party Reconsidered* (Baltimore: Black Classic Press, 1998), 169.

16. Omari L. Dyson, "Nesting the Black Panther Party in the Zeitgeist of Uncertainty," in *On the Ground: The Black Panther Party in Communities across America*, ed. Judson L. Jeffries (Jackson: University Press of Mississippi, 2010), 279.

17. Huey P. Newton, *Revolutionary Suicide* (New York: Harcourt Brace Jovanovich, 1973), 356.

18. Huey P. Newton, *Revolutionary Intercommunalism*, 28.

19. Huey P. Newton, *Revolutionary Suicide*, 359.

20. Zoé Samudzi and William C. Anderson, *As Black as Resistance: Finding the Conditions for Liberation* (Edinburgh: AK Press, 2018), 48.

21. David Hilliard and Donald Weise, eds., *The New Huey P. Newton Reader*, 214.

22. Huey P. Newton, *Revolutionary Intercommunalism*, 37.

23. Judson L. Jeffries, *Huey P. Newton: The Radical Theorist*, 81.

24. A. J. Williams-Myers, *Destructive Impulses: An Examination of an American Secret in Race Relations-White Violence* (New York: University Press of America, 1995), 50.

25. Kenneth B. Clark, *Dark Ghetto: Dilemmas of Social Power* (New York: Harper & Row 1965), 223.

26. Delio Vasquez, "Intercommunalism: The Late Theorizations of Huey P. Newton, 'Chief Theoretician' of the Black Panther Party," *Viewpoint Magazine*, June 11, 2018. https://www.viewpointmag.com/2018/06/11/intercommunalism -the-late-theorizations-of-huey-p-newton-chief-theoretician-of-the-black-panther -party/

27. David Hilliard, Keith Zimmerman, and Kent Zimmerman, *Huey: Spirit of the Panther* (New York: Basic Books, 2006), 236.

28. Jennifer B. Smith, *An International History of the Black Panther Party* (New York: Garland Publishing, 1999), 70.

29. Sean L. Malloy, *Out of Oakland: Black Panther Party Internationalism during the Cold War* (Ithaca: Cornell University Press, 2017), 112.

30. In "An Account of Group Knowledge," Raimo Tuomela argues that although a group can be conceived as an agent, it is not a mentalist understanding of agency by which they are expected to have a mind. For this reason, "mental attributes are only 'extrinsically' attributed to it." What it is for a group to believe, in the central case of a "group-socially normatively binding group belief," is for there to be grounds for reasoning and acting on the belief that are internal to the group, i.e., directed toward achieving the group ethos. A group's normatively binding belief depends on members' beliefs (directed toward this goal), since a group operates only through the functioning of its members. See Raimo Tuomela, "An Account of Group Knowledge," in *Collective Epistemology*, eds. Hand B. Schmid, Daniel Sirtes, and Marcel Weber (New Brunswick: Transaction Books, 2011), 77, 85.

31. George Jackson, *Blood in My Eye* (Baltimore, MD: Black Classic Press, 1990), 12.

32. George Jackson, *Blood in My Eye*, 105.

33. Stokely Carmichael and Charles Hamilton, *Black Power: The Politics of Liberation in America* (New York: Vintage Books, 1967); Stokely Carmichael, "From Black Power to Pan-Africanism," a speech delivered at Whittier College, Whittier, California on March 22, 1971; James A. Tyner, "'Defend the Ghetto': Space and the Urban Politics of the Black Panther Party," *Annals of the Association of American Geographers* 96 (2006): 105–118.

34. The peoples of Africa have scored outstanding successes in the struggle for national liberation. The first half of the 1970s ushered in the final stage of the downfall of the colonial system on this continent. For a long time, the imperialist

powers had hoped in earnest that decolonization in Asia and Africa would result in no more than a partial loss of political domination and that they would be able to retain the economic levers of exploitation of the peoples in the newly free countries and retain control over those countries' social processes. The neocolonialists refused to understand that the peoples' urge for genuine national independence and social progress was inexorable, that it was impossible to quell it with false promises. For most countries, the winning of political independence has become a starting point in the struggle for complete equality in the world community. See E. A. Tarabrin, "The Present Stage of the Anti-Imperialist Struggle," in *Neocolonialism and Africa in the 1970s*, ed. E. A. Tarabin (Moscow: Progress Publishers, 1975), 14–15.

35. Kwame Nkrumah, *Handbook of Revolutionary Warfare: A Guide to the Armed Phase of the African Revolution* (New York: International Publishers, 1968), 27.

36. Kwame Nkrumah, *Handbook of Revolutionary Warfare*, 27.

37. Kwame Nkrumah, *Handbook of Revolutionary Warfare*, 23.

38. David Hilliard and Donald Weise, eds., *The New Huey P. Newton Reader*, 268.

39. Mumia Abu-Jamal, *We Want Freedom* (Cambridge, MA: South End Press, 2004), 105.

40. Göran Hugo Olsson, *The Black Power Mixtape 1967–1975* (Chicago: Haymarket Books, 2013), 105.

41. David Hilliard, ed., *The Black Panther Intercommunal News Service* (New York: Atria Books, 2007), 269.

42. Judson L. Jeffries, *Huey P. Newton: The Radical Theorist*, 55.

43. David Hilliard, ed., *The Black Panther Intercommunal News Service*, 13.

44. David Hilliard and Donald Weise, eds., *The New Huey P. Newton Reader*, 268.

45. David Hilliard, ed., *The Black Panther Intercommunal News Service*, 270.

46. Judson L. Jeffries, *Huey P. Newton: The Radical Theorist*, 63.

47. Göran Hugo Olsson, *The Black Power Mixtape*, 103.

48. Charles E. Jones, ed., *The Black Panther Party Reconsidered* (Baltimore: Black Classic Press, 1998), 170.

49. Sean L. Malloy, *Out of Oakland*, 173.

50. Huey P. Newton, *Revolutionary Intercommunalism*, 32.

51. Frederic Jameson, "Periodizing the 60s," *Social Text* 9–10 (Spring 1984): 182.

52. Sean L. Malloy, *Out of Oakland*, 169.

53. John L. Martin and Matthew Desmond, "Political Position and Social Knowledge," *Sociological Forum* 25, no. 1 (March 2010): 2.

54. Nelda K. Pearson, "Social Action as Collaborative Transformation," *Women's Studies Quarterly* 27, no. 3–4 (Fall–Winter 1999): 102.

55. Amy A. Ongiri, "Prisoner of Love: Affiliation, Sexuality, and the Black Panther Party," *The Journal of African American History* 94, no. 1 (Winter 2009): 69.

56. Matthew W. Hughey, "The Pedagogy of Huey P. Newton: Critical Reflections on Education in His Writings and Speeches," *Journal of Black Studies* 38, no. 2 (November 2007): 213.

57. Huey P. Newton and Erik H. Erikson, *In Search of Common Ground*, 108.

58. Huey P. Newton and Erik H. Erikson, *In Search of Common Ground*, 212.

CHAPTER 10

1. I use the term "K. Cleaver" as an abbreviation of Kathleen Neal Cleaver in the rest of this chapter so that readers will not confuse her with Eldridge Cleaver, her former husband, whom she divorced in 1987.

2. Catherine Ellis and Stephen D. Smith, eds., *Say It Loud: Great Speeches on Civil Rights and African American Identity* (New York: The New Press, 2010), 68.

3. Janet Dewart Bell, *Lighting the Fires of Freedom: African American Women in the Civil Rights Movement* (New York: The New Press, 2018), 140.

4. Kathleen Neal Cleaver, "And the Beat Goes On: Challenges Facing Black Intellectuals," *Souls* 4, no. 2 (2002): 18.

5. Catherine Ellis and Stephen D. Smith, *Say It Loud*, 69.

6. Kathleen Neal Cleaver, "Women, Power and Revolution," in *Liberation, Imagination, and the Black Panther Party: A New Look at the Black Panthers and their Legacy*, eds. Kathleen Cleaver and George Katsiaficas (New York: Routledge, 2001), 125.

7. Patricia Hill Collins, "Learning from the Outsider Within: The Sociological Significance of Black Feminist Thought," *Social Problems* 33, no. 6 (1986): 14–32; and Patricia Hill Collins, "The Social Construction of Black Feminist Thought," *Journal of Women in Culture and Society* 14, no. 41 (1989): 745–773.

8. See Kelly Oduro, "Bringing the Marginalized into Epistemology," *Stance* 15 (2022): 69–77; Monica Allen, April Smith, and Sandra Dika, "Black Feminism and Black Women's Interactions with Faculty in Higher Education," *Oxford Research Encyclopedia of Education*, January 31, 2023, accessed January 17, 2024, https://oxfordre.com/education/display/10.1093/acrefore/9780190264093.001.0001/acrefore-9780190264093-e-1723?p=emailAeG.LfDlLQgBM&d=/10.1093/acrefore/9780190264093.001.0001/acrefore-9780190264093-e-1723; Brenda J. Allen, "Black Womanhood and Feminist Standpoints," *Management Communication Quarterly* 11, no. 4 (1998): 575–586.

9. Under feminist epistemological theory, the standpoint thesis asserts that the embodied knowledge, thoughts, and articulated views of Black women or women generally cannot be disputed. In "Black Feminist Thought as Methodology," Ashley Patterson, Valerie Kinloch, Tanja Burkhard, Ryann Randall, and Arianna Howard describe this as an epistemic disposition that is self-defined, self-affirming, and embraces an embodied way of knowing. This implies that Black women's subjective knowledge represents a standpoint epistemology that reinforces itself from within, regardless of whether the putative elements of its avowals correspond to the truth of reality. See Ashley Patterson, Valerie Kinloch, Tanja Burkhard, Ryann Randall, and Arianna Howard, "Black Feminist Thought as Methodology: Examining Intergenerational Lived Experiences of Black Women," *Departures in Critical Qualitative Research* 5, no. 3 (2016): 55–76, https://doi.org/10.1525/dcqr.2016.5.3.55; Tracy Bowell, "Feminist Standpoint Theory," *Internet Encyclopedia of Philosophy*, accessed January 22, 2024, https://iep.utm.edu/.

10. See for instance, the accounts narrated in Patricia H. Collins, *Black Sexual Politics: African Americans, Gender, and the New Racism* (New: Routledge, 2004); Paula J. Giddings, *When and Where I Enter: The Impact of Black Women on Race and Sex in America* (New York: W. Morrow, 1984); Judson L. Jeffries, *Comrades: A Local History of the Black Panther Party* (Bloomington, IN: Indiana

University Press, 2007); Jordan Elisabeth Matthews, "'Ain't I A Comrade?' A Critical Examination of the Treatment of Black Women Members of the Black Panther Party as It Relates to the Goal of Liberation," *The Macksey Journal* 3 (2022): 1–8.

11. Ashley D. Farmer, *Remaking Black Power: How Black Women Transformed an Era* (Chapel Hill: University of North Carolina Press, 2017), 51.

12. Mary Phillips, "The Feminist Leadership of Ericka Huggins in the Black Panther Party," *Black Diaspora Review* 4, no. 1 (Winter 2014): 189.

13. Kathleen Neal Cleaver, "The Feminist Role in a Race-Based Civil Rights Struggle," *Boston Sunday Globe* (1995): 1.

14. K. Cleaver expands on this idea in her essay on "Racism, Civil Rights and Feminism," stating that in many ways, the Southern-based struggle to end segregation during the 1950s and 1960s, which can be considered as a human or civil rights movement, was a women's movement, since if it were not for Black women, "there would have been no Montgomery Bus Boycott, few voting rights campaigns, far less marvelous educational impact—in short, the civil rights movement as we know it could not have occurred." She also emphasized how Black women contributed to the civil rights movement through their efforts within religious and social organizations by supporting the churches that sustained the movement and raising money for the National Association for the Advancement of Colored People (NAACP), Congress of Racial Equality (CORE), the Southern Christian Leadership Conference (SCLC), and other groups. K. Cleaver's analyses are focused on how all of these achievements were directed at achieving freedom and racial progress for the Black community as a whole. See Kathleen Neal Cleaver, "Racism, Civil Rights and Feminism," in *Critical Race Feminism: A Reader*, ed. Adrien Katherine Wing (New York: New York University Press, 2003), 48–49 (emphasis mine).

15. Kathleen Neal Cleaver, "Women, Power and Revolution," 123 (emphasis added).

16. Kathleen Neal Cleaver, "Women, Power and Revolution," 124.

17. Tracye A. Matthews, "'No One Ever Asks What a Man's Role in the Revolution Is': Gender Politics and Leadership in the Black Panther Party, 1966–71," in *Sisters in the Struggle: African American Women in the Civil Rights–Black Power Movement*, ed. Bettye Collier-Thomas and V. P. Franklin (New York: New York University Press, 2001), 232.

18. A personal experience she recounted further corroborated her stance on gender dynamics: "I'll always remember a particular mini-trial that took place at one of our meetings. A member of the Party was accused of raping a young sister, who was visiting from Los Angeles chapter of the Black Panther Party, and he got voted out of the Party on the spot. Right there in the meeting. In 1970 the Black Panther Party took a formal position on the liberation of women. Did the U.S. Congress make any statement on the liberation of women? Did the Congress enable the Equal Rights Amendment to become part of the Constitution? Did the Oakland police issue a position against gender discrimination? It is in this context that gender relations—a term that we didn't have back then—in the Black Panther Party should be examined." See Kathleen Neal Cleaver, "Women, Power and Revolution," 126.

19. Antwanisha Alameen-Shavers, "The Woman Question: Gender Dynamics within the Black Panther Party," *Spectrum: A Journal on Black Men* 5, no. 1 (Fall 2016): 33–34.

20. Tracye Matthews argued further that "while it can justifiably be argued that the BPP at various points in its history was a male-centered, male-dominated organization, this point should not negate the important ideological and practical contributions of its female members or of the men who resisted chauvinistic and sexist tendencies." See Tracye A. Matthews, "No One Ever Asks What a Man's Role in the Revolution Is," 233–234.

21. Kathleen Neal Cleaver, "And the Beat Goes On," 21.

22. Bryan Shih and Yohuru Williams, eds., *The Black Panthers: Portraits from an Unfinished Revolution* (New York: Nation Books, 2016), 83.

23. Janet Dewart Bell, *Lighting the Fires of Freedom*, 151.

24. Janet Dewart Bell, *Lighting the Fires of Freedom*, 152–153.

25. Kathleen Neal Cleaver, "Back to Africa: The Evolution of the International Section of the Black Panther Party (1969–1972)," in *The Black Panther Party Reconsidered*, ed. Charles E. Jones (Baltimore, MD: Black Classic Press, 2005), 154.

26. Cedric J. Robinson, *Black Marxism: The Making of the Black Radical Tradition* (Chapel Hill, NC: The University of North Carolina Press, 1983), 2.

27. Michael Ralph and Maya Singhal, "Racial Capitalism," *Theory and Society* 48, no. 6 (December 2019): 854.

28. Peter Hitchcock, "Racial Capitalism and the Grounds of Contradiction," *The Comparativist* 46 (2022): 53.

29. Siddhant Issar, "Listening to Black Lives Matter: Racial Capitalism and the Critique of Neoliberalism," *Contemporary Political Theory* 20 (2020): 49.

30. Whitney N. Laster Pirtle, "Racial Capitalism: A Fundamental Cause of Novel Coronavirus (COVID-19) Pandemic Inequities in the United States," *Health Education and Behavior* 47, no. 4 (2020): 504.

31. Cedric J. Robinson, *Black Marxism*, 2.

32. Kathleen Neal Cleaver, "Racism, Civil Rights and Feminism," 53.

33. Henry Louis Gates Jr., "Interview with Kathleen Cleaver," *The Two Nations of Black America*, PBS Frontline, Par. 24, accessed December 21, 2023, http://www.pbs.org/wgbh/pages/frontline/shows/race/interviews/kcleaver.html.

34. Rose Freeman, "The Black Panther Party, Malcolm X, and the Question of Revolutionary Politics Today: An Interview with Kathleen Cleaver," *The Platypus Affiliated Society*, July 25, 2018, accessed on January 3, 2024, https://platypus1917.org/2019/02/03/the-black-panther-party-malcom-x-and-the-question-of-revolutionary-politics-today-an-interview-with-kathleen-cleaver/.

35. Henry Louis Gates Jr., "Interview with Kathleen Cleaver," Par. 24.

36. Henry Louis Gates Jr., "Interview with Kathleen Cleaver," Par. 24.

37. Kathleen Neal Cleaver, "Women, Power and Revolution," 125.

38. Kathleen Neal Cleaver, "Life, Liberty and Babies," *The Women's Review of Books* 15, no. 9 (1998): 20.

CONCLUSION

1. Beverly M. Gordon, "The Necessity of African-American Epistemology for Educational Theory and Practice," *The Journal of Education* 172, no. 3 (1990): 90.

2. James B. Stewart, "Black/Africana Studies, Then and Now: Reconstructing a Century of Intellectual Inquiry and Political Engagement, 1915–2015," *The Journal of African American History* 100, no. 1 (Winter 2015): 111.

3. In this regard, Kwame Appiah notes that even though the call for inter-disciplinary or multidisciplinary scholarship is common today—especially in the abstract characterizations of human thinking, there has not been an equally extensive exploration of the question of how racism has misguided our more abstract reflections, of how the absence of Black voices has shaped our philo-sophical discourse. See Kwame A. Appiah, "African-American Philosophy?" in *African-American Perspectives and Philosophical Traditions*, ed. John P. Pittman (New York: Routledge, 1997), 31.

4. Paul C. Taylor, "A Future for Africana (Post-)Analytic Philosophy," *South Atlantic Quarterly* 108, no. 3 (Summer 2009): 505.

5. Paul C. Taylor, "A Future for Africana (Post-)Analytic Philosophy," 505.

6. Tina F. Botts, Liam K. Bright, Myisha Cherry, Guntur Mallarangeng, Quayshawn Spencer, "What is the State of Blacks in Philosophy?" *Critical Philosophy of Race* 2, no. 2 (2014): 226.

7. Tommy J. Curry and Gwenetta Curry, "On the Perils of Race Neutrality and Anti-Blackness: Philosophy as an Irreconcilable Obstacle to (Black) Thought," *The American Journal of Economics and Sociology* 77, nos. 3–4 (May–September 2018): 660.

8. Tommy J. Curry and Gwenetta Curry, "On the Perils of Race Neutrality and Anti-Blackness," 667.

9. Cornel West, *Keeping Faith: Philosophy and Race in America* (New York: Routledge, 1993), 35.

10. West conceives of this kind of critique as a prophetic criticism that suffers from a kind of Du Boisian double consciousness—of *being* deeply shaped by Euro-American modernity—which is what we get when Africans in the Americas confront their exclusion to remake and recreate themselves into a distinctly *new* people, a world-historical and monumental process in which oppressed and degraded people invent themselves in alien circumstances and with alien languages and products. See Cornel West, *Keeping Faith*, xii.

11. Cornel West, *Keeping Faith*, 39.

12. Lucius Outlaw, "African, African American, Africana Philosophy," in *African-American Perspectives and Philosophical Traditions*, ed. John P. Pittman (New York: Routledge, 1996), 76.

13. Beverly M. Gordon, "The Necessity of African-American Epistemology," 89.

14. Here, I agree with Lucius Outlaw's assessment that tracing the connec-tions between Black thinkers in different diasporic contexts is something that is obviously missing in the current work of African-American philosophers, namely, research work that is conducted with little or no knowledge of, or attention to, the history of philosophical activity on the African continent or elsewhere in the African diaspora. At the very least, this lack of awareness and attention may well contribute to deficiencies in our historically informed self-understandings and, to that extent, will have important implications for the work we do, whether or not we take our work to be distinguished, or at least conditioned in significant ways, by our being persons of African descent. See Lucius Outlaw, "African, African American, Africana Philosophy," 71.

Index

Adebayo Oluwayomi is an Assistant Professor in the Department of Philosophy at West Chester University.